Rachel Whiteread,
House, 1993.

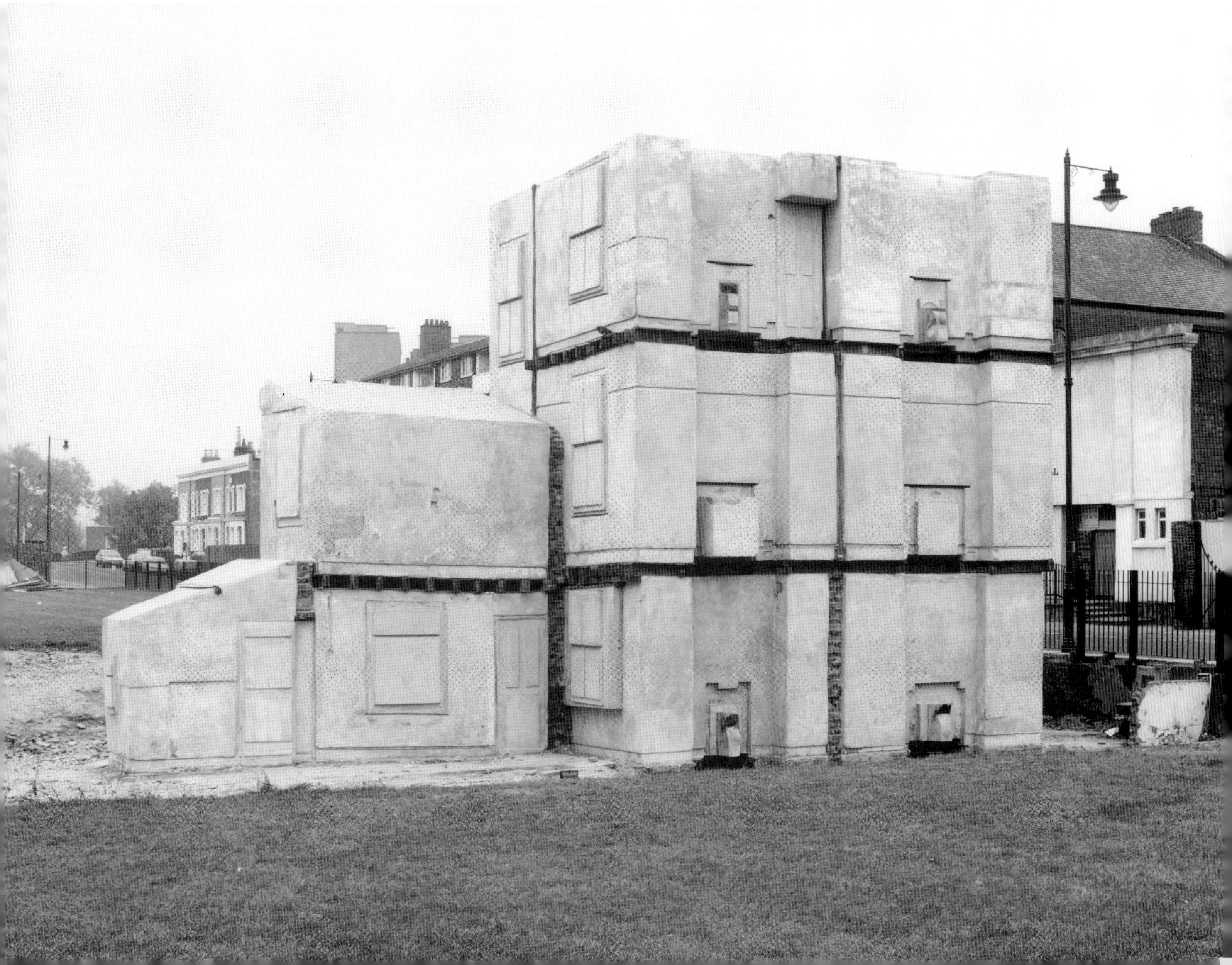

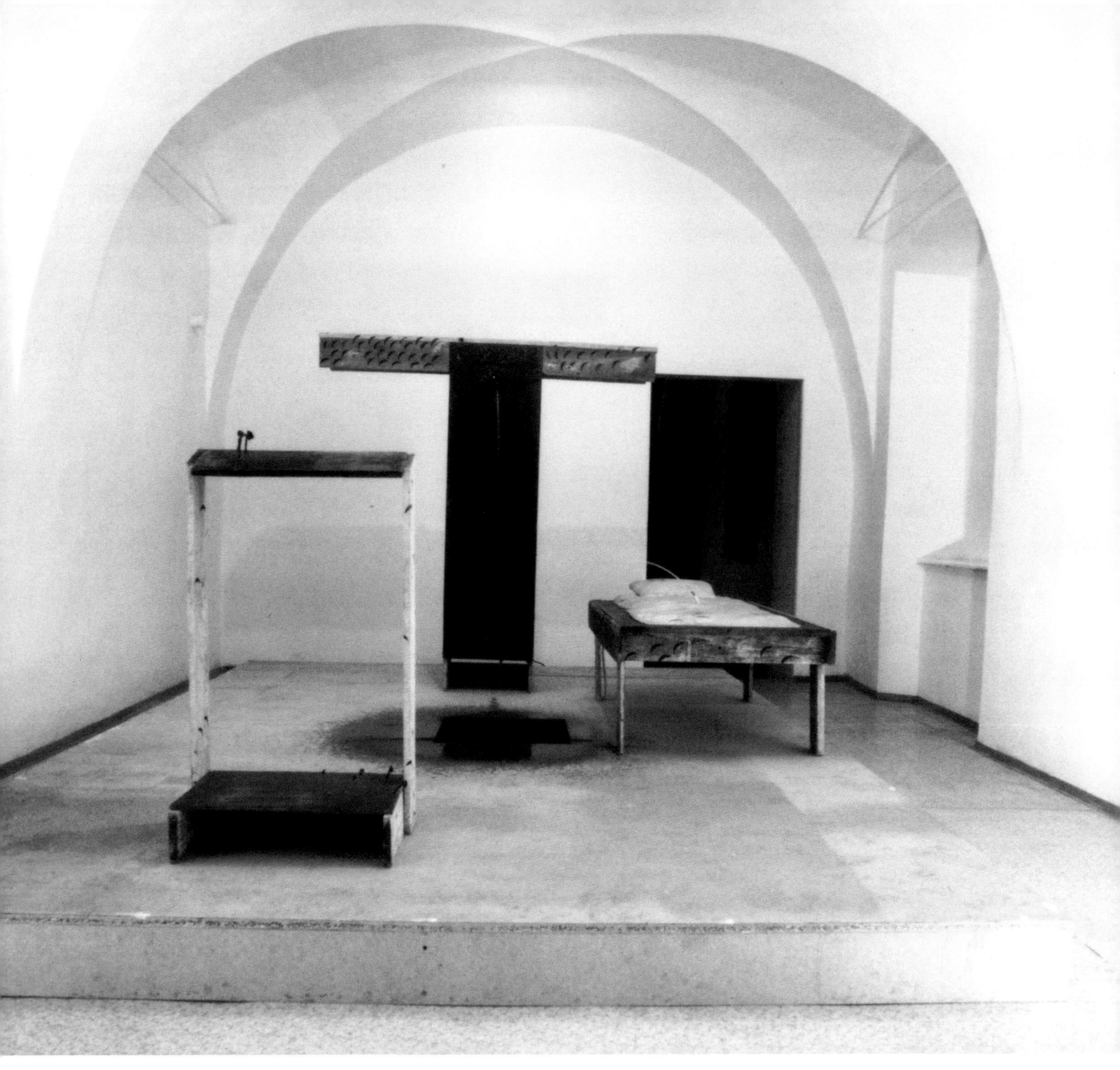

Mirosław Bałka,
When you wet the bed, 1987.

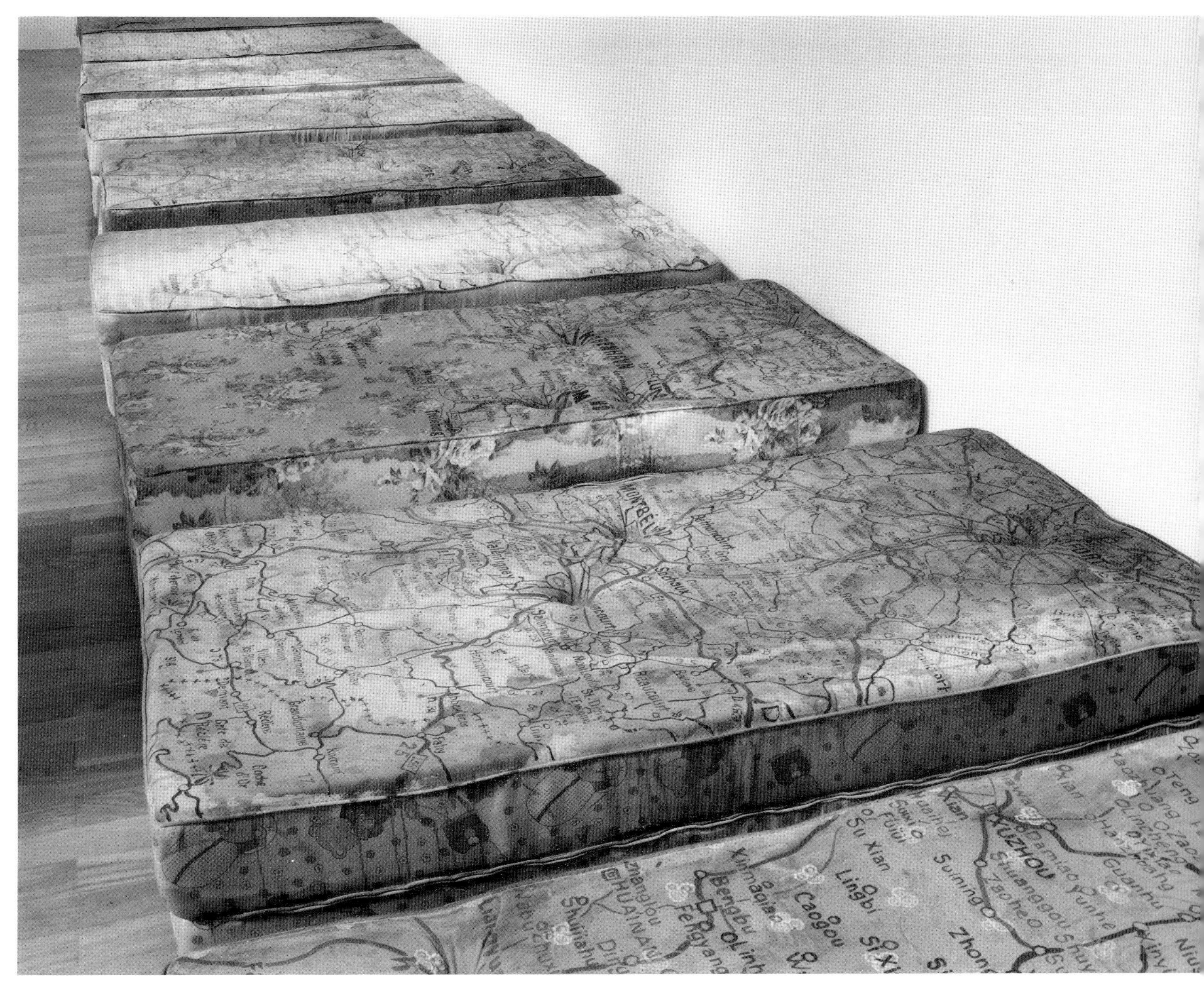

Guillermo Kuitca,
Untitled, detail, 1993.

Mike Kelley,
Educational Complex,
1995.

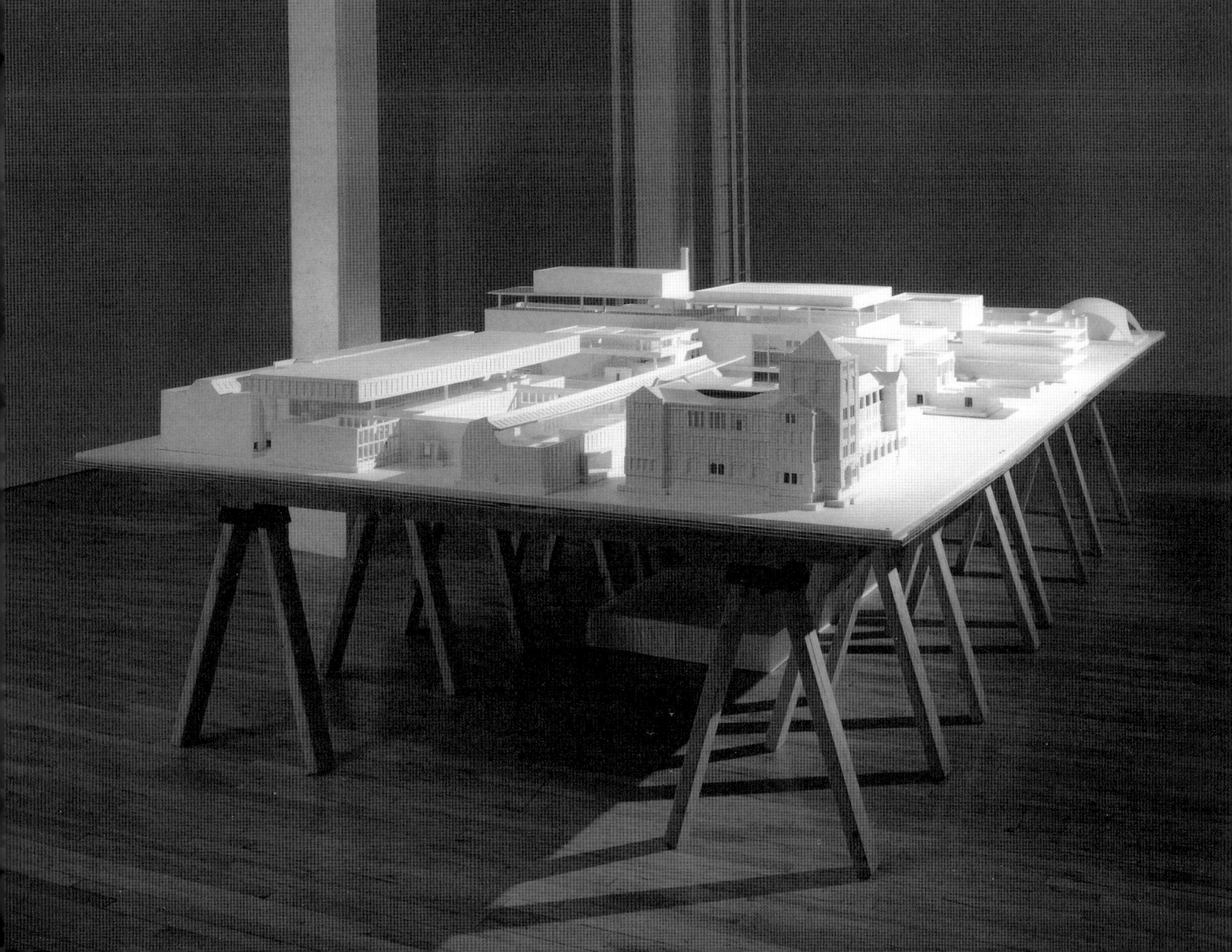

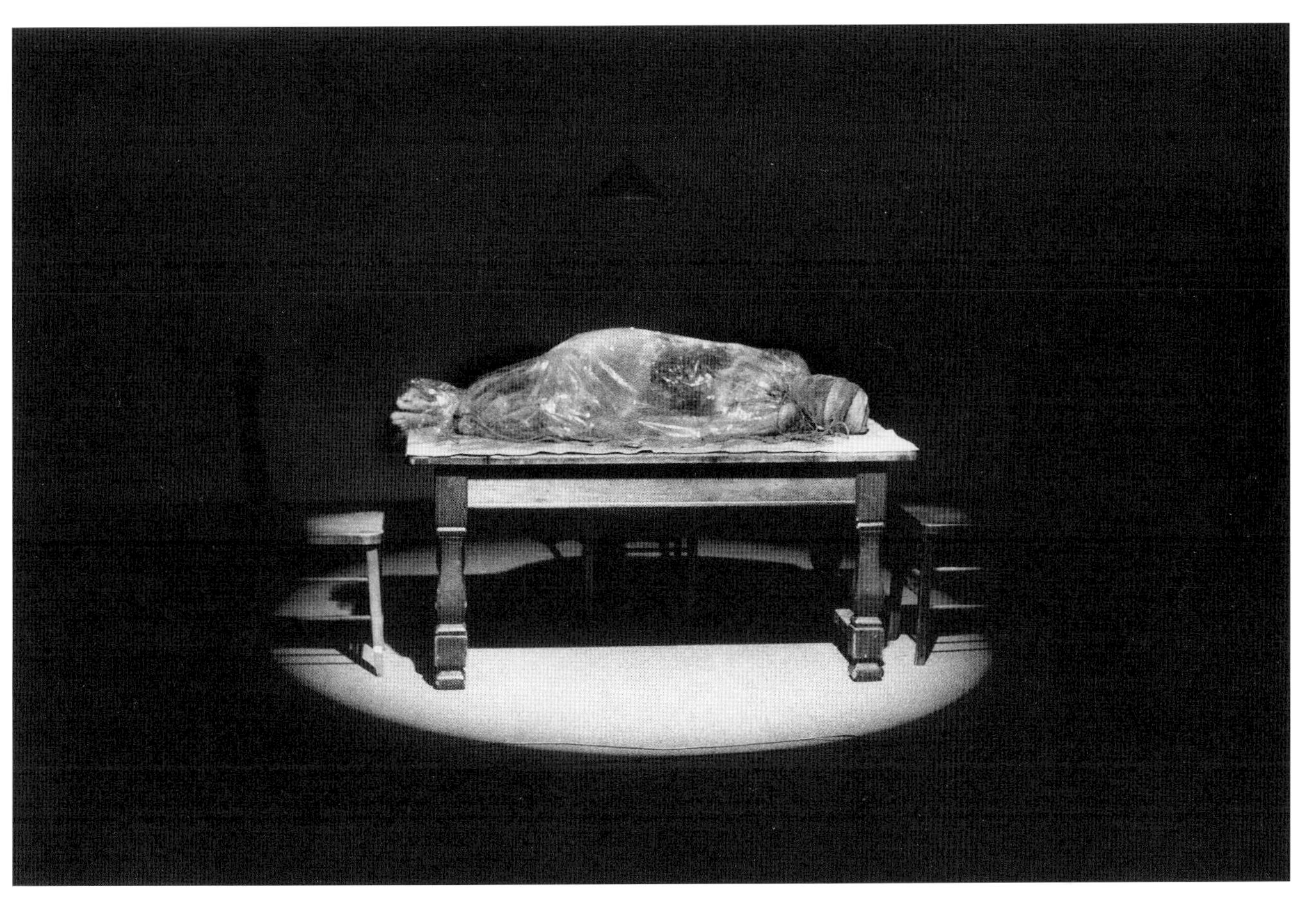

Mona Hatoum,
The Negotiating Table,
1983.

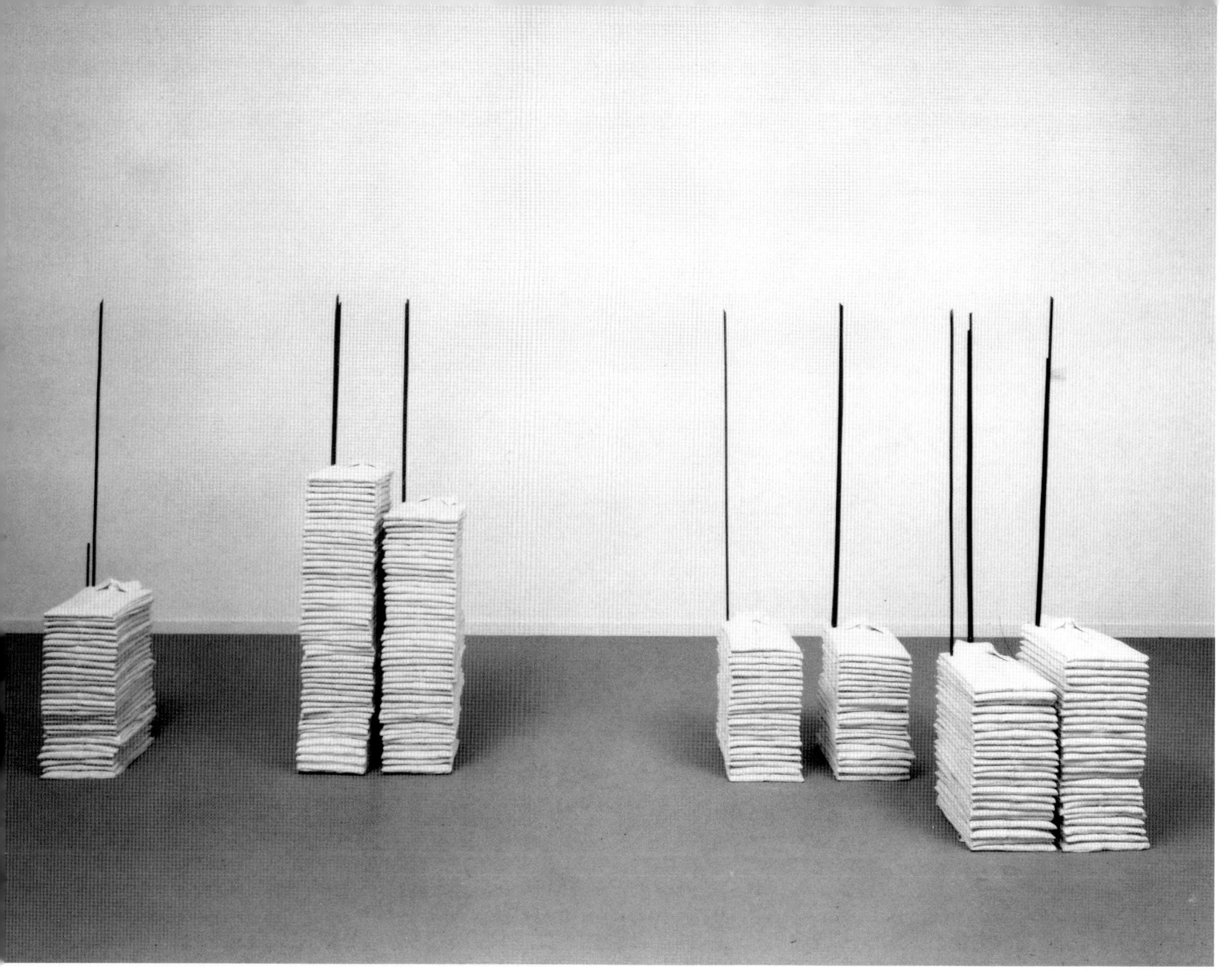

Doris Salcedo,
Untitled, 1989–93.

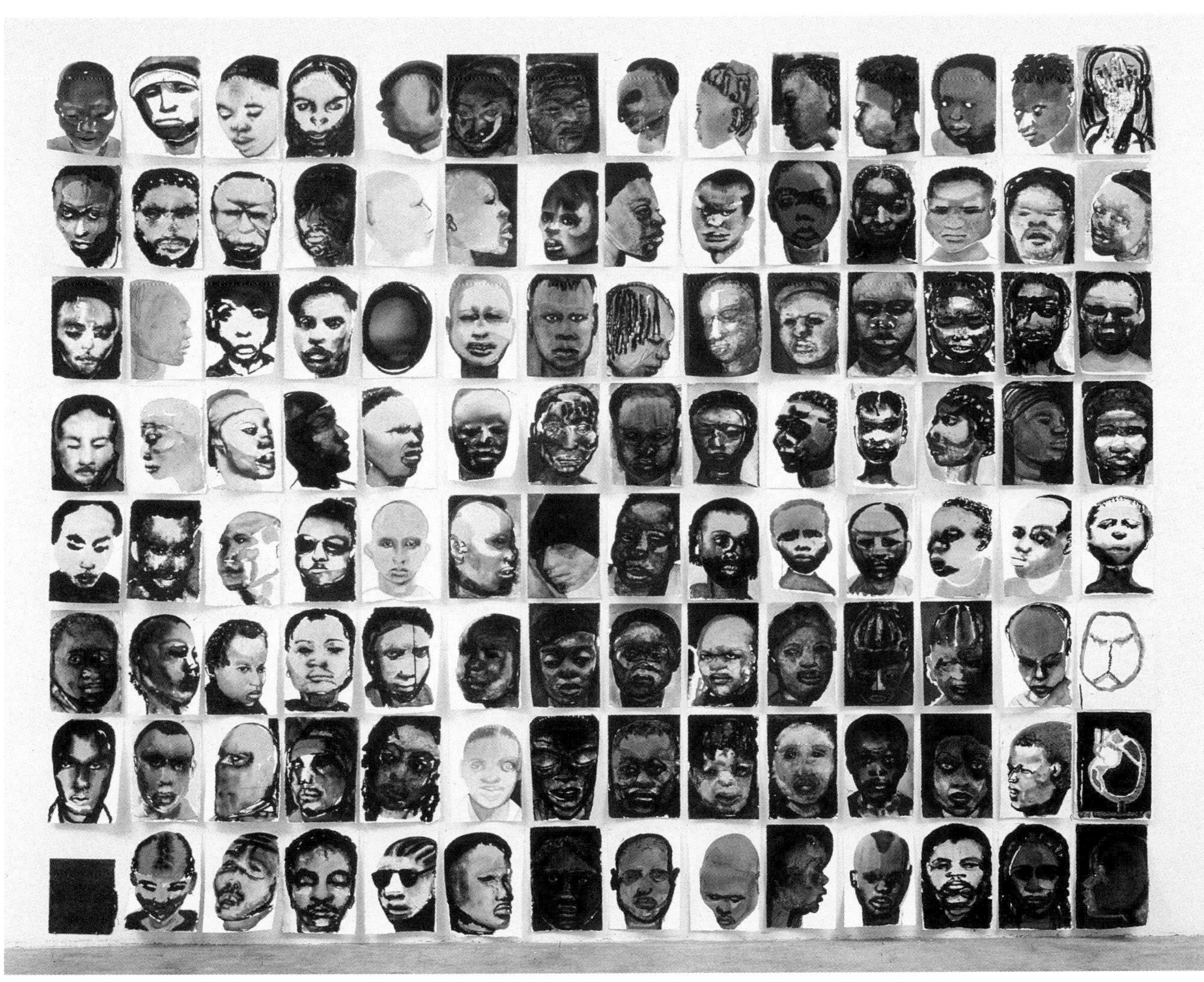

Marlene Dumas,
Black Drawings,
1991–92, cat. no. 2.

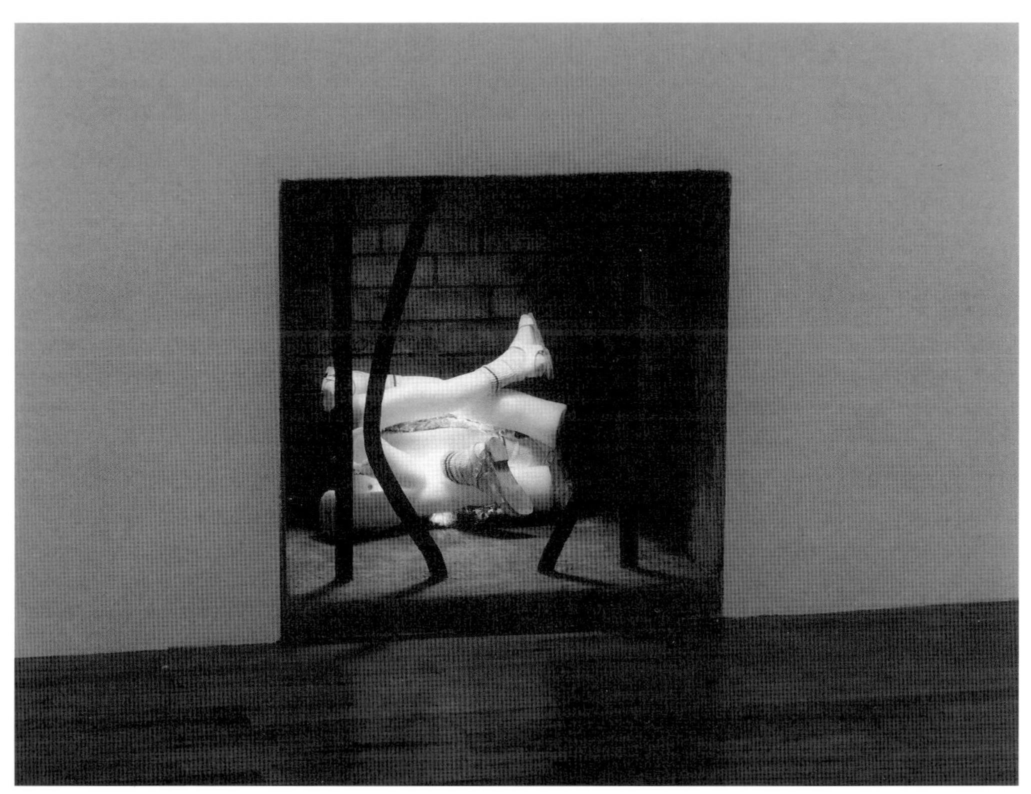

Robert Gober,
Untitled, 1994–95.

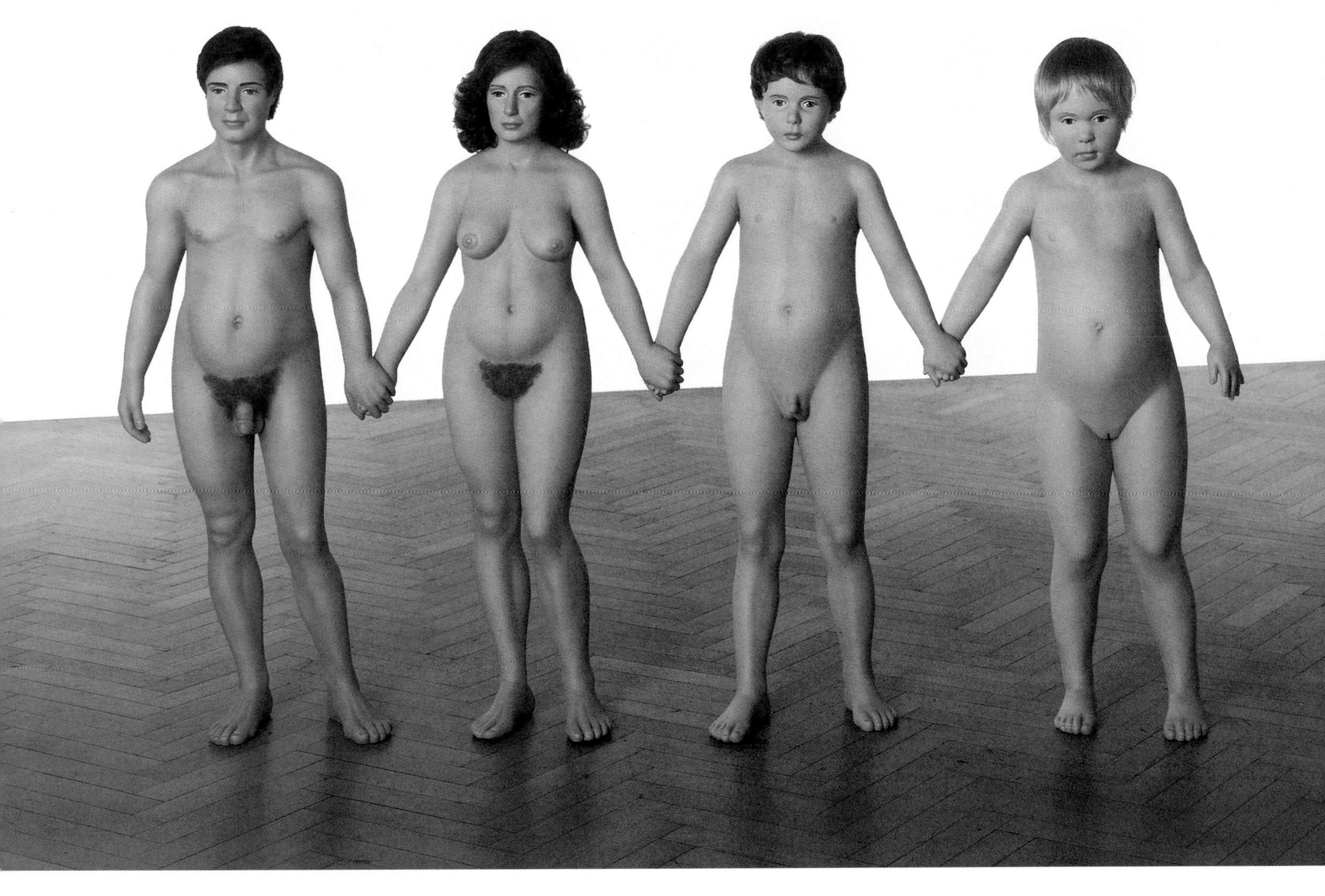

Charles Ray,
Family Romance, 1993.

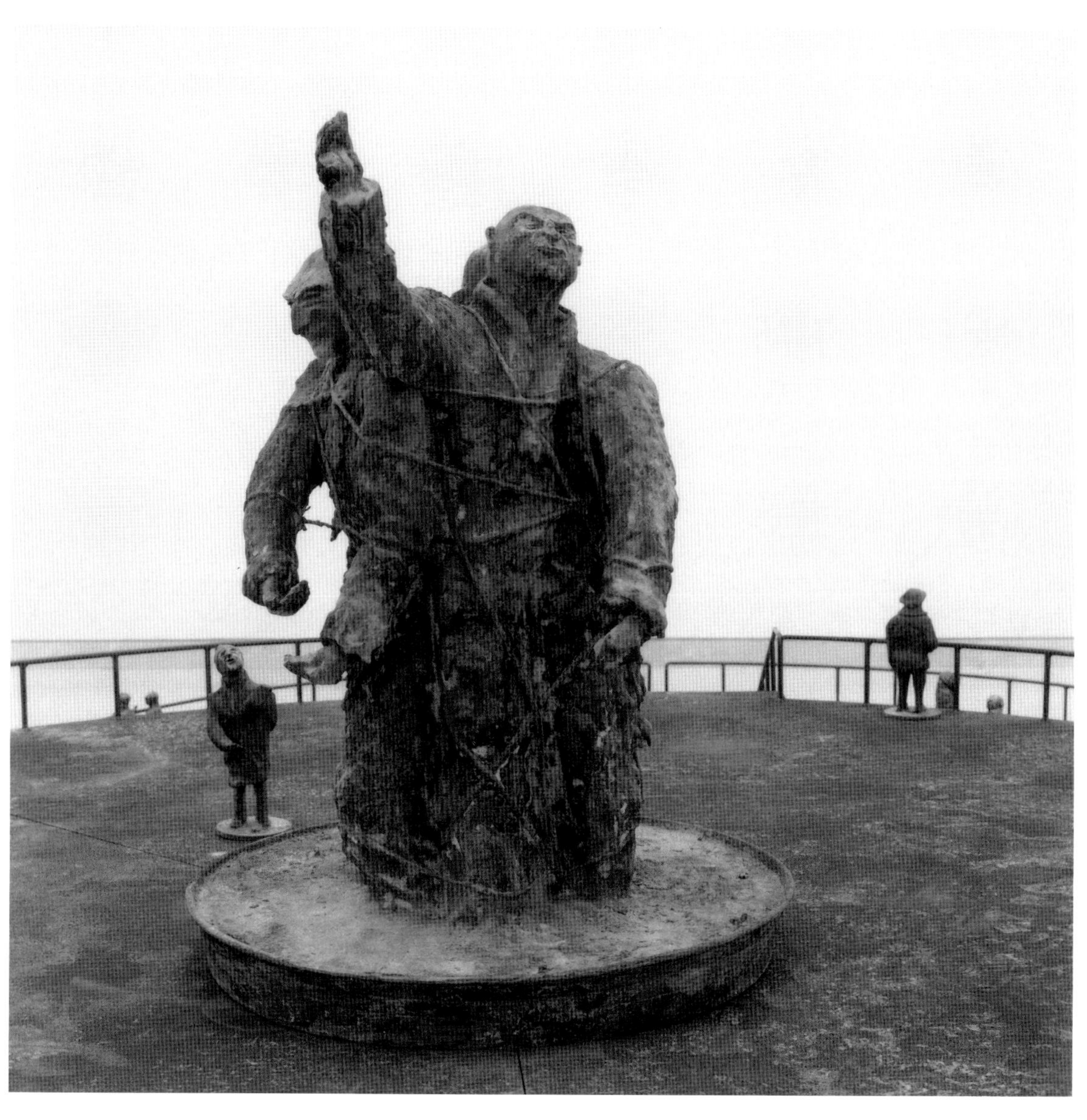

Thomas Schütte,
Grosser Respekt
(Large Respect),
1993–94, detail,
cat. no. 35.

DISTEMPER

Dissonant Themes in the Art of the 1990s

NEAL BENEZRA

OLGA M. VISO

Hirshhorn Museum and Sculpture Garden
Smithsonian Institution, Washington, D.C.
in association with
D. A. P./Distributed Art Publishers, New York

Published in 1996 by the Hirshhorn Museum and Sculpture Garden, Smithsonian Institution, Washington, D.C., in association with D.A.P./ Distributed Art Publishers, New York, on the occasion of an exhibition organized by the Hirshhorn Museum and Sculpture Garden and shown there from June 20 to September 15, 1996.

Major support for the exhibition was provided by a generous grant from the Lannan Foundation. Additional support was provided by Paul and Camille Oliver-Hoffmann, the British Council, The Henry Moore Foundation, the Institute for Foreign Affairs of the Federal Republic of Germany, and the Mondriaan Foundation Amsterdam.

Partial support for the publications accompanying the exhibition was provided by the Elizabeth Firestone Graham Foundation and the Washington Post Company.

Copyright © 1996 by Smithsonian Institution. All rights reserved. No part of this book may be reproduced or transmitted in any form or by any means, electronic or mechanical, including photocopying, recording, or any information storage and retrieval system, without the permission of the publishers.

Cover: Removal of the Statue of Lenin, Bucharest, Romania, March 1990.

Note to Reader: For complete captions, refer to the Catalog of the Exhibition (p. 127) or the List of Figure Illustrations (p. 130). Dimensions of works of art are provided by lenders; height precedes width.

Benezra, Neal David, 1953–
Distemper : dissonant themes in the art of the 1990s / Neal Benezra, Olga M. Viso.
p. cm.
Exhibition: Hirshhorn Museum and Sculpture Garden, Smithsonian Institution, Washington, D.C. June 20–Sept. 15, 1996.
Includes bibliographic references.
ISBN 1–881616–73–8 (pbk. : alk. paper)
1. Art, Modern—20th century—Exhibitions.
I. Viso, Olga M., 1966– .
II. Hirshhorn Museum and Sculpture Garden.
III. Title. N6487.W3H572 1996
709'.04'9074753—dc20

96–12624
CIP

The paper used in this publication meets the minimum requirements for the American National Standard for Information Sciences—Permanence of Paper for Printed Library Materials, ANSI Z39.48–1984.

Contents

Foreword

JAMES T. DEMETRION,
DIRECTOR

In November 1989 the Berlin Wall—that jagged and perverse symbol of politically induced schizophrenia—came crashing down amidst dancing and cheering crowds. The Cold War between the world's two "superpowers" had come to an end after more than four decades of the arms race, brinkmanship, confrontations, and stalemates. Euphoria reigned supreme, especially among the young and especially in the West (one wonders whether the ordinary citizens of Burundi or North Korea, for example, were euphoric). But the elation, if not the effects of the Wall's collapse, was short-lived—just a blip on the EKG of world history—as events moved relentlessly onward. Perhaps only jaded and aging pessimists understood that distemper and disquiet assert themselves as the usual condition of the world, and it was the euphoria that was abnormal and aberrant.

If one equates distemper with the norm (one is reminded of snafu, an acronym from World War II meaning—in its polite version—"situation normal, all fouled up"), the contrast between that sour mood and the ecstasy that prevailed in the autumn of 1989 is all the greater, and the ensuing and inevitable disillusion is all the more exaggerated and disheartening. The particular distemper of our times is reflected in various ways in the works of the ten artists represented in this exhibition. It may be worth noting that in 1989 those artists ranged in age from twenty-six to thirty-seven; the co-curators of this exhibition were twenty-three and thirty-six; and the undersigned was fifty-nine. Despite one's generational perception regarding the premise of distemper, and whether it is unique to our age or periodic, this exhibition captures a compelling mood that unites artists of distinct, imaginative, and varied careers. I am pleased that the Hirshhorn Museum can provide a context in which to view these works by artists from around the world.

I extend my gratitude to all of the Hirshhorn staff for bringing about the exhibition. Foremost credit must go to Neal Benezra, the museum's Director of Public Programs/ Chief Curator, who conceived the show and made the initial selection of the artists. His work load was eased considerably and the project was enhanced greatly by the arrival on staff in the spring of 1995 of Assistant Curator Olga M. Viso. She became a full partner in the undertaking, contributing in a substantial manner to the final selection of the artists and the works and to all aspects of the exhibition and the accompanying publications.

It is my pleasure, also, to extend my heartfelt gratitude to those foundations, corporations, governmental agencies, and individuals who provided the necessary financial and in-kind support without which this exhibition could not have been realized in its present form. The Lannan Foundation, in particular, awarded the Hirshhorn a most generous grant toward the exhibition and its related programming. Special thanks are extended to Patrick Lannan for his continued commitment to funding exhibitions of contemporary art, for which fundraising is often especially difficult. I am grateful, too, to Kathleen Merrill, the foundation's art program director, who was particularly encouraging of the project. In addition, I would like to thank Camille Oliver-Hoffmann, a trustee of the museum, and her husband, Paul, for their generous contribution toward the realization of this endeavor. I also acknowledge Ray Graham and the Elizabeth Firestone Graham Foundation for a grant toward the production of this catalog. The Washington Post Company, a benefactor of several Hirshhorn educational programs in the past, generously provided the printing of the exhibition's gallery guide. My thanks go to Rima Calderon for graciously offering her staff's time in overseeing the production of that important publication.

Additional support, for transportation- and travel-related costs associated with the exhibition, was provided by the British Council, The Henry Moore Foundation, the Institute for Foreign Affairs of the Federal Republic of Germany, and the Mondriaan Foundation Amsterdam. I am grateful to these organizations for their participation and assistance.

Preface and Acknowledgments

NEAL BENEZRA
OLGA M. VISO

Exhibitions devoted to contemporary art have become increasingly complex undertakings. Those representing the works of more than one artist soar exponentially in terms of organizational difficulty. The debt of exhibition curators to their own museum's staff is always enormous and generally insufficiently acknowledged, and we would like to begin our thanks with our colleagues at the Hirshhorn. One must inevitably start at the top. As indicated by his foreword, Director James T. Demetrion clearly questions some of the premises underlying the topic of this exhibition. That we nevertheless have proceeded with his full and enthusiastic support is a credit to his open-minded confidence in his staff. Former Deputy Director Stephen E. Weil often provided wise counsel and advice, as has Administrator Beverly Lang Pierce. In the early stages of the project, curators Amada Cruz, formerly on the staff of the Hirshhorn, and Phyllis Rosenzweig offered substantive and friendly recommendations. In developing this publication we were supported in exemplary fashion by Leslie R. Rabinovitz, a graduate student at the University of Southern California. Jane McAllister, Publications Manager, provided diligent and persistent editorial guidance and worked long hours on our behalf. Anna Brooke and the staff of the Hirshhorn library offered consistent and thorough support. The exhibition itself is the result of the experience and teamwork provided by Douglas Robinson, Chief Registrar, and Edward Schiesser, Chief of Exhibits, and their respective staffs, in particular, Penelope Brown and Bob Allen. The education and film programs were conceived and administered by Teresia Bush and Kelly Gordon, respectively. Sidney Lawrence, Head of Public Affairs, made an outstanding contribution in bringing the exhibition to public notice. As always, curatorial assistant Francis Woltz offered her enthusiastic support. Together with the Hirshhorn staff, we would like to thank John H. Brown and Janice Deputy for their determined fundraising efforts on behalf of this exhibition.

Beyond the Smithsonian we would like to offer our warm thanks to Sharon Helgason Gallagher, President, D.A.P./Distributed Art Publishers, for her determination to publish this catalog, and to Bethany Johns and Kathleen Oginski, whose design so effectively gives form to our ideas. On a personal note, we would like to acknowledge the important individuals in our lives, Maria Makela and John Gallagher, respectively, for their patience, thoughtful attention, and continual encouragement. Finally, a tremendous number of individuals offered support in a wide variety of ways, and we are pleased to name them here, with our sincere appreciation.

Carolyn Alexander
Paul Andriesse
Richard Armstrong
Roland Augustine
Steven Beyer
René Blouin
Ted Bonin
Dan Cameron
Bart Cassiman
Paula Cooper
Chantal Crousel
Jan Debbaut
Rosamund Felsen
Geoff Fischer
Konrad Fischer
Gary Garrells
Lawrence Gleeson
Marian Goodman
Louis Grachos
Kathy Halbreich
Selma Holo
Hudson
Frans L. E. Hulsman
Ghislaine Hussenot
Raphael Jablonka
Nicholas Ward Jackson
Marc Jancou
Annabella Johnson
Jay Jopling
Robert and Carrie Lehrman
Mike Le Tourneau
James Lingwood
Lawrence Luhring
Lisa Lyons
Alina Magnuska
Marvin and Elayne Mordes
Paola Morsiani
Philip Nelson
Steven Oliver
Sue Patterson
Janelle Reiring
Andrea Rose
Karsten Schubert
Fran Seegull
Natasha Sigmund
Steve Speil
Jack Tilton
Reyn van der Lugt
Helene Weiner
Angela Westwater
Donald Young

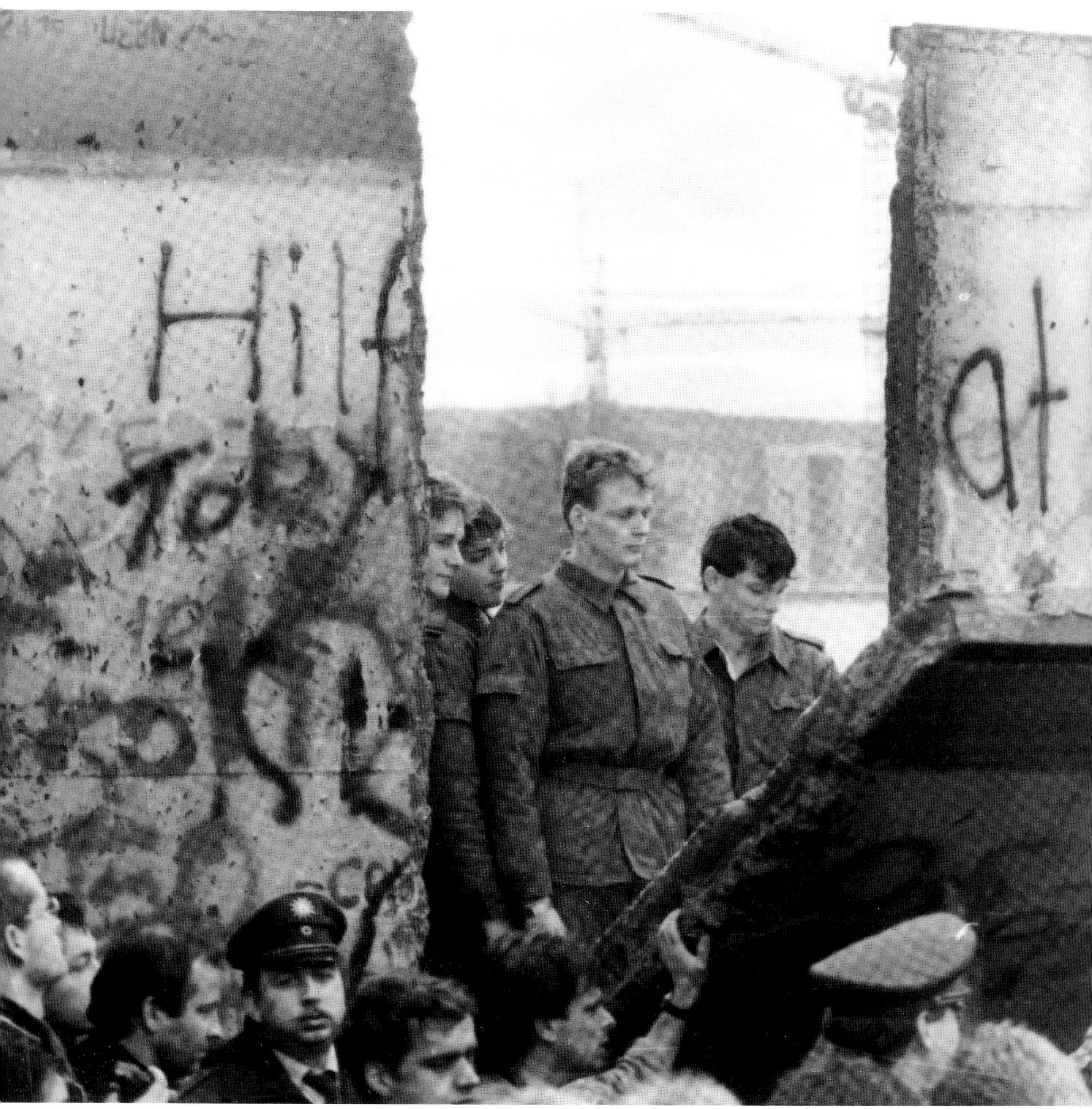

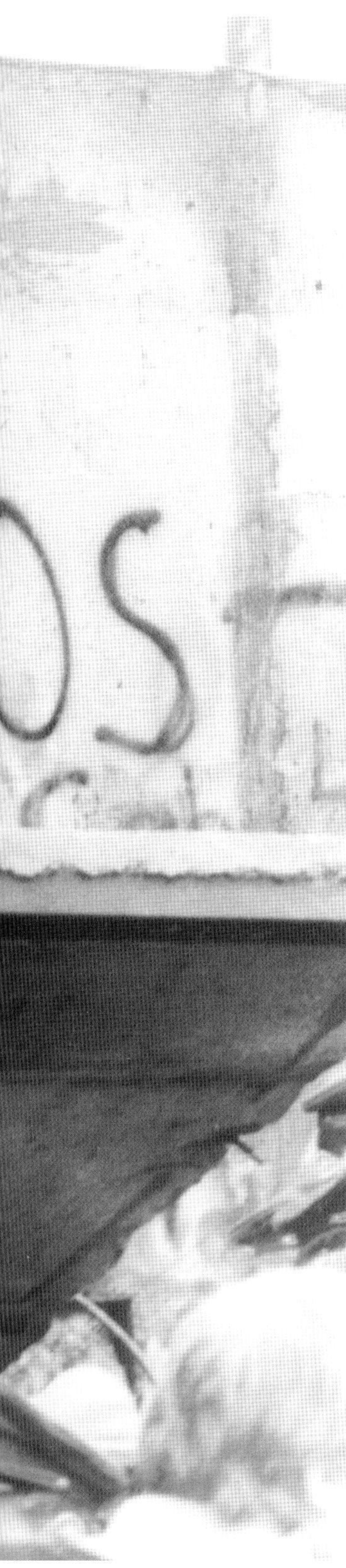

Fig. 1. Dismantling of the Berlin Wall, 1989.

Distemper:
Dissonant Themes in the Art of the 1990s

NEAL BENEZRA
OLGA M. VISO

In February 1989 the Soviet army ended its occupation of Afghanistan, a retreat that foretold the coming collapse of Communist Eastern Europe and the breathtaking fall of the Berlin Wall that autumn. By year's end, statues of Lenin were being dismantled throughout the Eastern bloc. In May 1989 a group of art students among the hundreds of thousands of citizens occupying Tiananmen Square in Beijing raised *The Goddess of Democracy*, a hastily constructed replica of the symbol of American freedom. Elsewhere and more recently, the end of apartheid in South Africa, the restoration of democracy in Chile and Argentina, and the temporary lessening of hostilities in the Middle East and Northern Ireland suggested that a "new world order" precipitated by the events of 1989 might be in the offing.

As early as the summer of 1989, an essay titled "The End of History?" by a policy planner in the United States Department of State, Francis Fukuyama, inspired impassioned commentary within a variety of political circles for its vision of the possibilities wrought by the fall of Communism. Fukuyama's article, which was published in the *National Interest*, and a subsequent book, *The End of History and the Last Man*[1] (1992), argued that current public events, particularly in Europe, represented a momentous shift in the public culture and history of the West. Contrary to the pessimism that Fukuyama considered to be characteristic of the preceding decades of the twentieth century, the events of 1989 augured great hopefulness for the 1990s and the twenty-first century beyond.

Briefly, Fukuyama's unabashed, even utopian, optimism seemed justifiable, as he gave voice to the ardor that so many shared: "What we may be witnessing is not just the end of the Cold War, or the passing of a particular period of postwar history, but the end of history as such: that is, the end point of mankind's ideological evolution and the universalization of Western liberal democracy as the final form of human government."[2] So strong was Fukuyama's enthusiasm that he concluded his article, rather remarkably, by commenting nostalgically on the challenges of the recent past: "The worldwide ideological struggle that called forth daring, courage, imagination, and idealism" will be replaced by the far more mundane demands of "economic calculation, the endless solving of technical problems, environmental concerns, and the satisfaction of sophisticated consumer demands," in which "there will be neither art nor philosophy, just the perpetual caretaking of the museum of human history."[3] For Fukuyama, writing precisely two hundred years after the French Revolution, the West seemed poised at the threshold of a new, if somewhat uninspired, golden age.

Yet events that have transpired in the 1990s are of a far different order from those Fukuyama envisioned. Only two years into the decade, columnist E. J. Dionne, Jr., wrote in the *Washington Post* of a series of problems that had been unleashed with the fall of ideological debates of past decades, among them, "the decline of national economies; the collapse of big ideas; the impulse to fragment; and the search for choices beyond government and the market." The world Dionne described was riven by tension and insecurity. If Fukuyama had been unapologetically optimistic, Dionne skeptically considered the changes that the end of Communism had brought:

> *With weakened national governments and with the old ideologies lacking the ability to explain everything, individuals and small groups throughout the democratic world are turning inward. On the left, for example, concerns over class and economics often give way to a focus on race, gender and culture. On the right, there is a renewal of nationalism and, in some cases, xenophobia.*[4]

The term Dionne affixed to this international state of mind—and which we have appropriated in part as the title and underlying premise of this exhibition—was "democratic distemper." While a disaffected state of the world may not be new—indeed the etymology of the word "distemper" has deep roots—its implications are intriguing in regard to contemporary art. "Distemper" appears as early as the fourteenth century in the context of natural science as "disturbing due proportion." Chaucer and Shakespeare both used the word to describe the misfunctioning of the body, and the expression has often been applied to human behavior to mean "disturbance of humour or temper; ill-humour; ill-temper; uneasiness; disaffection." By the seventeenth century the term had assumed a decidedly social and political thrust, as references to "civil and political distemper" abound.[5] Taken together, the meanings of "distemper" aptly conjure, we believe, a widespread malaise and disaffection prevalent in contemporary life and art.

As a starting point to discuss aspects of Western art of the 1990s, "distemper" is meant to suggest a social and cultural anxiety that permeates the West as the end of the millennium approaches. The ten artists in the exhibition—Mirosław Bałka, Marlene Dumas, Robert Gober, Mona Hatoum, Mike Kelley, Guillermo Kuitca, Charles Ray, Doris Salcedo, Thomas Schütte, and Rachel Whiteread—give form to this anxiety in their work. The artists range widely in their use of media and their approaches to form and content. Any attempt to classify so varied a group beyond this general spirit is invariably fraught with difficulty. Linking them, nonetheless, is a shared if diverse response to the political, social, and cultural circumstances of the Western world in the 1990s and the challenges of making meaningful art in this new context. Ultimately, the ten artists are brought together here to suggest a broad-based internationalism in which artists from many continents can be considered to share a creative purpose and humanistic intent that might bridge divisions of geography, ethnicity, gender, and other boundaries. Rather than continue to seek out and respect differences—as has been done extensively on the cultural stage in recent years—"Distemper" explores commonalities within diversity.

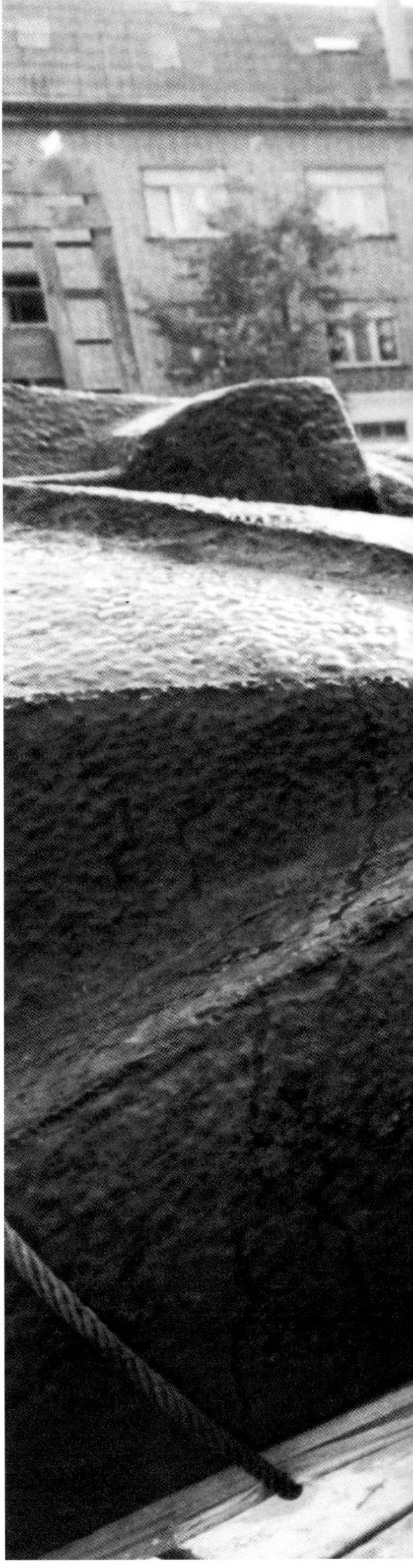

Fig. 2. Removal of the statue of Lenin, Valmiera, Latvia, October 1990.

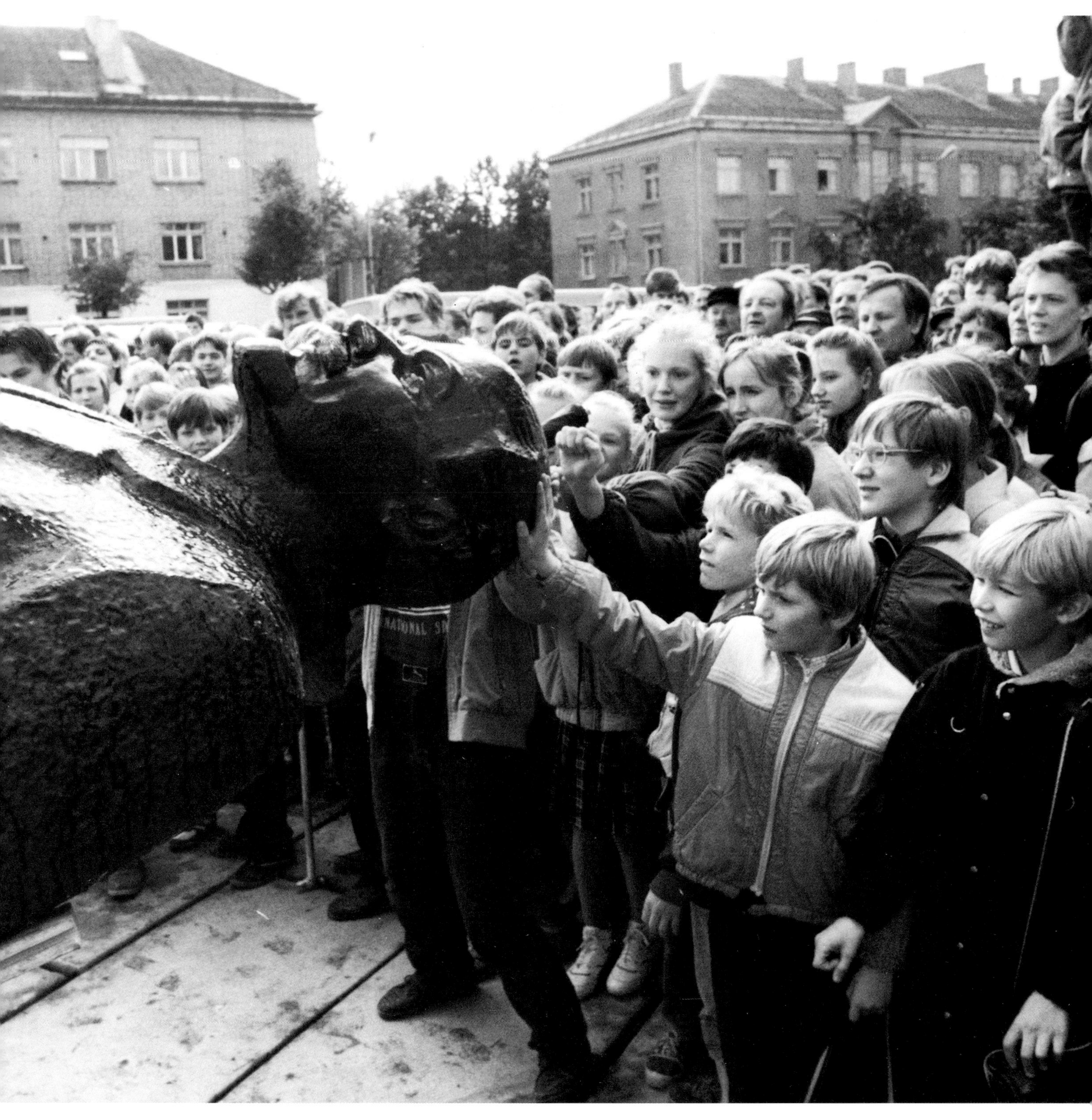

A number of general themes underlie the work in this exhibition. The first is the dissonant nature of time and memory. Registering moments of rupture between the past and the present, time is often rendered by the artists as if in a state of collision or suspension. The treatment of time, a potent underpinning in both the figurative and the nonfigurative works, shows a conflicted nostalgia for the past and a growing unease with the present. The artists' assertion of memory in their work may be viewed in light of a larger cultural crisis in the structure of time. In the face of deflated ideologies and an expanding information age that is furiously transforming the ways we live and remember, society's understanding of its past, present, and future is severely in flux.

Second is an evolving notion of beauty, a term long associated with the arts but one that in recent years has often assumed pejorative overtones. Many artists and critics since the late 1980s have dismissed work in which formal considerations seem to outweigh content. Several artists included in "Distemper" bring form and content into a tense and provocative balance that proposes a reconsideration of the understanding of beauty in the 1990s.

Third is the unusual manner in which some of the artists conjoin private existence with the public sphere through the ritualization of contemporary life. This theme is seen in the fascination with the objects and environments of daily existence—furniture, domestic architecture, and public spaces—as well as in the psychological implications of seemingly common experience.

The ten artists represented in this exhibition were born between 1952 and 1963 and came to artistic maturity in the 1980s. All bear witness to the shifting sands on which the art of that decade was based. In retrospect, the art of the 1980s is notable for several important and intriguing developments. The early years of the decade were driven by the power and passion of Neo-Expressionism, an international movement dominated by oversized canvases and emotional gestures, and by a bustling commercial market. Young artists emerging in the later 1980s, in direct reaction, moved away from such large and ambitious statements, and from painting generally. This generation viewed the medium with contempt, considering it a commodity to be bought and sold and thus incapable of social commentary. If painting and Neo-Expressionism were suspect, so too were the premises underlying modernism, and young Neo-Conceptualists at the beginning of the decade replaced it with work that brought together Minimalist aesthetics, a variety of photographic media, and a concentration on subject matter devoted to the body as a vehicle for a range of commentaries relating to identity.

While the directions of the late 1980s have influenced the artists in this exhibition, the works in "Distemper" diverge in several crucial respects. Working in the aftermath of political ideology, the artists represented here espouse no particular artistic doctrine. The effect has been liberating as artists are no longer burdened by traditional debates concerning originality versus appropriation, conventional media (painting and sculpture) versus time-based arts (film, photography, performance, and video), or the figure versus abstraction. Rather than engage in ideological critique and clichéd conceptual strategies, they look beyond the often hermetic debates of the art world in search of content and an aesthetic that are at once more public and more open-ended. Choosing to work with traditional media in often unconventional ways, the artists in "Distemper" perceive their roles as artists in a new manner. In general, they view themselves less as social critics and more as cultural barometers whose works measure and calibrate a general unease and uncertainty with the world at large.

Twilight Memory

> *Twilight is that moment of the day that foreshadows the night of forgetting, but that seems to slow time itself, an in-between state in which the last light of the day may still play out its ultimate marvels. It is memory's privileged time.*[6]
> —Andreas Huyssen, 1994

In his book *Twilight Memories: Marking Time in a Culture of Amnesia* (1995) cultural historian Andreas Huyssen considers memory one of the key concerns as this century ends. Huyssen makes the surprising statement that memory has, for all intents and purposes, replaced history. His claim seems paradoxical in a contemporary culture generally described as amnesiac, in which generational memory is seen as fading, elusive, and consonant with forgetting. The disturbing dismissal of the Jewish Holocaust as the substance of myth and legend by various segments of today's youth attests to the tenuous place of history and memory in our time. For Huyssen, the current obsession with memory is a symptom of a desire to counteract the proclivity to forget. In his view, that preoccupation is manifested in contemporary culture by the revival of period styles, the resurgent need for monuments and memorials, and the proliferation over the past decade of commemorative architecture and museums devoted to some of the major catastrophes of this century, most notably the Holocaust.

Huyssen further explains the present cultural engagement with the past as symptomatic of a crisis in the structure of temporality, or society's understanding of time and its place within the historical continuum. He sees the crisis as the result of failed ideologies and, in particular, of the deflation of the modern view of progress. For a world that no longer looks to the future with hope and expectation, the past seems equally blurred and confusing. Huyssen characterizes the current crisis in confidence in the same terms as Dionne, but he takes the notion further:

> *The twenty-first century looms like a repetition: one of bloody nationalisms and tribalisms, of religious fundamentalism and intolerance that we thought had been left behind in some darker past. The increasing two-way interpenetration of First and Third World adds yet another dimension. Rather than moving together, if at different paces, into the future, we have accumulated so many non-synchronicities in our present that a very hybrid structure of temporality seems to be emerging.*[7]

More than just another bout with pessimism, Huyssen contends that what we are living through is a transformation of the modern structure of time. The process is further complicated by the unknown exigencies of a high-tech world in which the past, present, and future are constantly being altered by the pace of newly introduced technologies.[8]

According to Huyssen, the changing worldview and the rise of the media age profoundly effect the ways in which we understand cultural memory. He observes that the more memory is stored on data banks and image tracks, the less our culture is willing and able to remember. Ultimately, he sees society's current assertion of memory as a struggle for history and a form of "temporal anchoring" against high-tech amnesia. It represents, to Huyssen,

> *the attempt to slow down information processing, to resist the dissolution of time in the synchronicity of the archive, to recover a mode of contemplation outside the universe of simulation and fast-speed information and cable networks, to claim some anchoring space in a world of puzzling and often threatening heterogeneity, non-synchronicity, and information overload.*[9]

An obsession with memory is prevalent in much contemporary art,[10] evidenced by many of the artists represented in "Distemper" who strive to give form to the fissure between the past and the present that Huyssen so eloquently describes. Temporal rupture is most apparent in the art of Mirosław Bałka, Robert Gober, and Doris Salcedo, whose works materially register the collision and contusion of memory through the physical conjunction of objects. The familiar forms on which their sculptures are based trigger deeply personal remembrances and associations in the viewer that connect personal and shared experience. The fleeting and transitory nature of the images and moments evoked resemble the qualities of twilight, giving credence to Huyssen's evocative metaphor.

In an effort to suspend the twilight of memory, Salcedo, for example, buries objects in concrete. She passionately struggles to delay the inevitable demise of the individuals whose memory the artifacts conjure. Rachel Whiteread similarly attempts to anchor the fleeting nature of the past in the present. Her casts of domestic interiors and the spaces around household objects give form to the transience and immediacy of life. Qualities of impermanence also inspire Guillermo Kuitca, whose paintings of domestic and public spaces blur the boundaries between the past and the present, between lived and structured experience. Their non-synchronous nature is further complicated by the artist's evanescent presence in the work.

Mike Kelley's engagement with memory is more analytical. Exploring themes of failure and sublimation, the artist excavates often painful experiences that have been deeply buried in the cultural psyche. In his recent work, Kelley tackles society's fascination with repressed memory by delving into his own past as a basis on which to investigate the issue. Thomas Schütte's "anti-monuments" also tap into a collective unconscious. Addressing the significance of public monuments in a post–Cold War world, Schütte questions the ability of traditional forms of commemoration to serve as effective carriers of memory and meaning in our time.

As Huyssen and the works in "Distemper" would suggest, today's "mnemonic convulsions"[11] are serving as a powerful stimulus for cultural and artistic creativity. Perhaps another symptom of the desire to connect with the past is seen in many artists' reengagement with more traditional forms of artmaking, as well as a renewed, albeit ambivalent, interest in aesthetic theories that have long since faded.

Fig. 3. Replica of the Statue of Liberty, Tiananmen Square, Beijing, May 1989.

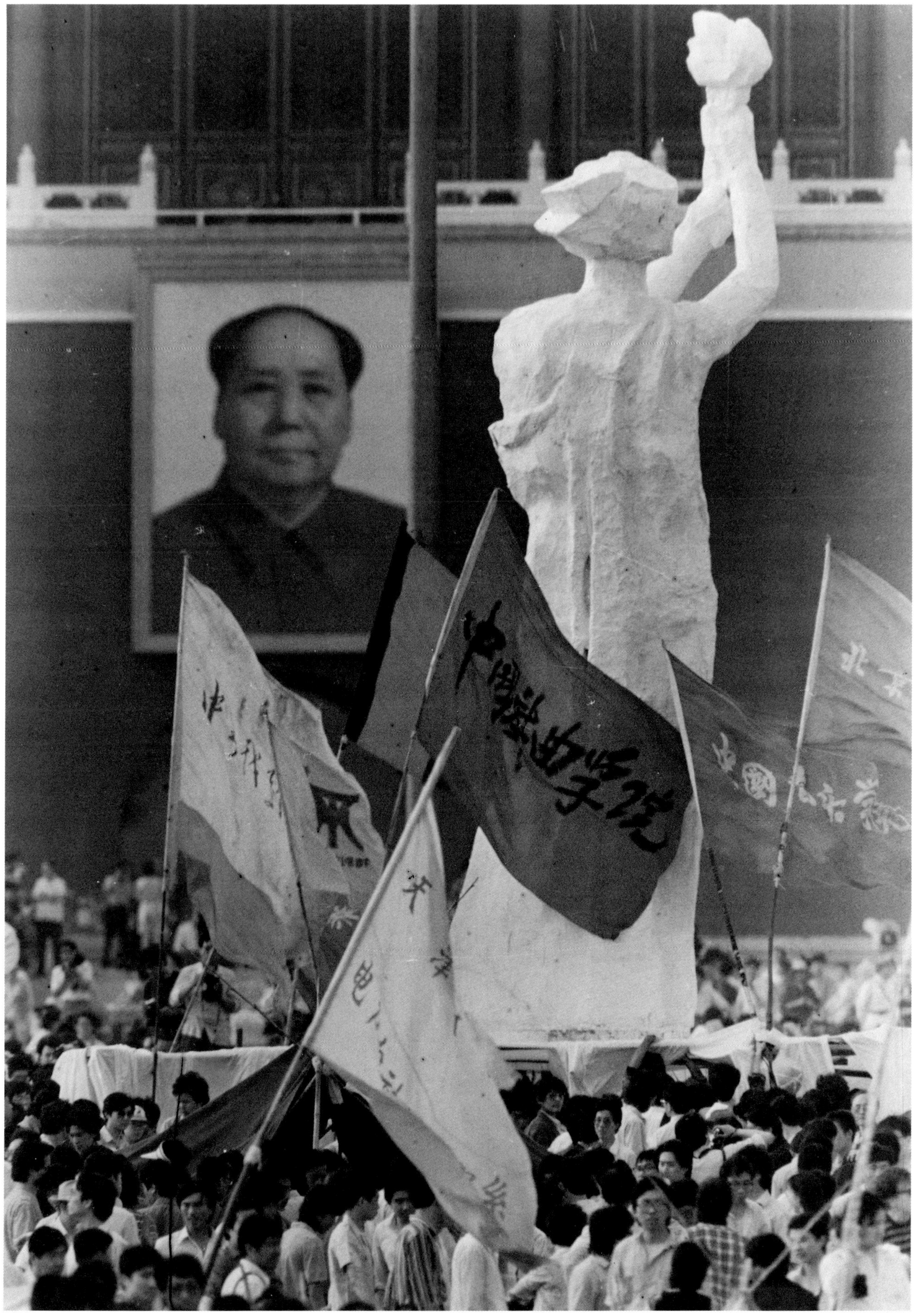
中国戏曲学院

Beauty: The Invisible Dragon

> *When politics is made the focus of art, beauty does not wait to be ousted from the process. Beauty deferentially withdraws, knowing its place. Beauty is not superfluous, not a luxury, but it is a necessity that waits upon the satisfaction of other necessities.*[12]
> —Peter Schjeldahl, 1994

While the word "beautiful" may not come immediately to mind when discussing works of art deemed anxious and despairing, the term curiously befits a great deal of the art included in "Distemper." This dissonance may be attributed to many of the artists' querulous encounter with aspects of the beautiful. The characterization of contemporary art in these terms seems suspect in an art world dominated since the late 1980s by content-driven political art in which beauty has had little, if any, resonance. Indeed, artists of the 1990s, piqued by an impassioned social consciousness, have often dispensed with qualities typically associated with the beautiful (harmony, visual pleasure, order, quality, and exactitude) to advocate an art that is, conversely, often discomforting and unsettling to look at, and didactic in its tenacious attack of stereotypes and biases generally held by society as "truth." In the current political climate, the concept of beauty in art has been supplanted by content and effectively relegated to embodying the ideals of an earlier age. Moreover, objects considered too pleasing to the eye have been associated with frivolity and the extravagance of the art market of the 1980s. Such does the general distrust of beauty persist today that the suggestion of a work's aesthetic value implies an unacceptable lack of meaning.

The divorce of beauty and content in recent art has troubled many artists and critics, most notably Dave Hickey, who in 1993 published a series of essays on the subject that characterized beauty as "The Invisible Dragon."[13] Questioning his own resistance to the idea of pleasure in contemporary art, Hickey explored the current critical focus. His essays trace the concept's historical context, which serve to remind us that beauty and content have coexisted for centuries in the history of art, including much of the present century. Using examples from the sixteenth and seventeenth centuries, he explains how beauty was employed by artists and their patrons to afford enjoyment as well as power. As a means to enfranchise audiences and advance shared values, the visually pleasing could also be irrevocably political. He explains, "Images argued for things—for doctrines, rights, privileges, ideologies, territories and reputations."[14] As Hickey further suggests, they often implied provocative and subversive content in the guise of the beautiful.

The implications of beauty today are vastly different from those in the past. In Hickey's view, we are currently being denied a direct appeal to beauty by a "therapeutic institution"—what he describes as a loose confederation of museums, universities, bureaus, foundations, publications, and other arts institutions governed by an overriding consciousness that has learned to doubt the appearance of images.[15] This distrust is born of an insistent need to justify art's place and function in society. The defensiveness in the art world may be attributed to many factors, including the debates about identity that emerged in the late 1980s and early 1990s in response to multiculturalism. Defensiveness has been further exacerbated by the raging political controversy concerning public funding of the arts that also began in the late 1980s. By constantly having to justify itself (or thinking that it must), the art world has curiously moved art away from the very objectives it sought to embrace. Rather than encourage the open-ended and inclusive, the contemporary art world has increasingly been accused of engaging in a closed dialog, and consequently has been labeled as self-serving in the desire for political correctness.

In his 1994 essay "Beauty," art critic Peter Schjeldahl builds on many of Hickey's ideas. In his words, much of the resistance to beauty may be "motivated by the disappointment with beauty's failure to redeem the world."[16] He insists that beauty need not be imprisoned by its former uses, and he proposes that it be seen as a fluid and changing concept that admits qualities of the unexpected and the bizarre. For Schjeldahl, it is the simultaneous experience of attraction and repulsion that makes the encounter with the beautiful jarring and memorable. One is reminded of the shock and intrigue that Edouard Manet's *Olympia*, 1863, caused in its time, when the artist's depiction of his model was widely viewed as ugly, common, and profane. Although our eyes have grown accustomed to his aesthetic, Manet heralded a reconsideration of what was considered beautiful in that age. His radicalism, as Caravaggio's before him, was the reintroduction of beauty in a vernacular sense.

The interpretation of beauty in terms of the familiar implies qualities of the present that distinguish it from the "historically freighted, abstract piety of Beauty," or beauty in the idealized, classical sense.[17] The vernacular conception recalls the writings of Charles Baudelaire, the French poet and critic, who, more than one hundred years ago, characterized beauty as encompassing the morbid and the perverse as well as the strangely familiar. In his seminal essay "The Painter of Modern Life" (1863), Baudelaire made a similar distinction between "general" beauty (as expressed by the classic poets and artists) and "particular" beauty, which he described as the "sketch of manners" of the present.[18]

Many of the artists of "Distemper" draw on the vernacular in an attempt to unearth beauty from that which is most familiar. Working with objects associated with the mundane aspects of everyday, lived experience, Mirosław Bałka, Guillermo Kuitca, Doris Salcedo, and Rachel Whiteread focus on the particular intimacy that exists between individuals and objects of daily use. A chair, a bed, and a floorboard register the marks of humanity over time. For Salcedo, it is the presence of life in such objects that makes them beautiful, and she (as her above-listed colleagues) struggles to recover those traces while tapping into collective memory. Charles Ray looks to the vernacular to connect with human experience, and in his most recent work he explores the dialectic of beauty with a clever yet disconcerting wit that distinguishes all his sculptures, including those inspired by mannequins. In Ray's hands the vernacular holds dual possibilities, providing a comfortable familiarity that is reassuring, as well as a glimpse into a reality that is odd, discordant, and even grotesque.

Following pages:
Fig. 4. Palestinian women carrying pictures of incarcerated relatives, Khan Yunis, Gaza Strip, June 1994.

These rich and complicated ideas of beauty in the familiar recall the nineteenth-century notion of the sublime in which beauty and terror were often curiously intermingled. First formulated by Edmund Burke in his *Philosophical Inquiry into*

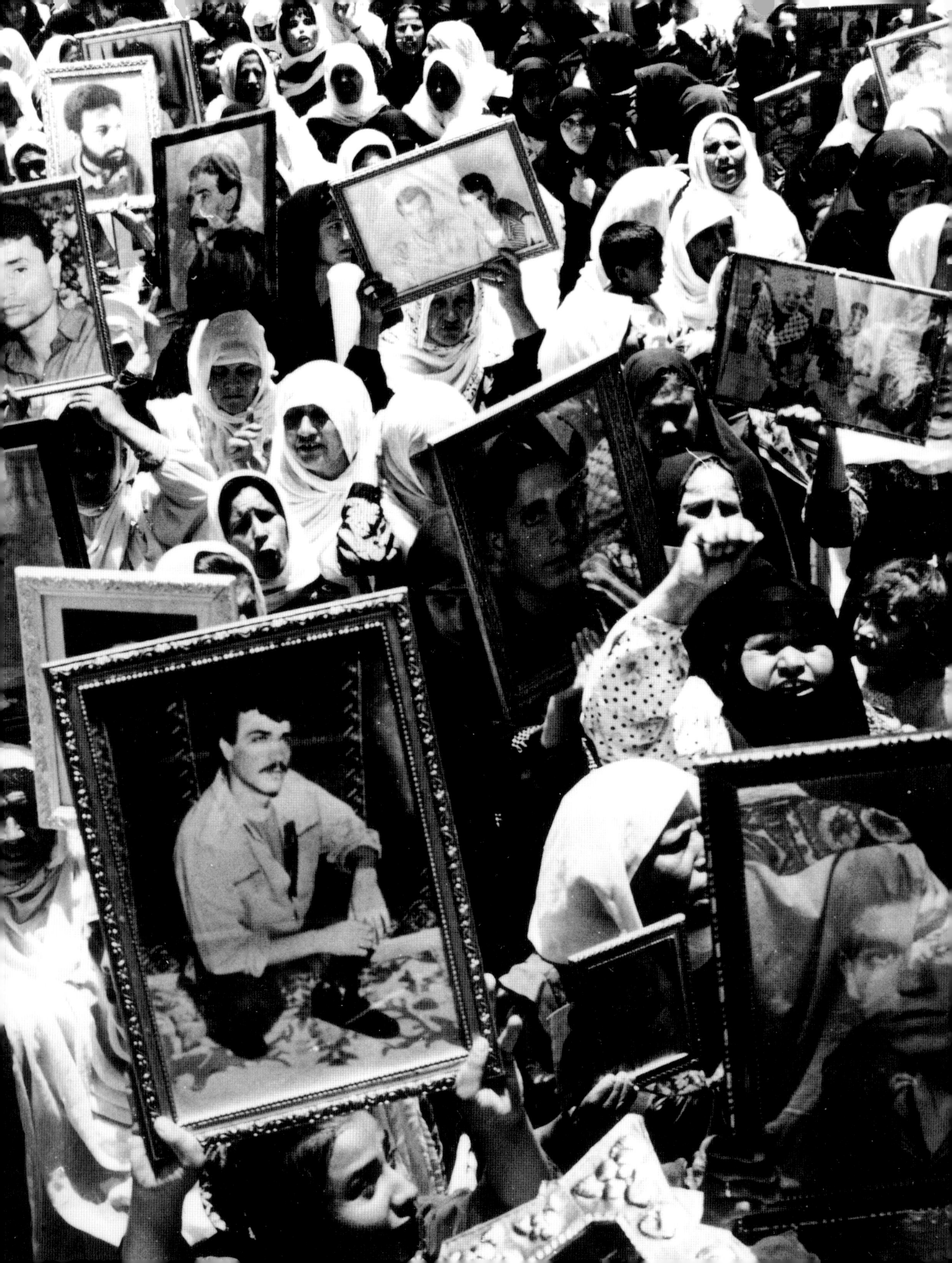

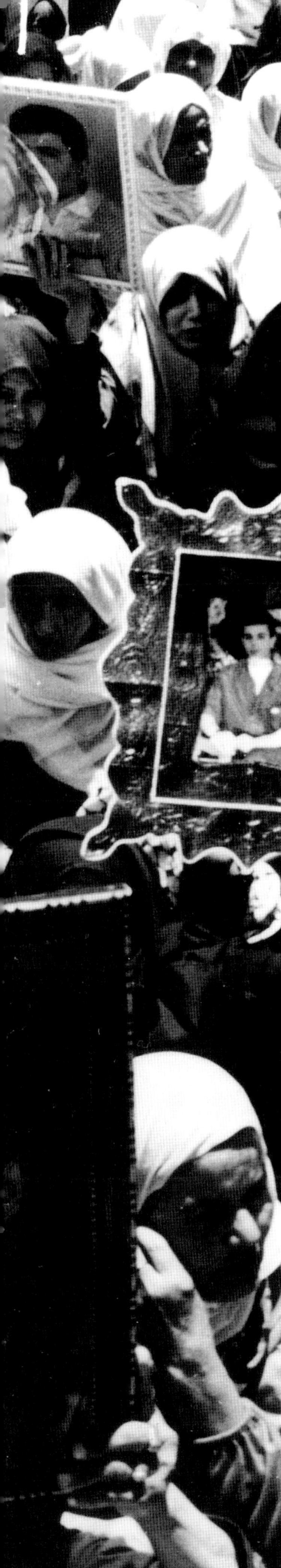

the Origin of Our Ideas of the Sublime and the Beautiful (1756), sublime beauty was typically associated with the awe-inspiring qualities in nature and thus called upon the viewer to ponder his or her spiritual existence in the world. For Marlene Dumas, the grotesque and the beautiful are irrevocably, even rhetorically, intertwined. As viewers, we are drawn to her sensuous figures painted in lush, lurid colors. Our deep engagement with her pictures, however, is gradually and assuredly interrupted by the visually discordant colors, the distortion of the body, and the unexpected, gruesome contexts in which the figure is often depicted. We are simultaneously seduced and repelled by their apparent subtlety and deepening complexity, for they propose to unmask the Western conception of beauty, much as Manet's *Olympia* did. The same sensation characterizes the work of Salcedo, whose battered furniture objects reverberate with a disquieting elegance. As we succumb to the rich, gritty surfaces, we are suddenly overtaken by a jarring sense of alarm, or a gnawing feeling of unease. As the fragments of human bone and past lives emerge from the surface of her sculptures, they take on a new dimension, revealing the sinister aspects of human nature that lie below the sensuous surface.

In the works of these and other artists included in "Distemper," one might say that beauty disarms the viewer. Once disarmed, disturbing content is slowly revealed. Mona Hatoum's sculptures and installations often bear this duality, and her inviting objects, often spare and minimal in their aesthetic, begin to take on macabre qualities. Both unstable and changing, the surfaces of her seemingly abstract sculptures teem and pulsate with life, evoking bodily images of evisceration and disembowelment. A similar intrigue draws us to Robert Gober's sculptures. The delicate pattern of the upholstered chair in his installation in this exhibition reveals a curious weave of ribbon and dismembered body parts. The corporeal presence triggers chilling thoughts of physical assault and tap deeply into our subconscious.

Content in the guise of the beautiful represents an important and even radical (re)direction for the art of the 1990s. The reassertion of the formal as consonant with meaning confirms Hickey's heralding of the reentry of the dragon, the mythical creature of ancient lore whose presence—as beauty—quietly hovers in the wings of the art world's critical consciousness.

A Reticent Public Voice

> *Hand in hand with skepticism about all Utopias goes, quite understandably, skepticism about the various types of manifestoes of the ideological mentality.*[19]
> —Václav Havel, 1985

In his 1985 essay "An Anatomy of Reticence," the Czech playwright-turned-president Václav Havel ruminates on the character of Eastern European public culture in the late twentieth century. The skepticism that Havel ascribes to the populace of Hungary, Poland, and the former Czechoslovakia, in particular, is born of the tortuous history of the region in this century, which has so often provided the battleground for competing armies and ideologies. The tragic failures of extravagant political and military ambitions and the grandiose utopianism that underpinned them have bred a broad-based and deep-seated cynicism. Although in times of peace, public monuments to such ambitions are often rendered invisible, in the midst of recent crises they have just as frequently signified the banishment of oppression or been the focus of dreams, as the iconoclastic treatment of images of Lenin throughout Eastern Europe and the appropriation of the quintessential symbol of American democracy to serve the dream of liberty in Beijing reveal.

Far from these self-conscious expressions of public sentiment, another form of public voice is being heard today. Havel describes the response of Eastern Europeans as distrustful of societal culture and filled instead with a "deepened sense of irony and self-irony, together with humor and black humor, and perhaps most important in this context, an intense fear of pathos and sentimentality, and of overstatement."[20] For Havel, this is a spirit of reticence. Although he wrote of such restraint well before the fall of Communism, his words have broader implications in time and place for the art of this decade. In essence, his worldview mixes hope and skepticism. Havel's fervent belief in the possibilities of culture and its art is tinged with irony, based on the shared experience and memory of the cataclysmic history of our declining century. Into the gap left by a communal, positivist culture, artists have come to assert the power of private experience, albeit without expansive ambitions or illusions regarding its exemplary nature or public implication. Reticence does indeed unite the work of several of the artists represented in this exhibition, who ritualize the experience of everyday life through their examinations of objects and environments that mediate between individual and public life.

The worldview engendered by this paradoxical conjunction of hope and skepticism can be seen in the presentation of private spaces and objects of daily domestic use in the context of art. This strategy is readily evident in the work of Mirosław Bałka and Rachel Whiteread, both of whom have postulated with quiet consistency the domestic environment as worthy of public consideration in the form of sculpture. Balka's work is the more intimate, as he has transformed the beds, tables, and floorboards of his family's former home and his current studio into the materials of his sculpture. Whiteread maintains a slightly more distanced stance, seeking out and reconstituting objects such as mattresses or bathtubs that are worn from years of use and redolent with psychological associations. There is little sentimentality and pathos to be found in the work of these artists. Partly, they evidence a prevailing Minimalist aesthetic, although it is a Minimalism of modesty and not mere formalism.

Other artists have explored similar territory in a related if somewhat more theatrical or political manner. Mona Hatoum, who began her career as a performance artist, in recent years has chosen objects such as bedsprings and cribs and imbued them with a nuanced but no less precarious human presence. She has done so by replacing a crib mattress with nearly invisible piano wire, for example, or by inserting red-hot heating elements in an upright bed frame. In other works, she has caused suspended bedsprings to move with painful slowness. In the process, Hatoum's objects have attained a quiet but thoroughly disconcerting power that combines the drama of her earlier performances with a newfound restraint.

Fig. 5. Dedication of the Vietnam Veterans Memorial, Washington, D.C., November 1982.

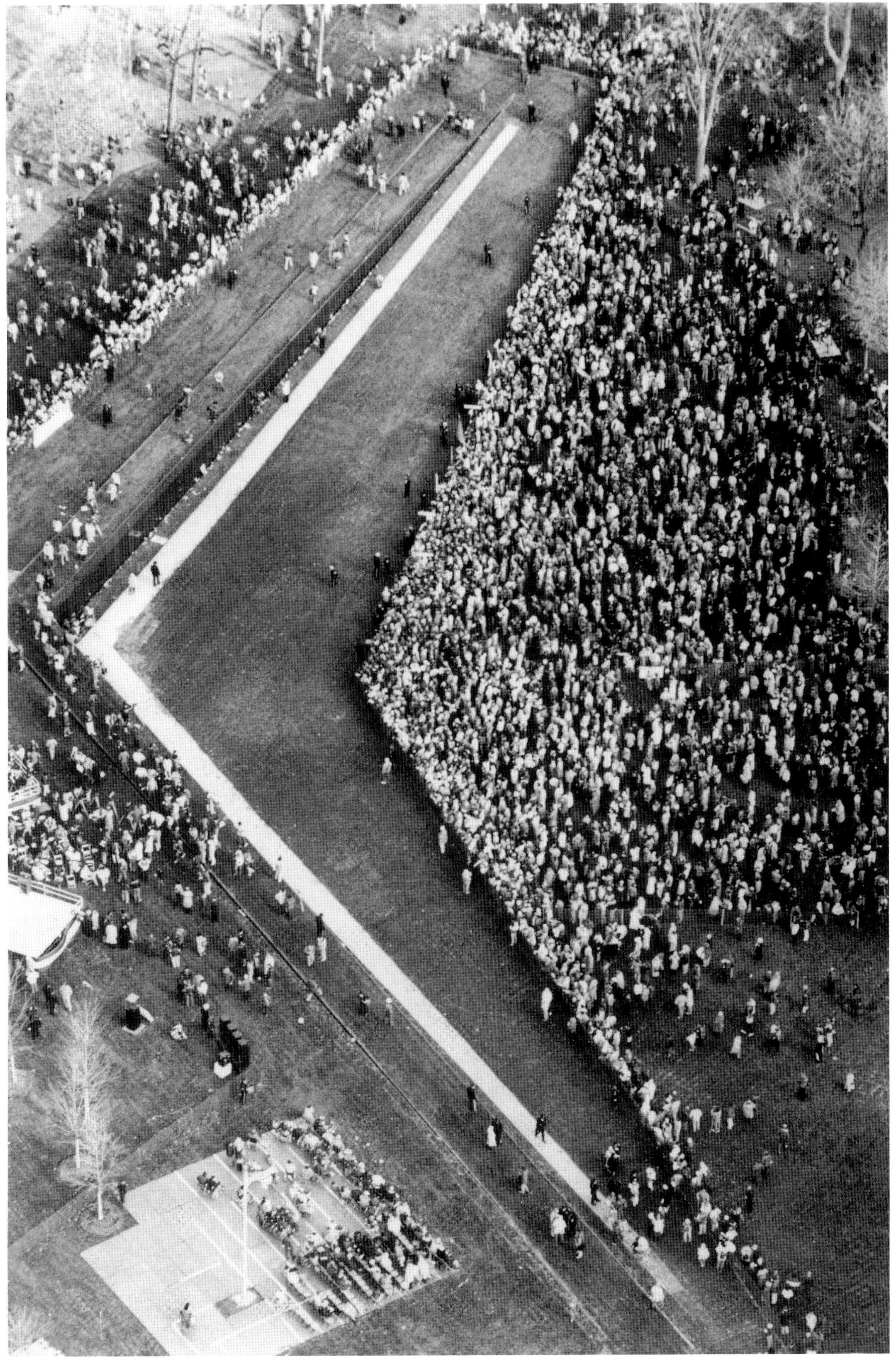

Similarly, Doris Salcedo has achieved a new type of political art, one based in a highly personal archaeology in which she "researches and excavates" a particular site of violence in her native Colombia. She then intervenes in the objects that are witness to the indescribable loss that family members have experienced. By embedding the most modest and barely visible fragments of bones or household items in the surfaces of her sculptures, she transforms mundane objects into vernacular reliquaries of the most profound authority.

Guillermo Kuitca attains a similarly redolent expression, through painted depictions of environments conspicuous for their absence of humanity. His is an architecture of allusion, in which humanity is relegated to memory. The presence of the figure in theaters, prisons, and even genealogical charts is reduced to implication and poetic inference.

One of the principal mechanisms employed by all the "Distemper" artists in projecting private experience into the public sphere is the intentional confusion of scale and of indoor and outdoor placement. Although a Surrealist such as René Magritte employed these devices throughout his career, he did so to thrust our most basic perceptions of physical reality into doubt. In the art of our own time, disconcerting shifts in scale and context function as more subtle expressive means, allowing artists to operate ironically to bar pathos or overt sentimentality from their work. The often skewed and unnatural proportions of Charles Ray's mannequin sculptures, for example, suggest the complexities and flaws in our relationships with others.

An unquestioned master of dissonant scale is Thomas Schütte. A student of the art of utopian artist ideologues such as Vladimir Tatlin, Schütte turns idealism against itself. His main vehicle in this faithless endeavor is the architectural model, through which he presupposes alternative forms of social interaction. Scale plays a crucial role in Schütte's deconstruction of the public monument, as his figures are often radically mis-scaled, not only in relation to their environments but also to one another. Clearly horrified by the public sculptures that have been erected by totalitarian and democratic regimes alike throughout our century, Schütte makes anti-monuments that force a reevaluation of the public role of art as we reach the millennium.

In assessing the new public voice represented by the ten artists in "Distemper," one must locate the balance implied between skepticism and hope and between irony and reticence. Thus when Mirosław Bałka or Rachel Whiteread directly transpose a domestic interior—in Bałka's case, an actual wood floor becomes a geometric metal floor sculpture, and in the hands of Whiteread, a Victorian interior is translated into a monolithic cast concrete cube, for instance—the effect is unsettling on a public level. When Kuitca presents an architectural ground plan of a cemetery or an elevation of a theater, his restraint is of the most evocative sort. And when Hatoum or Salcedo subtly alter or conjoin vernacular objects, their passion and anger at injustices done are only scarcely concealed. The impersonal muteness of the geometry that is their vocabulary is radically at odds with our shared awareness of the lives inscribed in these forms.

Ultimately, the artists included in this exhibition have, through their reassertion of painting and sculpture and their reevaluation of time-honored concepts of beauty and memory, demonstrated a faith in the traditional power of art. Yet, theirs is a hope well-tempered by the failed promise of our century. If the excesses of ideology and political and military ambition of the modern age have engendered a deep skepticism in our artists, we may also divine a quiet hopefulness in their reticence. In the words of Jorge Luis Borges, "The smallest of deeds presupposes the inconceivable universe, and conversely, the universe proceeds from the smallest of deeds."[21]

Notes

1. Francis Fukuyama, "The End of History?," *National Interest*, no. 16 (Summer 1989): 3–18, generated wide-ranging responses by such leading commentators as Allan Bloom, Pierre Hassner, Gertrude Himmelfarb, Irving Kristol, Daniel Patrick Moynihan, and Stephen Sestanovich, which appeared in the same issue of the journal. See also *The End of History and the Last Man* (New York: Avon Books, 1992). We are grateful to James T. Demetrion for bringing Fukuyama's work to our attention.

2. Fukuyama, "The End of History?," 4.

3. Ibid., 18.

4. E. J. Dionne, Jr., "Grumpy Days Are Here Again and a Democratic Distemper Is Worldwide," *Washington Post*, 12 July 1992, C2.

5. It should be noted that "distemper" possesses two other meanings as well. It refers to a disease in animals and to a painting medium in which pigment is combined with a thickening substance such as egg yolk. We are indebted to A. Clarke Bedford of the Hirshhorn's conservation staff for information in regard to the latter. For a complete etymological analysis of the term, see *The Compact Edition of the Oxford English Dictionary* (Oxford: Oxford University Press, 1971), 520–22.

6. Andreas Huyssen, *Twilight Memories: Marking Time in a Culture of Amnesia* (New York: Routledge, 1995), 3.

7. Ibid., 8.

8. Ibid., 7.

9. Ibid.

10. The exhibition "Doubletake: Collective Memory and Current Art," 1992, curated by Lynne Cooke and Brice Curiger for the Hayward Gallery, London, postulated memory and the tensions between our public and private selves as the premise by which to examine the works of diverse artists.

11. Huyssen, *Twilight Memories*, 7.

12. Peter Schjeldahl, "Beauty," *Art Issues*, no. 33 (May-June 1994): 28.

13. Dave Hickey, *The Invisible Dragon: Four Essays on Beauty* (Los Angeles: Art Issues Press, 1993).

14. Ibid., 17.

15. Ibid., 53.

16. Schjeldahl, "Beauty," 28.

17. Ibid., 25.

18. Charles Baudelaire, *The Painter of Modern Life and Other Essays* (London: Phaidon Press, 1964), 1.

19. Václav Havel, "An Anatomy of Reticence," *Living in Truth* (London: Faber and Faber, 1987), 178. The essay was written for a Peace Congress in Amsterdam, 1985, and originally published privately in Czechoslovakia. It was first published in English in 1986.

20. Ibid., 180.

21. Jorge Luis Borges, *Discusión* (Discussion) (Buenos Aires, 1932), quoted in *Mapping Out the Self: The Works of Guillermo Kuitca* (Rotterdam: Witte de With Center for Contemporary Art, 1990), 12.

Mirosław Bałka
A Privacy Which Can Be Public

For me the problem of art is not one of imagination, or of the invention of the new. It is rather a way of abstracting that which is well known, the familiar and the useful.... It is the problem of a privacy which can be public.[1]
—Mirosław Bałka, 1990

In approaching Mirosław Bałka's work for the first time from the West, one has a strong temptation to mythologize his life. His biography is compelling. Bałka grew up in Otwock, a small town near Warsaw, the grandson of a sculptor of funerary monuments who erected more than four hundred tombstones in the community cemetery. Bałka's father, an engineer, moonlighted by engraving the memorials that his own father had carved. Mirosław, remembering well the summer vacations spent hauling tombstones in a horse-drawn wagon to the Otwock cemetery where he would paint the engraved letters and numerals, credits his grandfather for encouraging his interest in art.

Bałka attended the Academy of Fine Arts in Warsaw from 1980 to 1985. His training there, where he concentrated on figurative sculpture, he has said, was "very academic, very realist. None of my teachers had any part in postwar or contemporary European art."[2] Bałka's graduation piece integrated self-portraiture and performance in a surprising way. Taking the rite-of-passage symbolism of graduation quite literally, Bałka invited the faculty and other guests to an abandoned farmhouse in the village of Zuków. Following a bus ride and a walk of several hundred yards down a country path, guests approached the house, where they were greeted by two young boys dressed for communion. The artist, a robust young man, six-feet three-inches in height, arrived on a small bicycle wearing gloves and white makeup. Inside the house was *Remembrance of the First Holy Communion*, 1985 (fig. 6). In the work, an adolescent male figure in painted burlap is mounted on a low platform with his hand resting on an adjoining table. Befitting his youth and the ceremonial act, he wears a jacket, shorts, and long white socks. Embedded in his chest is a red pincushion in the form of a heart, and mounted on the table

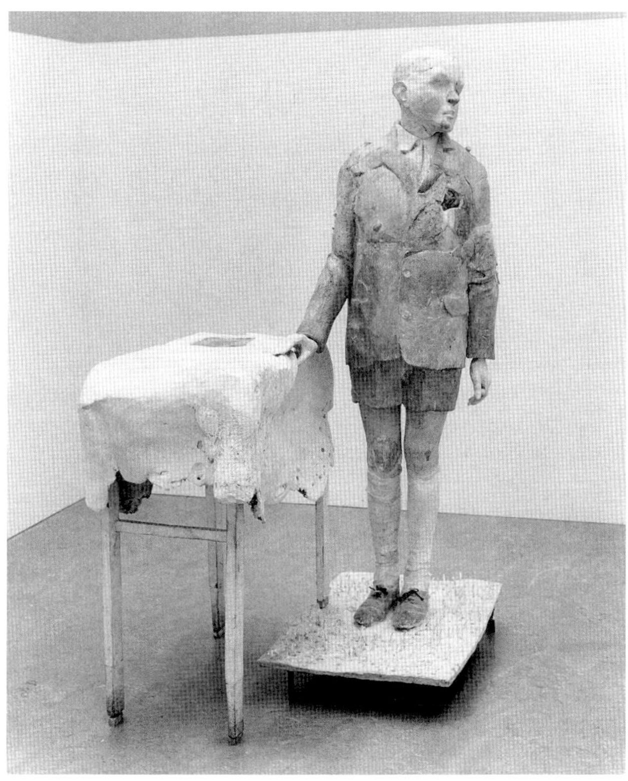

Fig. 6. *Remembrance of the First Holy Communion*, 1985.

is a photograph of the artist himself at his first communion.

The graduation piece introduced a wide variety of themes and components of Bałka's early sculpture. First is the location of the exhibition itself. Given Bałka's description of his staid professors, one can well imagine their dismay at the young artist's presentation far from the halls of the academy. And yet at that time—June 1985—Poland was in the fifth year of martial law following the advent of Solidarity in the summer of 1980. During those years, artists throughout Poland self-consciously withdrew from formal exhibitions in traditional spaces and instead held unofficial showings in churches, homes, and other sites. Bałka's ingenuity in staging his graduate show at such a remote locale was entirely consonant with his own independent nature and the rebellious spirit then prevailing in Poland.

Related to his ingenious siting is Bałka's practice, established from the outset, of creating a particular environment for his art. Although sculptors have long attempted to dictate the perception of their work, Bałka is intensely focused on establishing a psychological mood. He has consistently used architectural and sculptural methods—in this case a stagelike platform—to slow the pace at which we encounter his sculptures.

In conceiving *Remembrance of the First Holy Communion* and effectively staging his own rite of passage, Bałka poetically conjoined communion and graduation. The conflation of sculpture, performance, and autobiography in this exceptionally personal work would distinguish all of Bałka's early efforts. His direction at that time seemed to allude to the influential German artist Joseph Beuys, who in 1981 had donated a large body of archival work to the Muzeum Sztuki in Łódź. Those pieces would subsequently be exhibited in 1986 at the progressive Foksal Gallery in Warsaw, where Bałka himself would exhibit beginning in 1991. When asked about Beuys in an interview published that year, Bałka noted:

> *It is difficult to define any actual influence as I only recently had information about Beuys. But you could say my branch comes from the same tree. It's a tree which does not forget about its roots, which can be more important than the branches. Beuys showed how important autobiography is for the artist. I feel the same.*[3]

Bałka would continue to merge performance with sculpture through the late 1980s. These projects presented highly ritualized activities involving a variety of objects and sculpted animal forms. Yet, as his words suggest, Bałka is a profoundly private individual, and his quiet personality rather quickly recommended him away from the explicit personal involvement that performance requires and toward a sculpture of eloquent if silent allusion.

Initially, the figure predominated. Following *Remembrance of the First Holy Communion*, Bałka made *Fire Place*, 1986 (fig. 7, p. 24), a radically dismembered head and upper torso mounted above a simulated fireplace. The composition is situated on

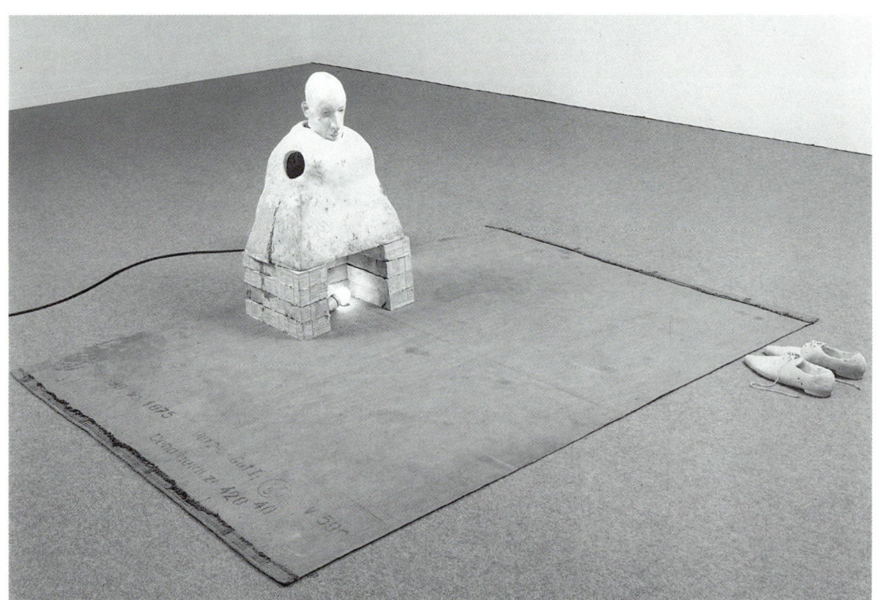

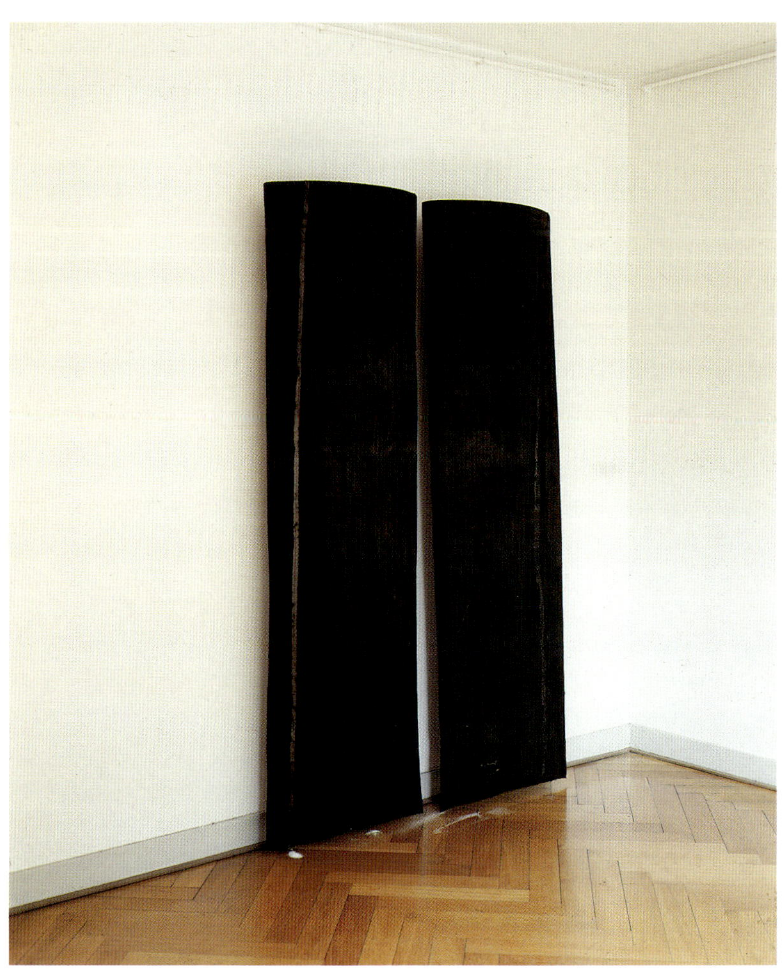

Fig. 7. *Fire Place*, 1986.

Fig. 8. *217 x 87 x 39, 191 x 57 x 37, 191 x 57 x 37*, 1992.

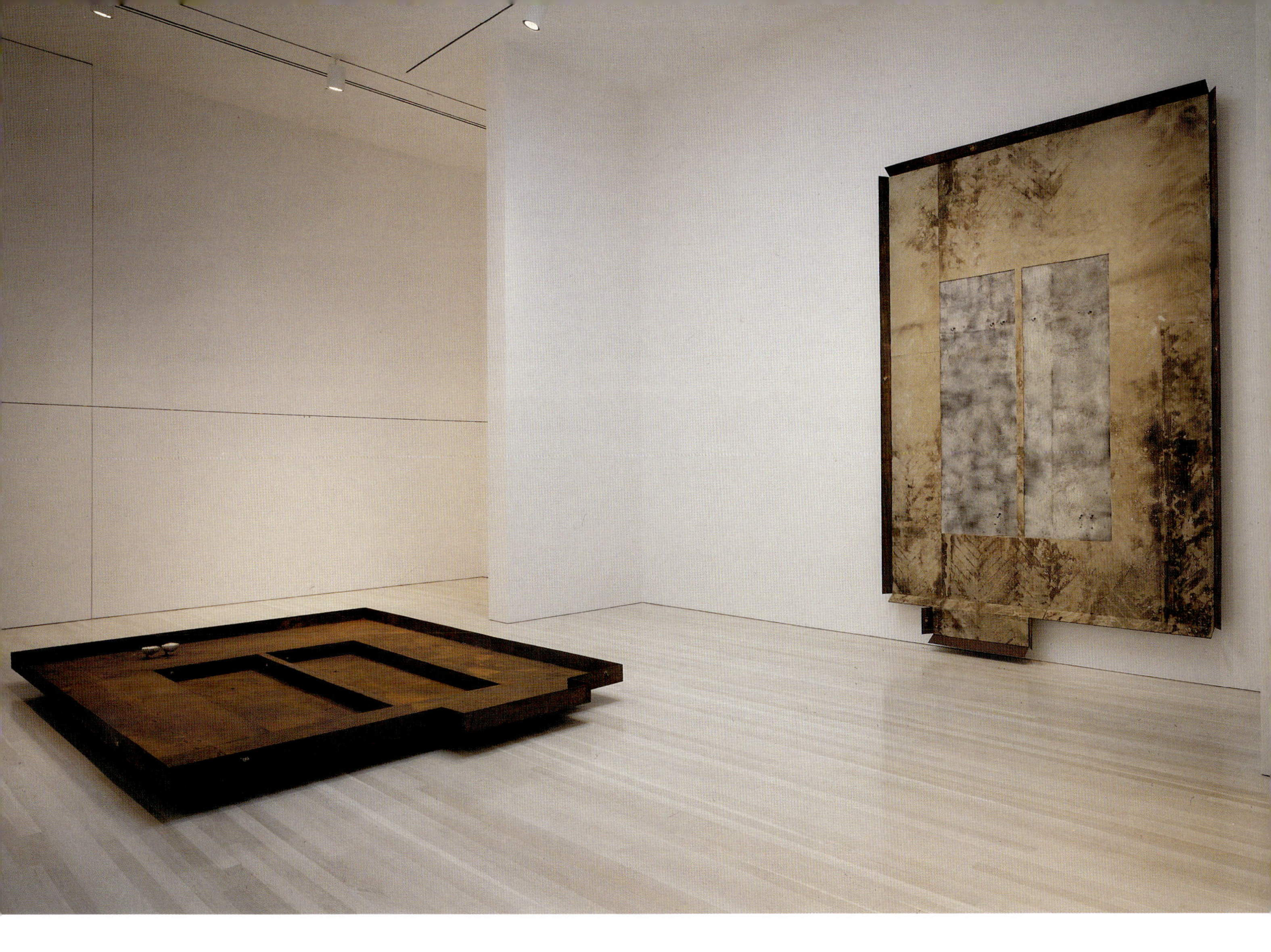

Fig. 9. *376 x 241 x 25* (on wall), and *350 x 230 x 23, ø0.4 x 810*, 1993.

a carpeted space just outside of which he placed two cement shoes. In addition to these freestanding sculptural environments, he completed a relief, *St. Adalbert*, 1987 (fig. 10), the title of which refers to a tenth-century Bohemian bishop who became embroiled in the politics of the moment but ultimately served as a missionary and lived as an ascetic monk. In Bałka's sculpture the white, headless figure is mounted horizontally on a black wall. A hatchet—the weapon of his martyrdom—is depicted in neon and mounted above the figure. Four neon loops suggest drops of fallen blood, which nourish a narrow trough of oats below.

Simultaneous with pursuing the somewhat diagrammatic, illustrational quality of *St. Adalbert*, Bałka was trying to achieve greater allusiveness in his work.

> *In my earlier works I employed the body in the very literal way.... After some time I satisfied my hunger for the form of the human body. I took interest in the forms that accompany the body and in the traces the body leaves: a bed, a coffin, a funeral urn.*[4]

A change began to occur in 1987, when Bałka made his first nonfigurative sculpture, *When you wet the bed* (illus. p. ii). The spatial environment in which he often placed his figures is here a raised platform on which stand three rough-hewn wooden objects: in the front is a simple framework resembling a prayer stall; to the side, an elevated bed with a plaster mattress and pillow; and at the rear, a tall, T-shaped object suggesting a crucifix. The latter two elements function as fountains, sending thin streams of fluid into a square depression in the platform. Religious allusions are omnipresent—prayer, baptism, crucifixion, and entombment among them. Ultimately, Bałka's spirituality is firmly grounded, not just in the religion of his upbringing but also in the mundane, daily processes of the body in which he finds the traces of life.

Since the late 1950s, beginning with the work of Robert Rauschenberg and continuing much more recently with the sculptures of Mona Hatoum and Rachel Whiteread, beds have been among the most richly metaphorical forms in contemporary art. As Bałka has noted:

> *The bed is where we spend at least a third of our lives, it's where we dream, where we make love, it's deeply private. But at the same time as soon as it's on public display it can remind one of a hospital or prison bed, a surgery table, something from an external situation. So there is a duality between public and private.*[5]

Thus, while Bałka continued to make figurative sculptures during the late 1980s, he was simultaneously exploring ways in which to make less literal, more allusive references to human experience. If certain materials referred poetically to himself and his environment, their symbolism encompassed the simple, ultimately greater, dramas of human life. As his words indicate, the symbolic nature of his work was not at the expense of its public implications, which subtly grew as his dependence on the figure lessened.

The nonfigurative aspect of Bałka's work, which he kept out of public sight until 1990, has deeply personal roots. In 1985, the year he left the academy, Bałka moved into a studio near his parents' home that became available following the death of a neighbor whom he had known. He would later note:

> *This is not an indifferent interior.... The room has given me a good deal. First of all, I have been able to concentrate on things that are quite invisible in what people call "objective interiors." I have found traces in this particular place. I have made works from old planks that I approached with all the respect that their private history deserved.*[6]

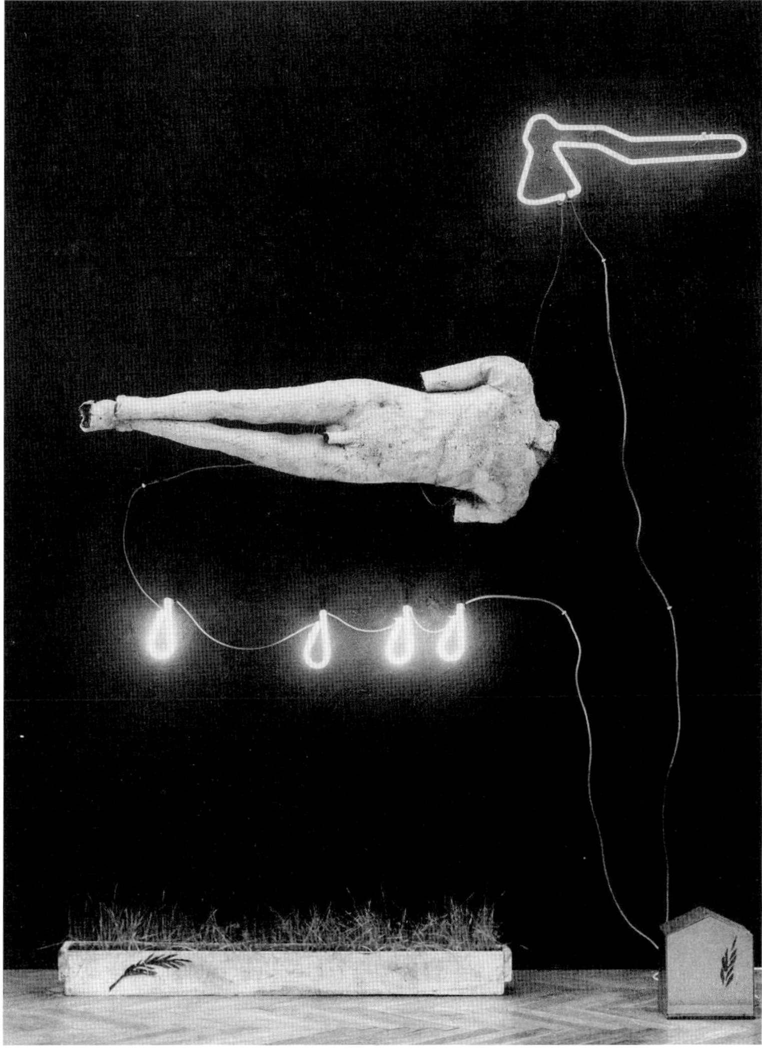

Fig. 10. *St. Adalbert*, 1987.

The place in which Bałka works is of utmost importance to him. In interviews he has acknowledged his interest in the art of the German Dadaist Kurt Schwitters, and one can liken Bałka's feeling for his surroundings to those of Schwitters for his *Merzbau*, the domestic studio in Hanover that in the late 1920s became the site of an ongoing environmental sculpture.[7] Yet, while Schwitters literally built into his studio, creating a sculptural grotto, Bałka is more of an archaeologist, extracting meaning from the layers of lives lived in a given interior. Bałka worked in that studio from 1985 to 1992, gradually transposing the objects, materials, and spirit of the modest, memory-laden interior into his art. While he continued to exhibit figurative pieces, he simultaneously was developing sculptures from old planks, bits of wallpaper and linoleum, as well as a variety of objects left in the house. Neither the smallest element nor the most unpromising material escaped Bałka's touch. He has stated:

> *For me the history of materials is more important than the history of art. I don't make any connection with Arte Povera, but rather base my decisions on my own private experience. These are the materials I encounter in my studio, they constitute my personal landscape.... I can spend hours deciding on which way I should cut a plank. For me it is a very important decision. I am looking for this kind of energy hidden in simple decisions.*[8]

Although Bałka began to make "abstract" sculptures as early as 1987, they did not become prominent in his public exhibitions until 1990. In three separate exhibitions in that year—"Good God" held at the Galerie Dziekanka in Warsaw in the spring; Aperto '90 at the XLIV Venice Biennale in the summer; and "Possible Worlds: Sculpture from Europe" at the Institute of Contemporary Arts and the Serpentine Gallery, London, in the fall—the figure was suddenly and startlingly absent. The sculptures Bałka now showed were seemingly simple, and in their modesty they made reference to functional objects, such as beds, benches, shelves, bookcases, and other household forms. If the absence of the figure implied a growing formalism—an impression furthered by the artist's titles, which consisted of the consecutive listing of the dimensions of each object composing a work—closer observation revealed that Bałka had now located remarkable ways in which to enrich the references in each piece.

Since the early 1990s, Bałka has exhibited widely, participating in major international group shows such as "Metropolis" in Berlin, 1991; Documenta IX in Kassel, 1992; and the Carnegie International 1995 in Pittsburgh. Given the subtlety of his work, however,

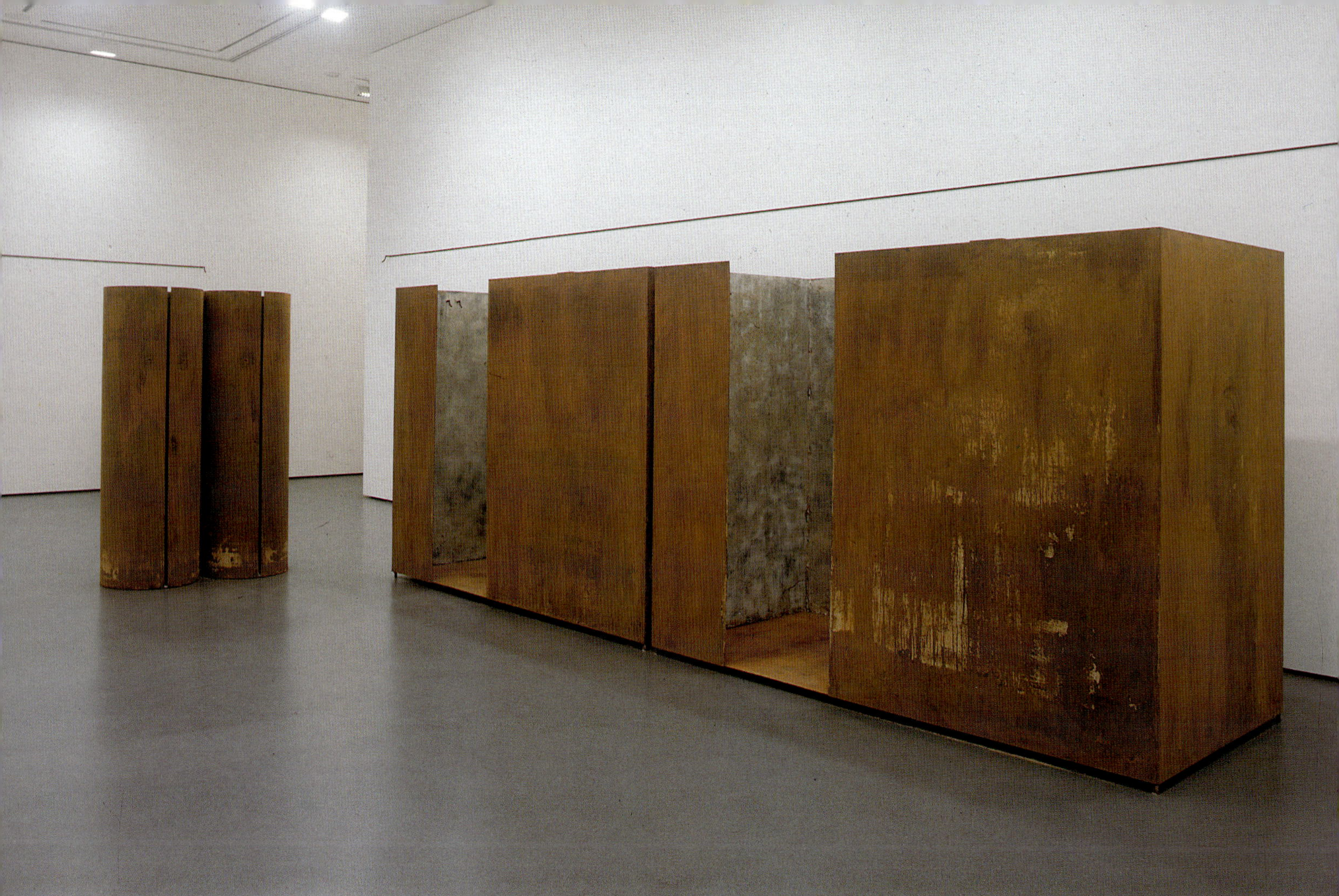

Fig. 11. *260 x 120 x 194, 250 x 120 x 194*, 1995.

Bałka's sculpture has been seen to best advantage in solo shows, particularly in intimate architectural settings.

One of Bałka's most compelling exhibitions was "Bitte," installed at the Museum Haus Lange, Krefeld, in 1992. The show offered Bałka the opportunity to conceive an installation for the Haus Lange, one of two adjoining brick houses designed by Ludwig Mies van der Rohe in Krefeld in 1930 and today used for public exhibitions. A beautifully scaled structure with a garden to the rear, the site encouraged Bałka to translate the domestic intimacy of his sculpture into a public exhibition space. One can scarcely imagine a better conjunction of sculpture and architecture. The modest interior, with its large windows, parquet wood floor, and domestic scale, served as an ideal location for Bałka and his work. Similarly, Bałka's sculptures were defined by their internal relationships, a series of dialogs that he carefully orchestrated among individual objects in an ensemble. His principal material, formerly wood, was now steel, sometimes in the form of plates, in other cases open or closed boxes, some wall-mounted and others set on the floor. Throughout, Bałka scaled the sculptures to his own height, 190 centimeters. The strength of the warm reddish brown steel and the human scale balanced the subtly placed interventions that Bałka made in these minimal forms. Floor sculptures were slightly elevated by legs, which in turn rested on small pools of salt. In many, Bałka made reference to a human presence, not just by virtue of the scale but also by the inclusion of small drains or slightly protruding pipes, discreetly placed to suggest body fluids. The references to death were unmistakable throughout, as Bałka also wall-mounted large fabric sacks—sometimes individually, sometimes in pairs—and filled them with ashes. The exhibition was dominated by the strong shapes and materials of the sculptures, but the more lasting impact derived from details implying human presence and absence: the manner in which the ash sifted through the sacks and onto the floor, the passage of air or body fluids through the small drains and pipes puncturing the steel boxes, and the inclusion of salt, which suggested bitterness but also the preservation of life.

In the year of the "Bitte" exhibition, 1992, Bałka's parents moved from the artist's childhood home in Otwock, a cramped, three-room house in which his grandparents had lived before them. The old house, where he had been reared with his sister, became Bałka's studio. The next year, 1993, his grandfather, Viktor, whose work as a stonemason had first introduced young Mirosław to art, died. The confluence of events called forth in Bałka memories of his youth and his extended family, and he turned to that powerful foundation in creating a new body of work.

In two exhibitions—the Polish pavilion at the 1993 Venice Biennale for which Bałka was the sole representative, and "Laadplatform + 7 Werken 1985–89" at the Stedelijk Van Abbemuseum in Eindhoven, The Netherlands, in 1994—Bałka again explored the idea of passage, this time in sculptures based on the dimensions of the Otwock home that was now his studio. The predominant sculptural motifs were large steel panels, sometimes wall-mounted, sometimes resting on the floor. Many were infused with soap or lined with carpet, and some were scaled to bear the imprint of Bałka's height. In each case, Bałka included a small protruding steel panel, a precise reference to the threshold over which one enters the family-home-turned-studio, and yet another suggestion of passage.

The imprint of the home/studio was the sculptural form that predominated in those installations, but the pungent smell of soap also permeated the exhibitions. On entering the pavilion in Venice, one traversed a long corridor with its walls lined with a layer of soap scaled, once again, to Bałka's height. In the Eindhoven installation, Bałka's most comprehensive exhibition to date, the Otwock studio sculptures were preceded by seven figurative installations made between 1985 and 1989. The viewer proceeded from the old works to the new only by passing through another soap-lined corridor. As Jan Debbaut, director of the Van Abbemuseum noted, "You do not have to have been brought up in Poland for it to evoke childhood memories; everyone of our generation has had to wash with this sort of soap when young."[9] Indeed, if Bałka had begun with a participatory rite of passage in 1985, he had now engaged us again in a highly personal, eloquent, and yet ultimately silent dialog about the passage of time and the traces each of us leaves in the world.

Notes

1. Quoted in Iwona Blazwick, "Mirosław Bałka," *Possible Worlds: Sculpture from Europe* (London: Institute of Contemporary Arts and Serpentine Gallery, 1990), 16.
2. Ibid., 18.
3. Ibid., 17.
4. Quoted in interview by Jaromir Jedlínski, "Conversation between Mirosław Bałka and Jaromir Jedlínski," *Mirosław Bałka* (Eindhoven: Stedelijk Van Abbemuseum, 1994), 64.
5. Quoted in Blazwick, *Possible Worlds*, 16.
6. Quoted in *Von angesicht zu angesicht—Face to Face: Ars Baltica Prolog 1991* (Kiel, Germany: Kunsthalle zu Kiel, 1991), 61.
7. See Bałka's comments on Schwitters in Blazwick, *Possible Worlds*, 18.
8. Quoted in ibid., 16.
9. Quoted in Jedlínski, *Mirosław Bałka*, 13.

Marlene Dumas
On Beauty

(They say) Art no longer produces Beauty

She produces meaning

but

(I say) One cannot paint a picture of

or make an image of a woman

and not deal with the concept of beauty.[1]

—Marlene Dumas, 1995

The art, life, and words of Marlene Dumas combine to constitute one of the most intriguing stories in contemporary art. Born and educated in South Africa, an émigré to The Netherlands, and there a student of painting as well as psychology, Dumas renders the figure with a fresh eye and hand and a directness that belie the complex implications of her choice of subjects and medium. Offering a stunning reconsideration of current assumptions about the role of beauty in art, Dumas's work breaks the seal on a Pandora's box of unaccustomed, even taboo, subjects and hypocritical attitudes in contemporary art and society, and feminizes figure painting in the process.

Born in Capetown, South Africa, in 1953, Dumas attended the University of Capetown from 1972 to 1975. Her vivid childhood recollections offer a startling impression of that country and the experience of growing up as a White female under apartheid and a rigidly conservative social system. Dumas's family attended a Dutch Reformed Church twice each Sunday, partaking in the strict rituals of church doctrine. The media in South Africa was carefully controlled by the government; television became available only in 1976, the year after Dumas graduated from college; and images in the print media were heavily censored. For Dumas, apartheid was as much a deeply felt personal challenge and artistic obstacle as it was a political and social issue.

> *The fact that I suddenly realized that because I was white in South Africa I was one of the oppressors greatly confused me. I personally don't see myself as a real oppressor, but I'm part of the oppression nevertheless. It gave me a feeling of real distrust in relation to myself: to see myself not as a "sweet young girl" but an oppressor is quite a leap, and at the same time it makes the problem of the way you regard things acute.*[2]

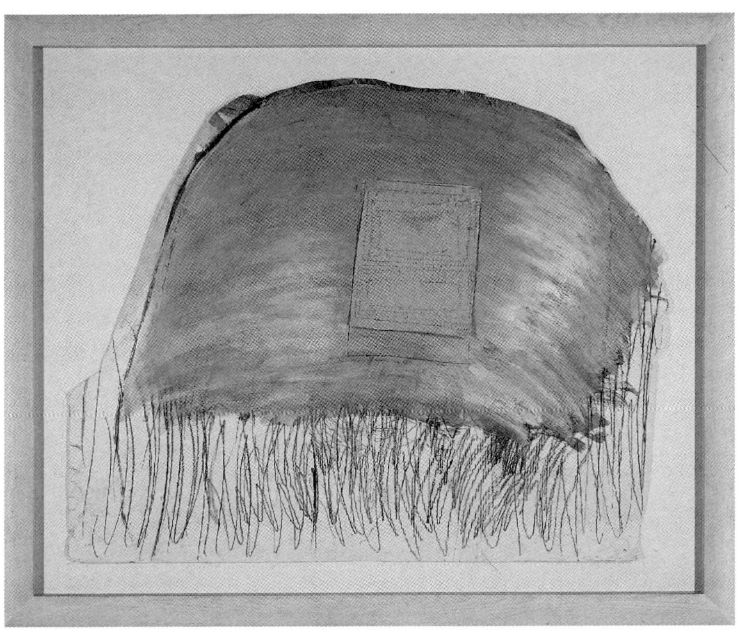

Fig. 12. *The Answer to the Marriage Proposal,* 1977–78.

Although Dumas has seldom made apartheid an explicit subject of her work, one senses in her evident self-awareness that the burden remained with her in Amsterdam, where she relocated from Capetown in 1976. This is most apparent in a self-portrait of 1984, *The Banality of Evil* (fig. 13, p. 32). Based on a candid photograph made of the artist seated in an automobile,[3] the painting boldly recasts her head into a whitened death mask crowned by a shock of orange hair. The image combines the empathetic observation of facial detail and psychological implication of the early twentieth-century painter Paula Modersohn-Becker with the disembodied coloration of the German Expressionist Emil Nolde or, more recently, Andy Warhol. In the painting and its title—which Dumas drew from Hannah Arendt's *Eichmann in Jerusalem: A Report on the Banality of Evil* (1963)—the artist willingly implicates herself in the crime of apartheid while suggesting that the most profound immorality may lurk in entirely benign human settings.

At the University of Capetown, Dumas made drawings, collages, and a few sculptures in addition to paintings. Her interest in depicting the figure—which was out of step with the international vogue for abstraction—was nearly quashed by the censorship of the media there. While nude Black women could be depicted in print, for example, all such images of Whites were banned. Similarly, about art school, Dumas said:

> *It was clear that no one was inspired by the nude drawing classes anymore. The women (of colour) who posed at the university had been there for many years. Being a model had become their occupation. They had posed themselves into (still-life-like) generalized subjects, devoid of erotic (or any kind of) energy.*[4]

Dumas recognized that if she were to mature as an artist she would need to move from South Africa. Soon after leaving school she moved to Amsterdam, and soon thereafter she entered Ateliers '63 in Haarlem, one of the leading art schools in The Netherlands. There her instructors included the sculptor Carel Visser and two noted conceptualists, Jan Dibbets and Ger van Elk.[5] Dumas's little-known work of the late 1970s and early 1980s is indebted to that formidable trio of artist-instructors. The figure is largely absent from the work she made at that time, and in the informality of her methods—freely collaging together scrap and torn paper with photographic reproductions and evocative, abstract line drawings—Dumas demonstrated an affinity for the work of each of those artists. She often added printed reproductions to the collages, which she occasionally installed directly on the floor or combined with pieces of stone for mounting on a wall.

Dumas's career evolved quickly: in 1978, the same year she graduated from art school, she was included in an exhibition of young Dutch artists at the Stedelijk Museum in Amsterdam; in 1979 her first solo show was held in a Paris gallery; and in 1982 she would be included in Documenta VII in Kassel. Yet, Dumas's path also took an unexpected turn. Simultaneous with her busy

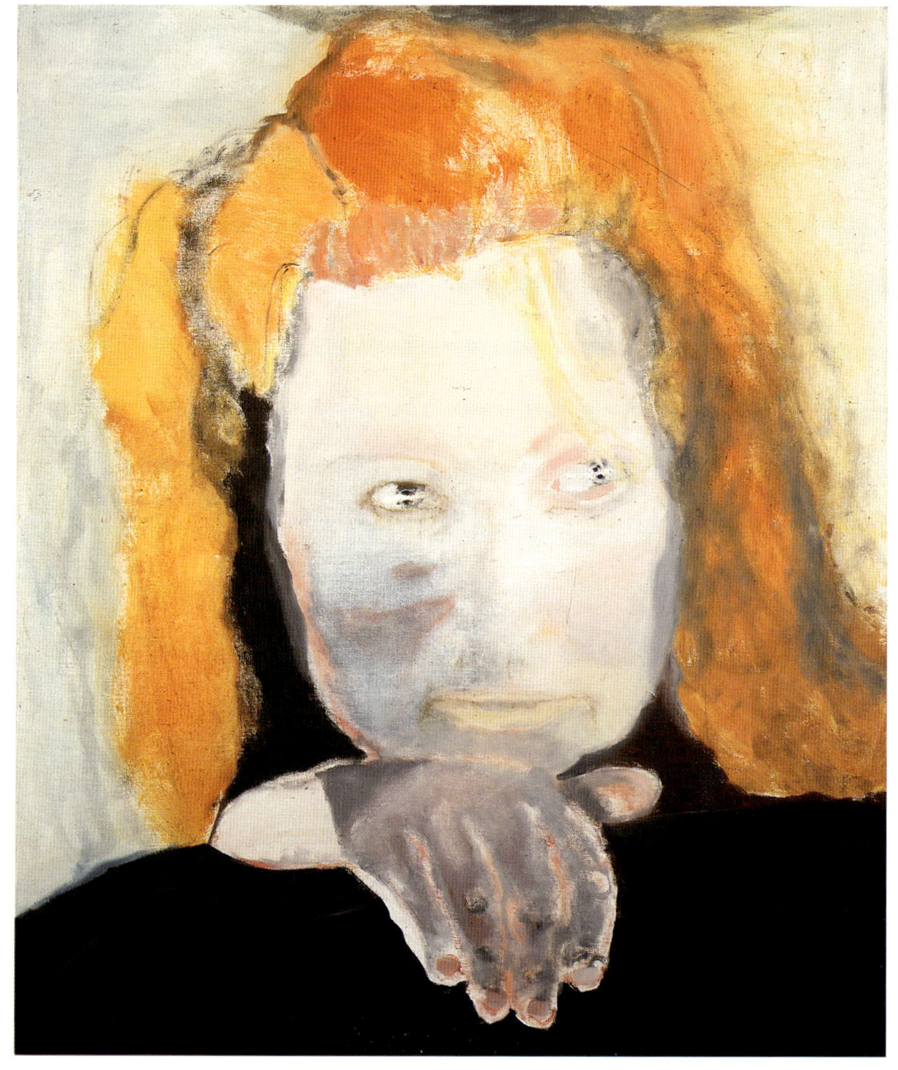

Fig. 13. *The Banality of Evil,* 1984.

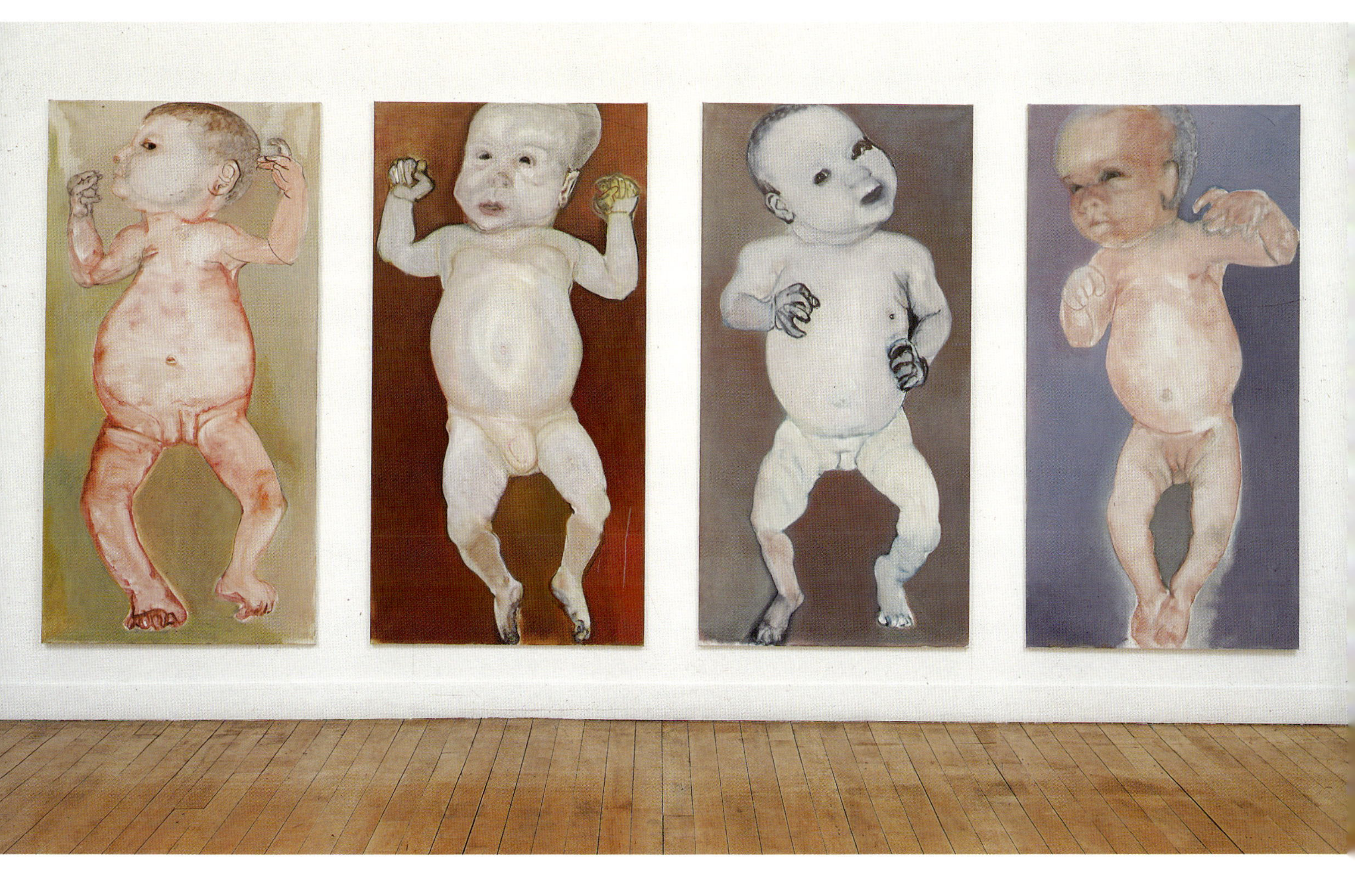

Fig. 14. *The First People (I–IV)*, 1991.

exhibition schedule, she enrolled at the University of Amsterdam, where she studied psychology in 1979–80. Although she stopped short of a formal degree, finding the course of study too quantitatively based for her intuitive and intellectual interest in the field, Dumas was greatly influenced by her reading. By 1983 she had returned to the figure in paintings and drawings.

The self-portrait *The Banality of Evil*, 1984, is related to the major body of work Dumas created from 1984 to 1986: a series of nearly square, tightly cropped paintings, mostly of female heads. Although some are devoted to specific individuals—for example, *Martha—Sigmund's Wife*, 1984, a portrait of Sigmund Freud's wife, the former Martha Bernays—others are not identified by either likeness or title, despite their specificity. The series was exhibited in Amsterdam at the Galerie Paul Andriesse in 1985 under the title "The Eyes of the Night Creatures." This was among the first of many instances in which Dumas gave titles to her shows. An outspoken person, she has also, characteristically, authored texts for catalogs. As she would later note, "I want to speak for myself ... to participate in the writing of my own history."[6] In the publication for the Galerie Paul Andriesse, Dumas included several short statements, one of which reads in part:

> *The aim of my work ... has always been to arouse in my audience (as well as myself) an experience of* empathy *with my subject matter ... more so than* sympathy. *Sympathy suggests an agreement of temperament, and an emotional identification with a person. Empathy doesn't necessarily demand that.*[7]

Although Dumas's practice of layering color over a likeness produces a subtle psychological distance, perhaps of greater impact is her use of photographs or reproductions in the conception of her work. Elsewhere in the "The Eyes of the Night Creatures," Dumas remarked, "My people were all shot by a camera, framed before I painted them. They didn't know that I'd do this to them."[8] Dumas's manipulation of existing images is clear from the format of the paintings of the mid-1980s. In each painting the tightly cropped head fills the flattened pictorial field, a method she derived from film. Dumas would later describe the effect she was seeking:

> *I have used the close-up only for the human face. This method achieves an intimidating and confrontational effect which was what I wanted. Images combining intimacy (or the illusion of that) with discomfort. Eyes no matter where the gaze is directed have strong impact. It is self-evident that the quick cheap thrills of immediate psychological impact can also turn out to be very tedious.*[9]

Dumas continued to assign referential titles to individual works and to her shows. In 1987 and 1988, she titled her exhibitions at the Galerie Paul Andriesse, "The Public Versus the Private" and "Waiting (For Meaning)," respectively. The dominant motif in Dumas's work at that time changed from frontal, bust-length images to the reclining figure. Again, the majority are women and, arguably, metaphorical self-portraits, but male subjects occasionally appeared as well. Dumas would reveal several of the sources for that body of work, when in 1992 she included numerous illustrations of a wide variety of horizontal figures in the exhibition catalog *Miss Interpreted*. These include celebrated works from art history—Hans Holbein's *Dead Christ*, 1521, and Henry Fuseli's *Nightmare*, 1781—as well as reproductions of Michael Jackson or women in calendar spreads.[10] In Dumas's painting *The Particularity of Nakedness*, 1987, a reclining male nude is reminiscent of the work of Egon Schiele, yet it is less fraught with tension and more languorous in its sensuality.

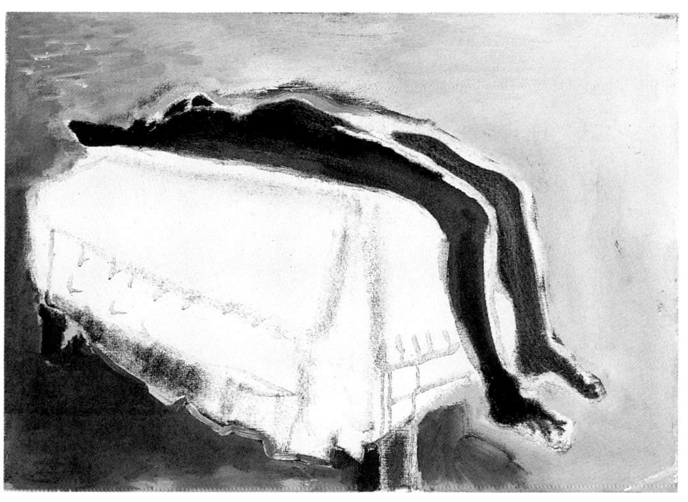

Fig. 15. *Waiting (For Meaning)*, 1988.

From the time she made the painting, Dumas was keenly aware that she was inverting the accustomed practice of male artists rendering female nudes. She was not interested in conventional, idealized notions of beauty and the tradition of the nude in art history. As suggested in her title, she was far more concerned with the nakedness—or presence—of the unclothed figure, as exemplified by Edouard Manet's landmark painting *Olympia*, 1863.

Dumas's empowerment of her subjects and her self-conscious reversal of the male-artist/female-model relationship are noteworthy in the series of reclining female figures she made in the late 1980s. The first was *Waiting (For Meaning)*, 1988 (fig. 15), a small painting of a woman outstretched on a bed. The combination of image and title suggests that the figure lies awaiting inspiration, recalling depictions throughout art history of Danaë lying on a bed soon to receive Zeus in the form of a shower of gold, thereby becoming the mother of Perseus. In the companion painting, *Losing (Her Meaning)*, 1988, Dumas replaces the bed with a pool of water and inverts the figure as if to drown her. Dumas's unmistakable point here is that the role of the female model throughout art history—that is, to serve as an object of inspiration but ultimately to be exploited and discarded—may be likened to that of the woman generally.

Also from 1988 is *Defining in the Negative*, a series of eight drawings of female nudes in a variety of studio poses.[11] In each, Dumas includes inscriptions that refer to several contemporary male artists. The words uttered, which overtake the image in their overall impact, are those of the models. In effect Dumas has lent the models her own voice, as a ventriloquist might, allowing them the impudence to "talk back" to each painter to censure his work and motivation. In the same vein Dumas composed a chart in 1989, which was reproduced in the catalog for a survey exhibition of her work organized by the Kunsthalle Bern titled "The Question of Human Pink." Here, she characterized painters of the human figure and their importance for her. In part a diatribe against Neo-Expressionism, Dumas's list is also a citation of positive influences, among them Holbein, Manet, and Nolde, as well as Gustave Courbet, Lucian Freud, and Rembrandt. Only three women artists appear on Dumas's list—Diane Arbus, Frida Kahlo, and Alice Neel. In her paintings and writings of the time, one senses the artist's lonely feeling of responsibility as a woman painter seeking to feminize a figurative tradition thoroughly dominated by male artists.

As a woman painting the figure, Dumas found herself in an awkward position in the late 1980s. On the one hand, figurative painting was the province of male painters, and predominant among them were the Neo-Expressionists. Obviously unsympathetic to both the self-consciousness of their processes and what she considered to be the sexist ramifications of their work, Dumas sought an art that would redefine the role of the figure in painting and which might also reconsider existing definitions of beauty. Elsewhere, however, the body as metaphor and subject in the art of the late 1980s had become hotly disputed, politicized terrain, with many artists treating it in an overtly ideological way. Women artists of her own generation, in particular Jenny Holzer and Barbara Kruger, employed the medium of language to rail against a male-dominated

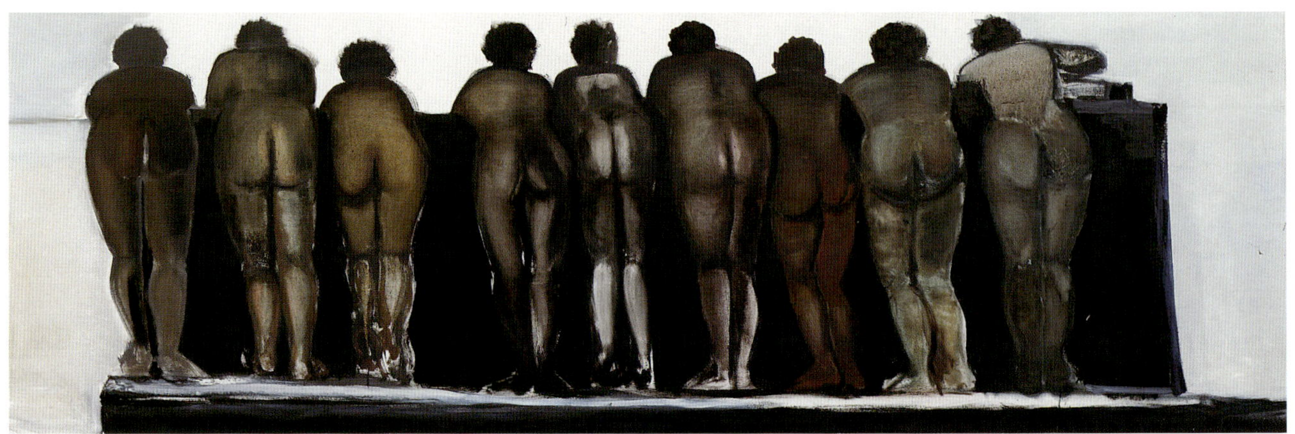

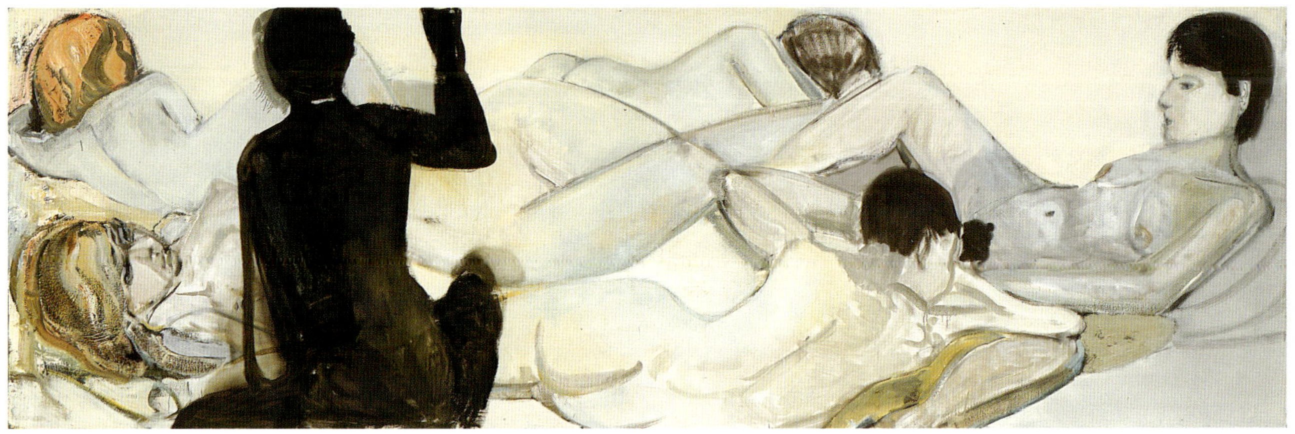

Groupshow II, 1993,
cat. no. 3.

Indifference, 1994,
cat. no. 5.

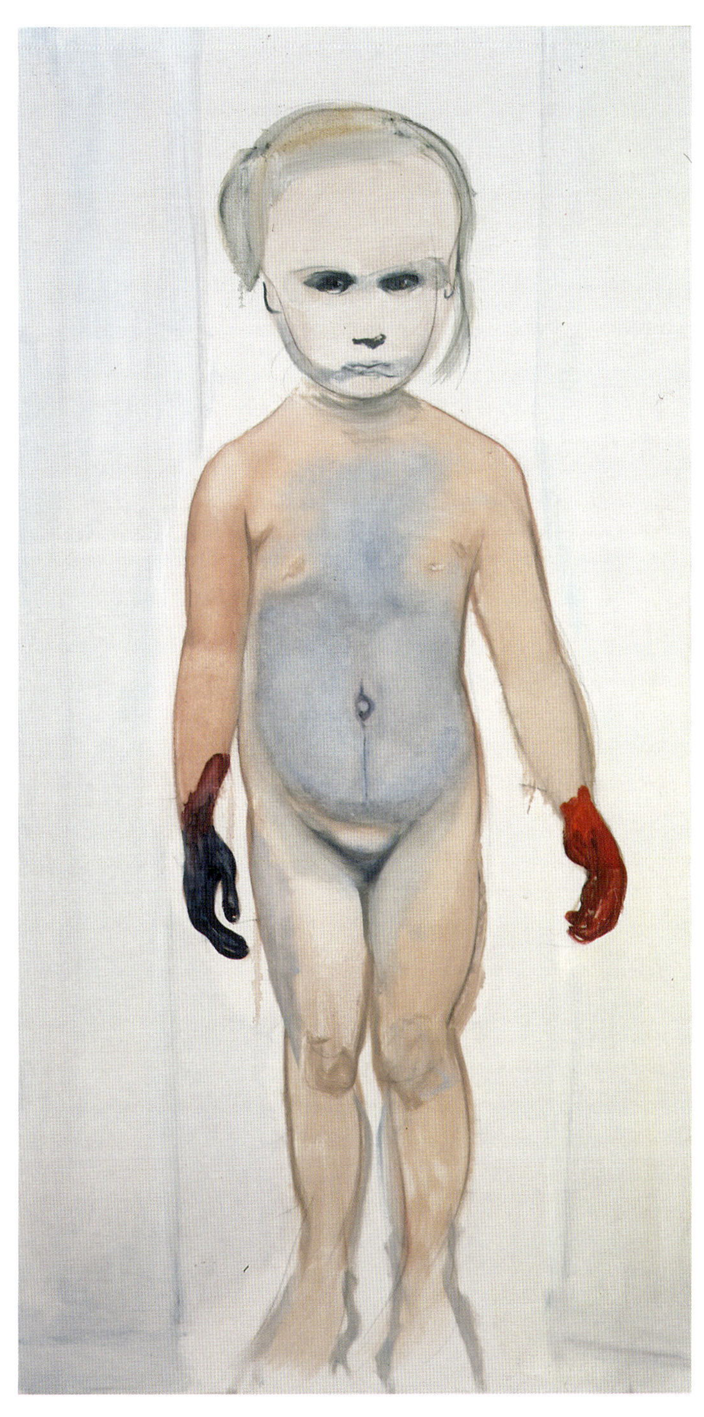

The Painter, 1994,
cat. no. 6.

art world and society at large. Although unquestionably sympathetic to their position, Dumas never abandoned painting and never gave her work over to ideology, preferring instead to maintain the balance she had struck between her images and words.

In 1987, Dumas gave birth to a daughter, Helena, and a remarkable body of work followed. The most compelling is *The First People (I–IV)*, 1991 (fig. 14, p. 33), a series of four large canvases devoted to newborn infants. The paintings are disconcertingly powerful on a number of levels. Each is large, in fact, many times greater than life-size, and each is composed vertically. The infants are thus seen from an aerial vantage point, seemingly frozen outside any spatial context and cropped by the frame. An idealized image, which one associates with depictions of young children, is altogether absent; these are unattractive, squirming little beings with gnarled fingers and toes, bloated bellies, and wrinkled flesh. As any new parent will readily admit, this is precisely how newborns really look. Dumas's shocking treatment of the figure confounds conventional wisdom, leaving us with a body that is shockingly grotesque and real.

In the early 1990s, Dumas returned indirectly to the subject of apartheid, commenting on the received media images of the struggle for freedom among South Africa's Black majority. *Black Drawings*, 1991–92 (cat. no. 2, illus. p. vii), is a single work composed of 112 small drawings of Blacks, the majority of them men, who are depicted in india ink on paper. Dumas arranged the drawings into a grid and mounted them on a wall, in a manner reminiscent of the photographs of Bernhard and Hilla Becher. And yet, whereas the Bechers—and, for that matter, Thomas Ruff—have considered their subjects in an analytical, almost clinical way, Dumas's process is open-ended, and the resulting work is both more empathetic and politically charged than theirs. Within a tight Minimalist grid, Dumas has retained great range in characterization, with each head depicted with a different degree of realism. Dumas would later describe her intentions in that work: "Among other things, it was an attempt to exhibit my own unease, fear and admiration for the individuals grouped together under the term "Black."[12] On a basic level, Dumas's words lay bare the complexity of her feelings for her homeland. By extension, viewers are called upon to question the stereotypical images transmitted by the media regarding the struggle against apartheid in South Africa—the inspiring photogenic likeness of Nelson Mandela on the one hand, and a barrage of pictures of angry and often violent Black men and women in the townships on the other. Dumas's work reminds us that the implications of the received images of the South African struggle are far more complex than we might realize.

In her most recent work, Dumas has returned to the relationship between artists and models, and to the controversial subject of beauty. Following on *Black Drawings*, Dumas completed *Models*, 1994, another wall-mounted grid of ink-on-paper drawings, in this case, a panoramic catalog of female beauty drawn from the history of art, advertising, and the media. Dumas's roaming encyclopedia is breathtaking, ranging from images drawn from Rembrandt and Johannes Vermeer, to figures from film,

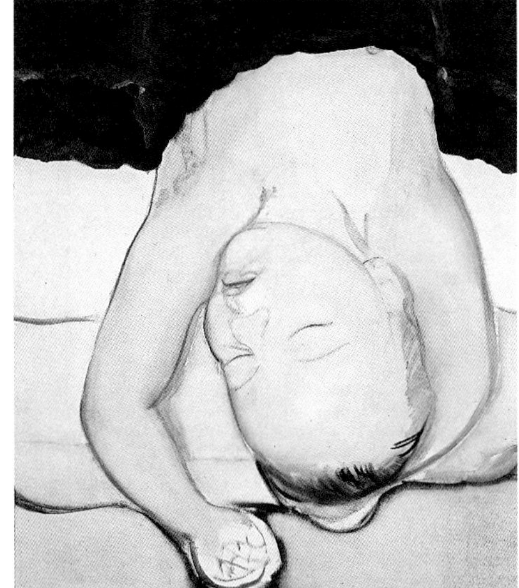

Cupid, 1994, cat. no. 4.

fashion, and music, among them Brigitte Bardot, Billie Holiday, and Claudia Schiffer.[13] The following year, Dumas broadened her roster of women even further. Chosen as one of three artists to represent The Netherlands in the 1995 Venice Biennale, Dumas exhibited a body of paintings called "Magdalena," 1995. The title refers to Mary Magdalene, the biblical "fallen women" who was transformed into a saint. With each painting devoted to a tall, slender, and quite aggressive woman, the series conflates the idealized, media-derived "beauty" of the fashion model with the confrontational, socially unacceptable "beauty" of prostitutes, all the while referring to the role of women in Western tradition.

Dumas's proclamation that "one cannot paint a picture of or make an image of a woman and not deal with the concept of beauty" strikes to the heart of her assumptions and intentions in these recent works. Just as Dumas is an avowed opponent of all images that would reduce human emotion and motivation to simple good and evil, she also seeks to root out any simpleminded or monolithic understanding of beauty. Beyond that, Dumas's attitude is informed by the recent efforts of many artists, critics, and theorists to politicize the imaging of the body. Just as evil may reside in banal circumstances, for Dumas, beauty is a most impure substance and may be found in the most unlikely subjects.[14]

Cold Woman, 1995, cat. no. 7.

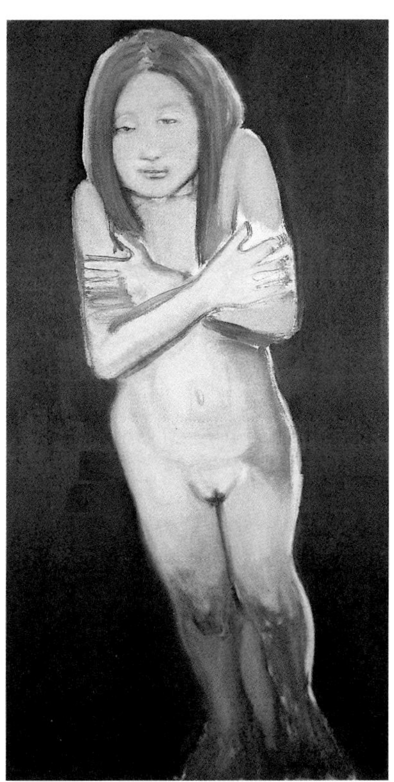

Ultimately, even the motives of the female painter are open to question in Dumas's withering critique, as is apparent in *The Painter*, 1995 (cat. no. 6, p. 37). In size and execution it is an unselfconscious, even modest, work and yet it may be Dumas's signature image to date. A seemingly innocent, young female artist stands before us, bearing bloodied hands rather than a loaded brush. The clear implication is that women artists are as capable as their male counterparts of impure motives, and that the imaging of the figure is a complex undertaking no matter the gender or generation of the artist. *The Painter* seems an apt summation of Dumas's drive to unmask hypocrisy in all its forms, even when it resides close to home.

Notes

1. Quoted in *Marlene Dumas: Models* (Salzburg: Salzburger Kunstverein, 1995), 23.
2. Quoted in Marja Bosma, "Talking to Strangers," *Dutch Heights: Art and Culture in the Netherlands* 3 (September 1990): 14.
3. This photograph is reproduced in *Marlene Dumas/Francis Bacon: Det unika med att vara en människa/The Particularity of Being Human* (Malmö, Sweden: Malmö Konsthall, 1995), 79.
4. Quoted in *Marlene Dumas: Miss Interpreted* (Eindhoven, The Netherlands: Stedelijk Van Abbemuseum, 1992), 42.
5. I am indebted to Paul Andriesse for this and other unpublished biographical information.
6. Quoted in Ingrid Schaffner, "'Erotic Displays of Mental Confusions': Marlene Dumas at the Van Abbemuseum," *Kunst en Museum Journaal* 3, no. 6 (1992): 26.
7. Quoted in *The Eyes of the Night Creatures* (Amsterdam: Galerie Paul Andriesse, 1985), n.p.
8. Ibid.
9. Quoted in *Marlene Dumas: Miss Interpreted*, 34.
10. These images are reproduced together under the title "Bank," in *Marlene Dumas: Miss Interpreted*, 85–100.
11. *Defining in the Negative* is reproduced in *Marlene Dumas: Miss Interpreted*, 14.
12. Quoted in *Das 21. Jahrhundert* (Basel: Kunsthalle Basel, 1993), 124.
13. See Ernst van Alphen, "Facing Defacement: 'Models' and Marlene Dumas's Intervention in Western Art," *Marlene Dumas: Models*, 67–68.
14. See Dave Hickey, The Invisible Dragon: Four Essays on Beauty (Los Angeles: Art Issues Press, 1993), and Peter Schjeldahl, "Beauty," *Art Issues*, no. 33 (May-June 1994): 24–28.

Robert Gober
Plumbing Robert Gober

I thought of the drains as metaphors functioning as traditional painting, as a window into another world. However, the world that you enter into through the metaphor of the drain would be something darker and unknown.[1]
—Robert Gober, 1990

In 1994–95, Robert Gober completed several new object sculptures for an exhibition at the Museum für Gegenwartskunst in Basel. Although apparently disparate—a chair, an oversized tissue box, and an untraversable corridor—each work shares a common reference: a drain or pipe. For *Chair with Pipe*, 1994–95 (cat. no. 9, p. 44), Gober fabricated a rather standard-model living-room armchair, to which he added a handmade slipcover bearing a printed pattern resembling deckchair fabric with interwoven images of male arms and legs. *Untitled*, 1994–95, is an outlandishly oversized tissue box, also handmade, and in this case painted with a floral pattern. Each sculpture is impaled by an industrial-gauge culvert, a corrugated pipe commonly used in flood control.
The largest sculpture in the Basel exhibition was *Untitled*, 1995, a long, narrow domestic corridor, complete with paired doorways and sewer drains of the type found in every American street. Running underground beneath the drain was a sewer filled with running water, leaves, and beer cans.

At first glance, plumbing might seem an odd point of departure for a discussion of Gober's work. Yet, pipes, drains, running water, and the presence and absence of fixtures and fluids are among the most enduring of his subjects. They are also among the most meaningful, for in exploring seemingly mundane subjects and imbuing them with surprise, mystery, and allusion, Gober has defined a special direction for himself as an artist of private impulse whose sculptures have public implication.

Gober's images of plumbing appeared quite early in his work. Soon after graduating with a bachelor's degree in art from Middlebury College in Vermont in 1976, he moved to New York, where he labored in various forms of construction. Gifted with his hands, Gober worked as a carpenter, building all manner of objects, including

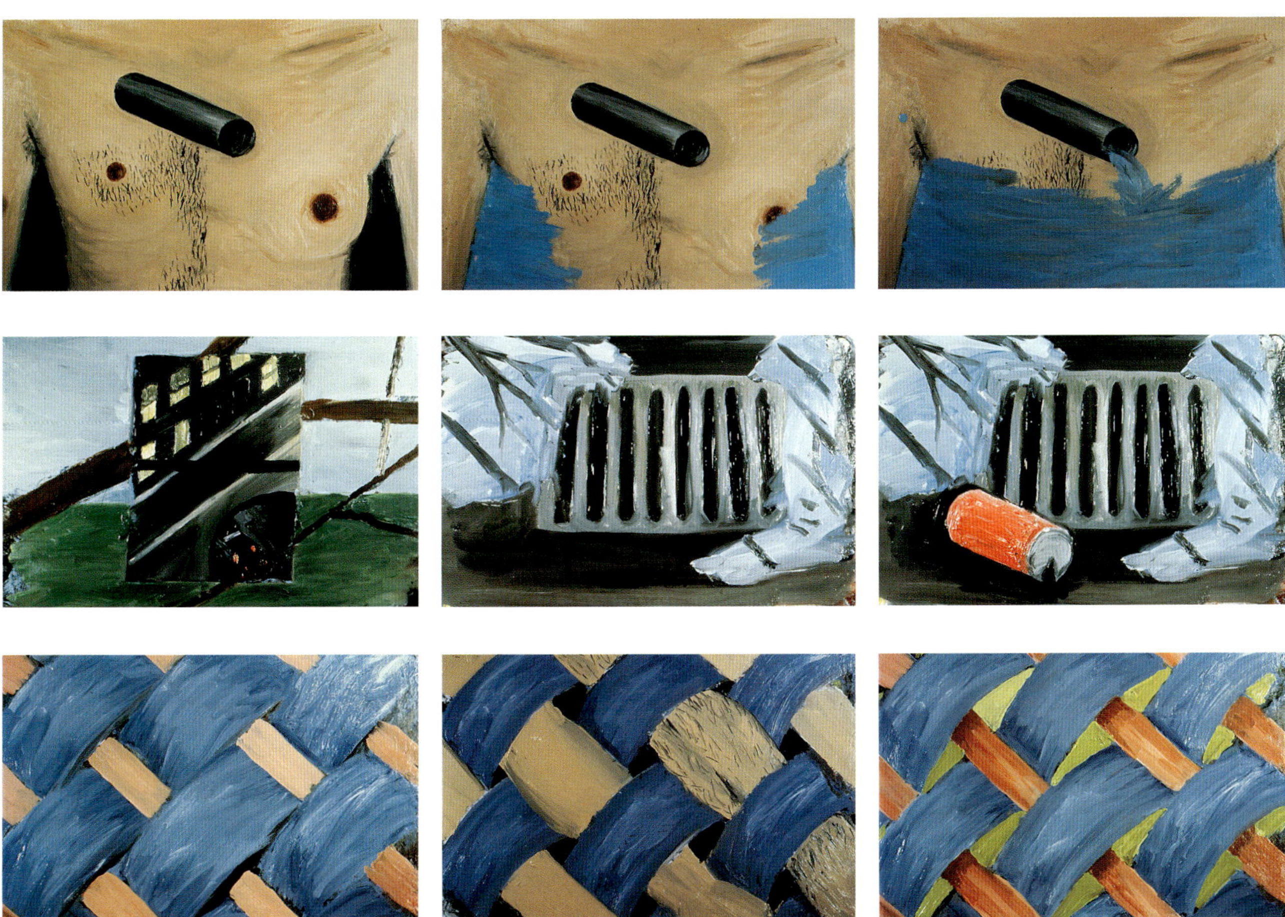

Fig. 16. *Slides of a Changing Painting,* detail, 1982–83.

dollhouses, and stretcher bars for several painters. Gober's arrival in New York coincided with the beginnings of Neo-Expressionism. "I had a kind of allergic reaction to it. So, in a way, my intuitive response to that gluttonous situation was to make a surfeit of paintings that really didn't exist."[2] If Gober was disinterested in his paintings as finished objects, he was obsessed with recording the images he was conceiving.

> *I had this little board on a table, about 11 x 14 inches on which I painted on and off for a year. I had my camera and lights mounted over it. I would paint, take a slide, add more paint, take a slide, scrape the paint off, take a slide. I took thousands of slides over the course of a year and then edited them down and showed them with a dissolve, basically a memoir of a painting. Looking back now, many of the images proved to be germane, uncannily so.*[3]

Slides of a Changing Painting, 1982–83 (fig. 16), proved to be nothing less than a genetic image bank for the artist. The slides reveal torsos, dresses, forests, arms, and legs—motifs that have reverberated in Gober's work ever since. Some of the most riveting and disconcerting ones deal with plumbing: kitchen and street drains, some of them accompanied by beer cans or covered over by autumn leaves and branches. Equally powerful is a series of images of a culvert protruding from a human chest of mixed gender; over the course of several slides, the pipe spills out water that gradually covers the chest, effectively drowning the body.

Simultaneous with *Slides of a Changing Painting,* Gober was sculpting animal and human figures in plaster, as well as miniature houses and churches. By 1985 he was exhibiting the objects that gave rise to his early notoriety: sinks, generally of minimal

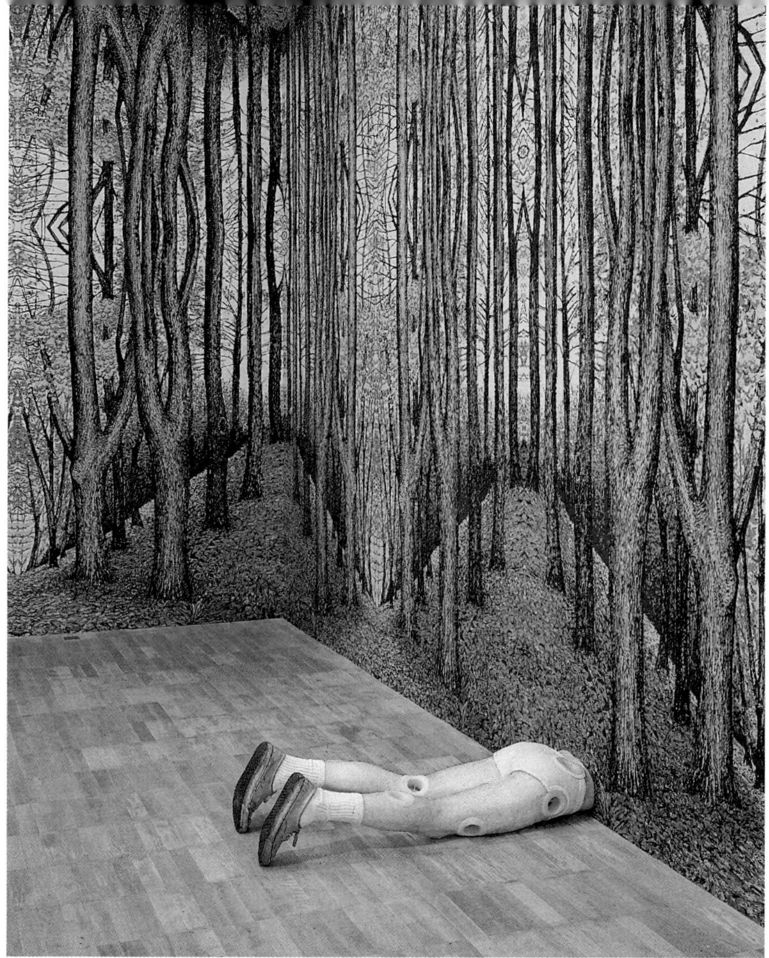

Fig. 17. *Untitled*, 1991. Installation, "Robert Gober," Galerie Nationale du Jeu de Paume, Paris, 1991.

but at times baroque form, mounted on walls. From the outset the sinks were conspicuous for their dysfunctional character, as they bore orifices but neither plumbing fixtures nor running water. The absence of function allowed a kind of Surrealist transposition, for not only did the sinks seem to metamorphose anatomically, but they also came to suggest various states of mind. When they were first shown in New York at the Paula Cooper Gallery in the fall of 1985, John Russell described the show in the *New York Times* as a "very impressive debut.... What is in life an indispensable but anonymous appliance, constantly in use but never thought about, and still less looked at, turns out to secrete within it reserves of eloquence that none of us had expected."[4]

Gober's work was quickly mated with the sculpture of other young object-based artists—in particular Jeff Koons and Haim Steinbach—who were pursuing a Neo-Conceptual critique of consumer society as it grew exponentially in the late 1980s. But Gober was miscast in that role. The distinction could be discerned in his craft, for while the others most often purchased objects and then composed them, Gober was adeptly constructing his pieces. His skill and ingenuity were immediately evident in the sinks, and critics were soon commenting on the labor-intensive nature of his sculpture. Gober, however, has downplayed that aspect, stating, "I think I have a knack for making things that look like they take a long time to make, but it's a trick. It doesn't actually take me that long."[5] Of far greater consequence is Gober's fascination with certain images and the amount of time he allows himself to ponder them before bringing them into his work. "It's more a nursing of an image that haunts me and letting it sit and breed in my mind, and then, if it's resonant, I'll try to figure out formally [if this] could this be an interesting sculpture to look at."[6]

Gober's memory echoes with associations. The result is that certain of his sinks assume the psychological character of portraits: for example, sinks used by his grandmothers, his father, or the artist himself.[7] The combination of memory, patience, and dexterity in his working process is striking when considered against so much contemporary art that is media based and ultimately temporal. Gober's resilience, his willingness to bring an idea to term over the course of sometimes several years, has yielded work that is consummate from conception to completion. The conceptual clarity and the directness of the realization of the image are so precise that we can scarcely imagine the work in any other form.

Gober began to shift focus around 1986. Until then, his sculptures had most often been mounted on walls in a rather traditional manner or occasionally installed in corners. But in sculptures such as *The Disappearing Sink*, 1986, or *Two Partially Buried Sinks*, 1986–87, Gober placed part of the work beyond view, embedding it either in a wall or underground. While on the one hand

Gober was literally bringing the sinks to a conclusion by burying them, he was also introducing narrative and theatrical aspects into his practice. Simultaneously, his exhibitions became ensembles, groups of works to be seen in concert with one another and suggestive of domestic arrangements. For an installation at the Paula Cooper Gallery in 1987, Gober showed a crib folded into an X shape and a living-room chair with a slipcover bearing a floral pattern. The odd distortions of form and treatments of surface, and Gober's placement of the sculptures in discomforting relationships to one another, gave the gallery the eerie feeling of a Diane Arbus photograph, with the domestic interior now inhabited by objects rather than individuals.

As Gober's work veered toward increasingly complex environments during the late 1980s and early 1990s, drains came to play a lead role. They first appear in *Untitled*, 1987–88, a small plaster stool with short wooden legs. Compact in size, sitting low to the floor, and with the drain inserted squarely in the seat, the piece suggests a bidet. Gober went to great lengths to design and fabricate a drain to his particular specifications, taking molds of the one in his kitchen, adding a cruciform element, and ultimately casting it in pewter.[8] Another exhibition at the Paula Cooper Gallery, in 1989, marked a breakthrough for the artist. The former painter now papered the gallery with images of male and female genitalia—employing this surrogate painting medium as a set design against which sculptures would be seen and considered. Into the wallpaper he embedded a row of drains, and in the center of the space Gober installed *Wedding Dress*, 1989, a life-size, hollow gown. In that context, the drains created a secret place, full of metaphor and mystery, and were far more allusive than the other objects and images in the room.

In 1989–90, Gober made his first sculptures of legs, specifically male legs, with shoes and socks, and pants pulled up a bit too high so as to reveal the calves. Gober set the sculptures on the floor and attached them to walls, a reference perhaps to the omnipresent homeless sprawled on the sidewalks of New York. The image of the disembodied leg had resonated in Gober's mind for some time, in the form of cropped legs that he had seen while seated in stalls in mens' rooms or while flying on planes.[9] The image had a much older derivation, as well. Gober recalls:

> *My mother ... used to work as a nurse in an operating room, and she used to entertain us as kids by telling stories about the hospital. One of the first operations was an amputation, and they cut off the leg and handed it to her. Stories like that had a big impact.*[10]

Slowly the legs extended to include torsos and buttocks, some of them imprinted with sheet music, others bearing candles, and some drains. Some of these are perversely humorous, some elegiac, but one is utterly bone chilling. This is *Untitled*, 1991 (fig. 17), a cast of a male body from the waist down. Stripped to his underwear, shoes, and socks, the figure is ravaged with gaping plastic drains as if they were, in fact, bullet holes. When Gober affixed the piece to a gallery wall papered with a densely forested scene for an exhibition at the Galerie Nationale du Jeu de Paume, Paris, in 1991, the allusion to death could not have been more clear.

The dismay and resignation in this work was borne of the AIDS crisis. The slightly wacky humor that had at times inhabited his sculpture to this point was now replaced with a mood far more macabre. Although language seldom plays a critical role in his art, during this time he twice resorted to words. Invited by the art journal *Parkett* to author a piece on the impact of the disease on the New York art world, Gober wrote:

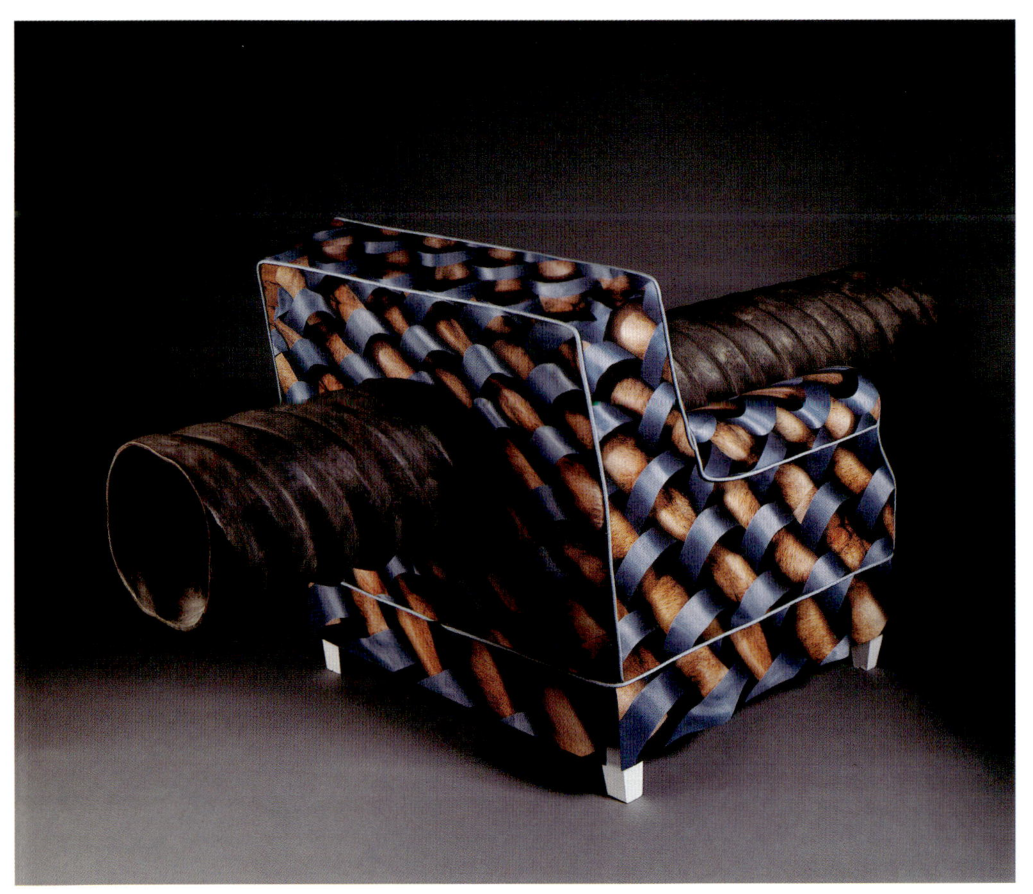

Chair with Pipe, 1994–95, cat. no. 9.

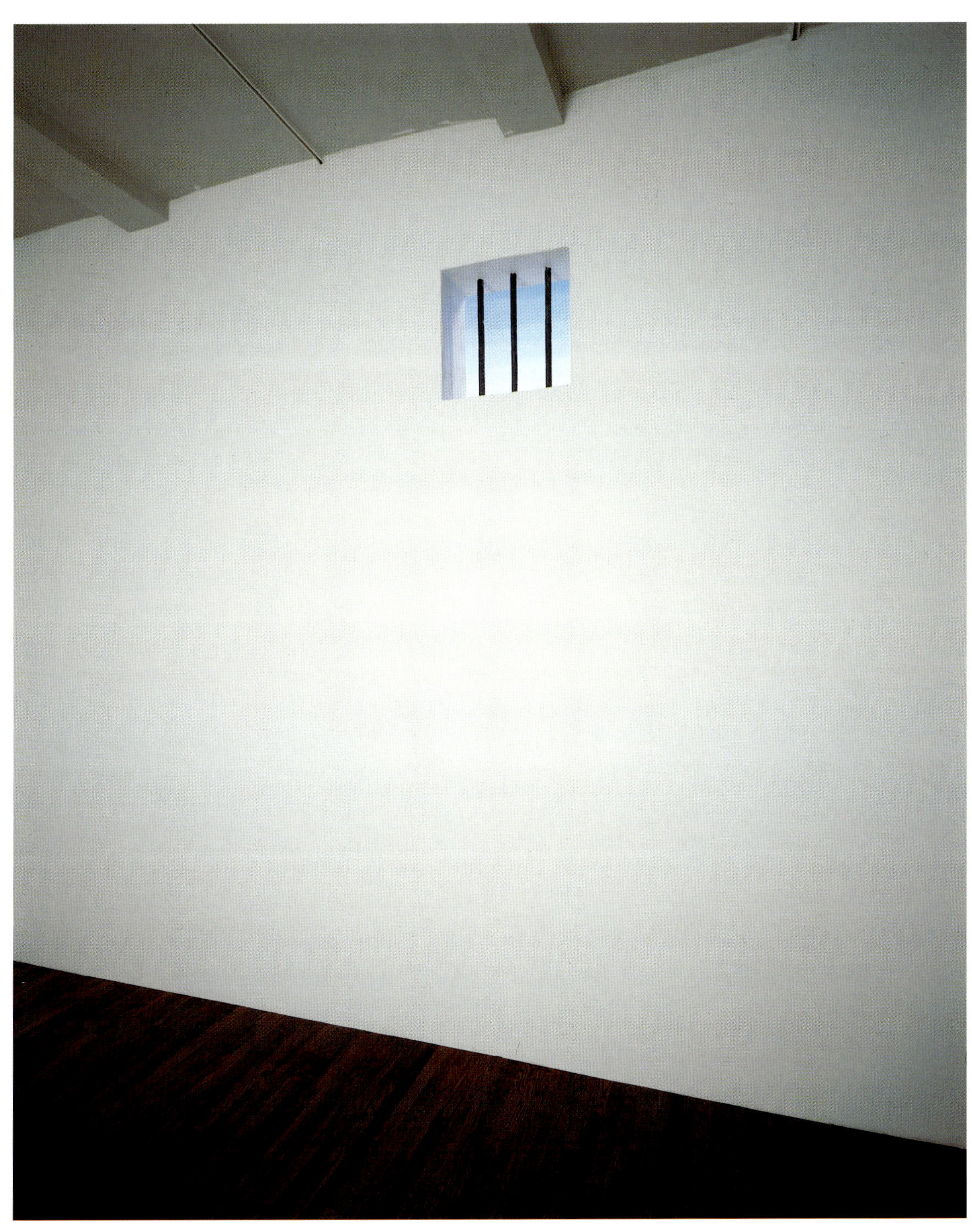

Prison Window, 1992,
cat. no. 8.

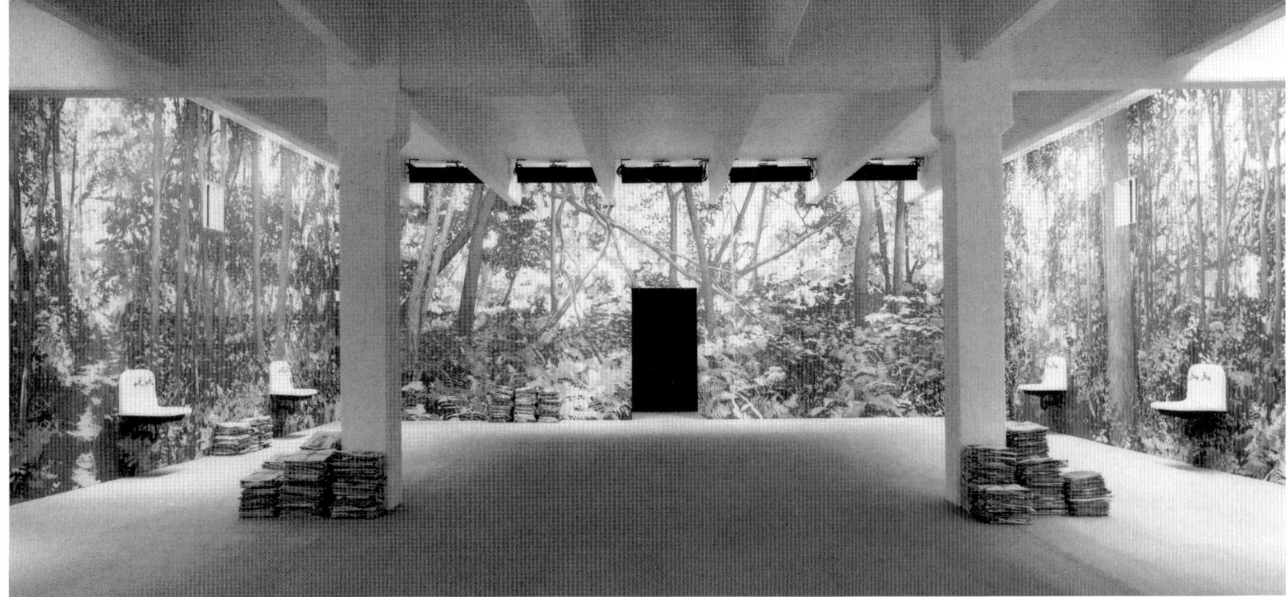

Fig. 18. Installation, "Robert Gober," Dia Center for the Arts, New York, 1992–93.

If people aren't themselves sick, they know someone who is, or they are struggling to assimilate the loss of someone who was. For me, death has temporarily overtaken life in New York City. And most of the artists I know are fumbling for ways to express this.[11]

In 1991, Gober transformed a page from the *New York Times*. Backdating it to 1960, six years after his birth, he inserted—among weather reports, lottery results, and wedding announcements—a small notice from his Connecticut hometown describing his own childhood death in an apparently accidental drowning while the backyard pool was being drained. Significantly, this explicit autobiographical reference came at a highly charged moment of public concern about AIDS, when the artist allowed himself to grieve publicly through his work.

Many of Gober's working ideas at that time culminated in an exhibition at the Dia Center for the Arts in New York in the fall of 1992 (fig. 18). There he composed an environment within the larger, darkened industrial exhibition space. Entry into the installation resembled descent into a murky, subterranean space. Although the room was painted with an Edenic forest scene, the bars on the windows set high on the walls, the stacks of old newspapers (some of which were replicas by Gober bearing self-referential images) tied with string and ready for disposal, and the rat bait all combined to suggest a family basement. In the mythology of the American home, light-filled attics are crowded to overflowing with pleasant memories—dusty scrapbooks, family photographs, trophies, and other mementos. But basements are eternally damp, dark inhospitable grottoes lined with wood paneling or old wallpaper in halfhearted attempts to lighten the mood—rooms where objects are stored or simply discarded after use. If the attic is the locus where memory is preserved, the basement is where less idyllic objects are cast out to be forgotten or purposely excluded from memory. At the Dia Center exhibition, Gober's sinks for the first time bore fixtures from which water trickled without end. While some interpreted the running water and the forest setting as illusory waterfalls in Eden,[12] more likely the images evoked the relentless dripping of basement plumbing in poor repair, the faucets and drains emblematic of matters unattended to in domestic life.

The Dia installation marked a momentary culmination in Gober's interest in spectacle, in terms of all-consuming room environments. Since then he has concentrated the theatrical dynamism of his former installations into individual objects. One of the most powerful of these recent works is *Untitled*, 1994–95 (illus. p. viii), in which frail sculpted children's legs, bearing only white socks and sandals, are set into an alcove representing a domestic fireplace, replete with prerecorded crackling sounds from within. In other recent works, the artist has merged the domestic environment with the world outside, such as in *Untitled (Man in Drain)*,

1993–94 (fig. 19), which consists of a street grate set into the floor. If Gober's Dia installation introduced a dank world of subterranean basements and discarded memory, the current works present a netherworld of dripping sewers. Floating beneath the grate is a man's chest with water flowing through a drain embedded in his sternum. While, on the one hand, the piece unconsciously satirizes Carl Andre's floor plans of the 1960s—in which art was reduced to the lowest possible psychological and sculptural profile—Gober also stages an unspeakable drama just beyond our reach.

It is from this context that Gober's new sculptures, dominated by corrugated rain culverts, rammed violently through tissue boxes and covered armchairs, have emerged. Formerly small domestic drains are now culverts and street drains, large enough to sweep a person away. The disjunction between the tissue box, which dispenses the most delicate and transient of objects, bound for a simple use and then disposed of, and the gaping pipe is imaginable only in a nightmare or perhaps a René Magritte painting. The once-benign armchair, a place of comfort and repose, is now covered in fabric printed with interwoven deckchair mesh and images of Gober's own arms and legs; impaled by the culvert, the tangle of limbs seems poised to be swept through the pipe and into a sewer beyond. Throughout, the expansion of the drain, previously in his sculptures a small household item of symbolic import, to a subterranean sinkhole through which figures may be lost, marks the transition of Gober's work from witty anecdote to macabre vision.

Notes

1. Quoted in Richard Flood, "Robert Gober: Special Editions, An Interview," *Print Collectors Newsletter* 21, no. 1 (March-April 1990): 8.
2. Quoted in "Robert Gober: Interview with Richard Flood," *Robert Gober* (London: Serpentine Gallery, 1993), 14.
3. Ibid.
4. John Russell, "Art: Jan Hafstrom Opens Season of New Names," *New York Times*, 4 October 1985, C24.
5. Quoted in *Print Collectors Newsletter*, 9.
6. Ibid., 6.
7. Gary Garrells, "New Sculpture," in catalog of the same name (Chicago: Renaissance Society at the University of Chicago, 1986), n.p.
8. Quoted in *Print Collectors Newsletter*, 7–8.
9. Quoted in *Robert Gober*, 13.
10. Quoted in Gary Indiana, "Robert Gober: Success," *Interview* 20, no. 5 (May 1990): 72.
11. Robert Gober, "Cumulus from America," *Parkett*, no. 19 (1989): 169.
12. See Lynne Cooke, "Disputed Terrain," in *Robert Gober*, 16.

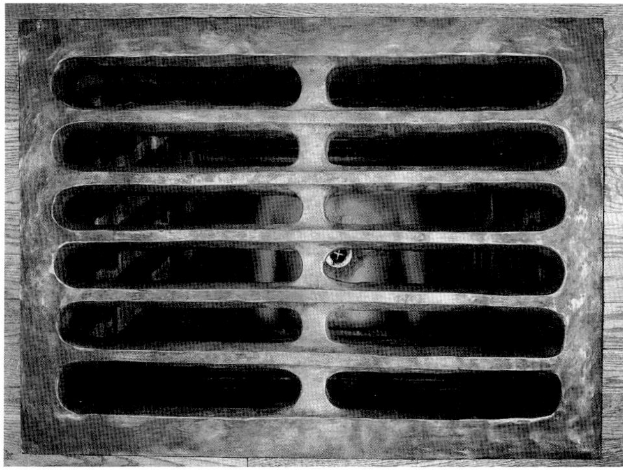

Fig. 19. *Untitled (Man in Drain)*, 1993–94.

Mona Hatoum
Direct Physical Experience

The body was always very much the focal point. Originally, when I did performance, I used the body—my body—as a metaphor for social systems. Now I'm trying to set up situations where the viewer has a direct physical experience with the installation and becomes completely implicated in it.[1]

—Mona Hatoum, 1995

Over the last fifteen years, Mona Hatoum has moved seamlessly between performance to videotape to installation to sculptural object. While she initially employed her own body as the raw material and her own experience as the narrative content of her work, in recent years she has explored a more metaphorical but no less powerful direction. In absenting herself from her work, Hatoum has extended and broadened the associative implications of her installations and directly engaged the viewer in the process. Despite their deceptively minimal means, Hatoum's recent sculptures and the spatial environments they inhabit yield a memorable and psychologically charged body of work.

Born in Beirut, Lebanon, in 1952, Hatoum is the third daughter of Palestinian parents. Her family had fled Palestine in 1948 following the founding of Israel, and their vivid if largely unspoken memories of the circumstances of their emigration remain with their daughter to this day. Hatoum, who attended Beirut University College in the early 1970s, was visiting London in 1975 when civil war broke out in Lebanon. Unable to return to her family's adopted home for several years, she too became an émigré, in England. Resourceful and hoping to become an artist, Hatoum enrolled in the Byam Shaw School, a small London art school with an international student body, where she remained for four years, through 1979, before she was admitted to the Slade School. Although she was engaged with Minimalist aesthetics at the time, Hatoum's experience at the Slade propelled her in an activist direction. While she had felt at home at the Byam Shaw School, at the Slade she encountered ethnic, class, and gender structures that were pronounced and complex. As a result, rather than retreat into purely aesthetic concerns, Hatoum loaded her sculptural installations with physical challenge, experimenting with electricity, for instance,

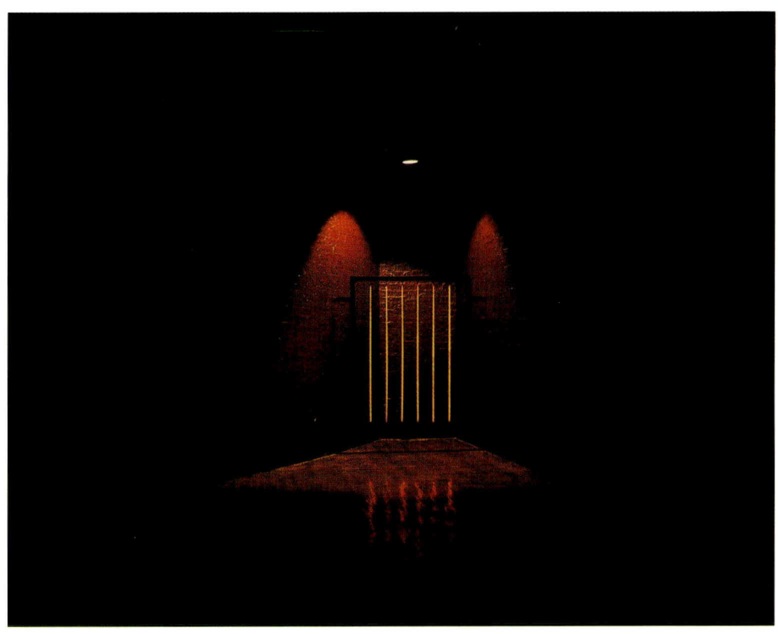

Fig. 20. *The Light at the End*, 1989.

in ways that were deemed unacceptable for presentation by the school authorities. Those developments led her to focus first on performance and later on videotape, in work based equally on a rejection of the art establishment as she had experienced it at the Slade and a passionate concern for the political circumstances of Third World peoples.[2]

Several of Hatoum's early performances involved acts of exceptional physical endurance, as she employed her body as a metaphor for the suffering of others. For *Under Siege*, which she performed in London in May 1982, she stripped herself of clothes and caged herself in a mud-filled Plexiglas container approximately the size of a bedroom closet. For seven grueling hours, Hatoum futilely attempted to stand up, each time slipping and falling to the bottom. The following year she performed *The Negotiating Table* (illus. p. v) in Ottawa, Canada. For this, she lay motionless for three hours on a table wrapped in a blood-stained, entrails-covered body bag. Two empty chairs were placed near the table, with tape-recorded news accounts of the civil war and peace negotiations in the Middle East played into the space. Perhaps Hatoum's most literal performance, if not also the most powerful, was *Variation on Discord and Divisions*, which she debuted in New York in 1984: In a shallow architectural space lined in newspapers, the darkly hooded Hatoum performed a variety of acts, including tracing the lines of her eyes, nose, and mouth with a knife, finally piercing the cloth covering. Other elements of the performance involved her scrubbing an apparently blood-stained floor, and seeming to pull entrails from her own body.

In a 1987 interview, Hatoum clarified her intentions in these works:

> *In fact I can think of only one piece which referred specifically to the invasion of Lebanon. It was entitled* The Negotiating Table *and it was more like a "tableau vivant." ... I made this work right after the Israeli invasion and the massacres in the camps which for me was the most shattering experience of my life. But in general my work is about my experience of living in the West as a person from the Third World.*[3]

In the same interview, Hatoum described performance as a medium based in "communication and a direct rapport or interaction with the audience without the mediation of an art object."[4] Yet a work such as *Variation on Discord and Divisions*, which Hatoum performed on several occasions in North America, had its drawbacks. The obviously strenuous, physical nature of her work, and the lengthy preparation required, even for the relatively small audience that actually experienced it, began to take a toll. As early as 1983, Hatoum had made *So Much I Want to Say* (fig. 21), a videotape of five-minute's duration, featuring a series of close-up stills of the artist's face covered by a hand that attempts to restrain her from repeating the words of the title. Here, Hatoum translated the prolonged duration of several of her performances into closely related serial or repeated images. In the process, she distilled the immediacy and power of her performances into videotape while carefully controlling the form and content. From here, Hatoum's work would evolve from a spectacle of physical endurance and a narrative of inevitably autobiographical and political implication toward an expression of quiet but relentless power. By the late 1980s, videotape was Hatoum's principal medium.

Hatoum's breakthrough work was *Measures of Distance*, 1988 (fig. 22). A videotape of fifteen-minute's duration, the work focused on a series of images the artist made of her mother during a visit to Beirut in 1981 and on the subsequent letters that they exchanged. The essence of the videotape is the sound of Hatoum's voice reading her mother's words aloud, heard against a visual backdrop showing the correspondence handwritten in Arabic. Hatoum photographed the letters so as to make them look like barbed wire, then layered them over indistinct stills. Her mother's letters describe her longing for the happiness and security of Palestine, which was "paradise compared to Beirut," and the difficulty of their departure in 1948, which she likens to being "stripped of her soul, identity, and sense of pride." She explains the worsening situation in Beirut after 1981, which made it difficult for her to visit family members within the city or even to venture outside her home to post letters. Throughout, the political implications of *Measures of Distance* are grounded in Hatoum's relationship with her mother. During the course of the 1981 visit, her conversations with her mother were deeply personal, touching upon matters of identification, separation, intimacy, and even sexuality. Hatoum had videotaped elements of their encounter, and in the finished work she included footage of her mother showering. Such was the power of this experience and her feeling of responsibility to her mother, that Hatoum required eight years to integrate the letters and the videotape into her work. When it was complete, she felt liberated artistically, as the process of publicly presenting a fully personal, even intimate, narrative in which she "said all that could be said," freed her of the self-imposed obligation "to tell the whole story" in future work.[5]

Fig. 21. *So Much I Want to Say*, 1983.

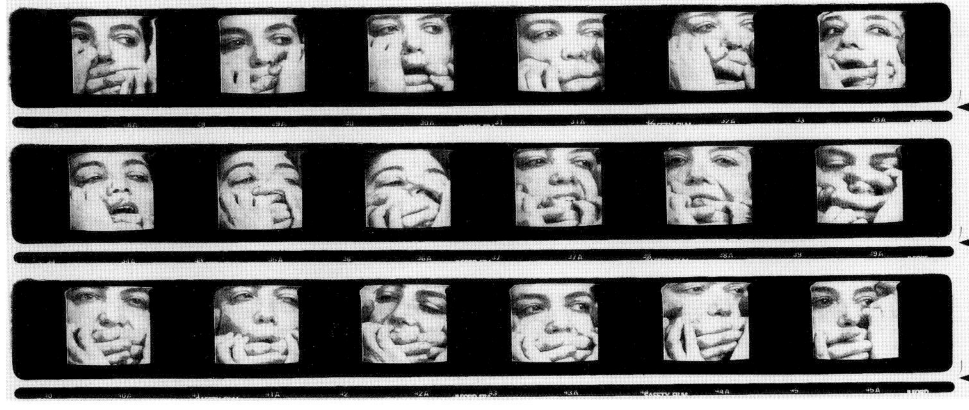

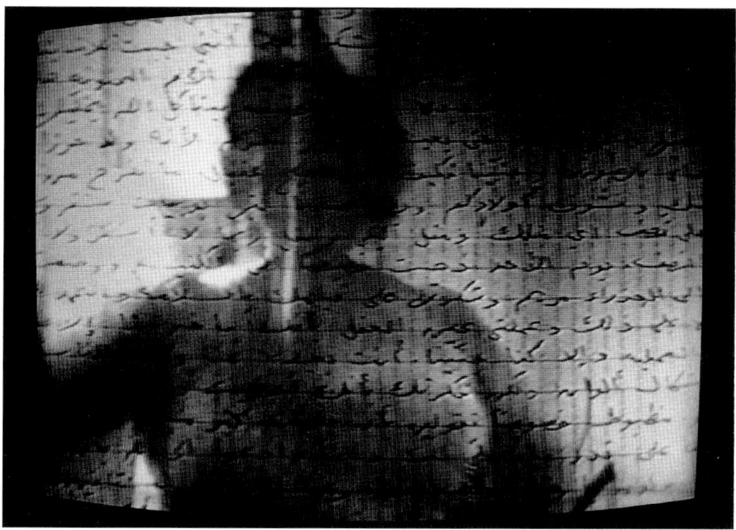

Fig. 22. *Measures of Distance*, 1988.

This new possibility became evident almost immediately. In 1989, Hatoum made *The Light at the End* (fig. 20). Installed in a darkened, wedge-shaped space, the piece consists of a series of six glowing electrical elements configured in an upright position in midair. These bright orange rods are scaled to the human body and mounted in an angled iron framework as if to suggest a suspended bed frame. Illuminated theatrically by a single spotlight and positioned at the concave end of the gallery space, the structure serves to attract and repulse. We are drawn unavoidably into Hatoum's web only to realize that real danger lurks in the highly charged sculpture. It is a work of consummate power, combining the drama of Hatoum's earlier performances with the newly evolved restraint of the videotapes. Hatoum described the work in an 1989 interview:

> *In* The Light at the End *I adopt a "minimal" aesthetic, but unlike minimal sculpture, the piece is referential and reverberates with meaning and associations. The theme of a divide, a psychic and physical barrier, has been central to my work, often referring to social, political and historical divisions. This is partly a personal metaphor but I think my most successful work has managed to distance itself from any personal or historical specificities.*[6]

If *The Light at the End* reflects Hatoum's nascent Minimalist sensibility and her early student experiments with electrical current, it also extends the formalist foundations laid by the light sculpture of Dan Flavin. No longer obliged "to tell the whole story," Hatoum here exchanges the terrible power of the body caged, bound, or shrouded, for an object and an environment of metaphorical but equally compelling meaning.

Hatoum has lived a somewhat peripatetic life in the West: she has traveled widely, as a performance artist in the early 1980s, and as an artist-in-residence, lecturer, and professor more recently. From 1989 to 1992 she was a Senior Fellow at the Cardiff Institute of Higher Education, a position that culminated in 1992 in the exhibition "Dissected Space." Hatoum completed two major new works for that show, both of which continue the direction introduced in *The Light at the End*. The references to bed frames and divided spaces in that installation are apparant in *Short Space*, 1992, which is composed of three parallel rows of hanging bedsprings, each suspended from a horizontal beam. Each row is raised and lowered by a motorized pulley system, reversing direction at the point at which it touches the ground. The movement proceeds in an achingly gradual manner, filling the gallery space with an air of chilling discomfort. The other piece, *Light Sentence*, 1992, is also made from existing objects, in this case, metal mesh lockers. As with *Light at the End* and *Short Space*, Hatoum worked with translucent objects, and in all three works one can scarcely escape the reference to fences and imprisonment. In *Light Sentence* the small cubic lockers are stacked six-feet high in a U-shaped configuration. In the center is a single suspended lightbulb, which—as in *Short Space*—descends until it grazes the floor and then starts back up again. The shadows that the light casts through the lockers on the walls behind destabilize the space, creating an unnerving atmosphere for the viewer.

These three major works—*Light at the End*, *Short Space*, and *Light Sentence*—

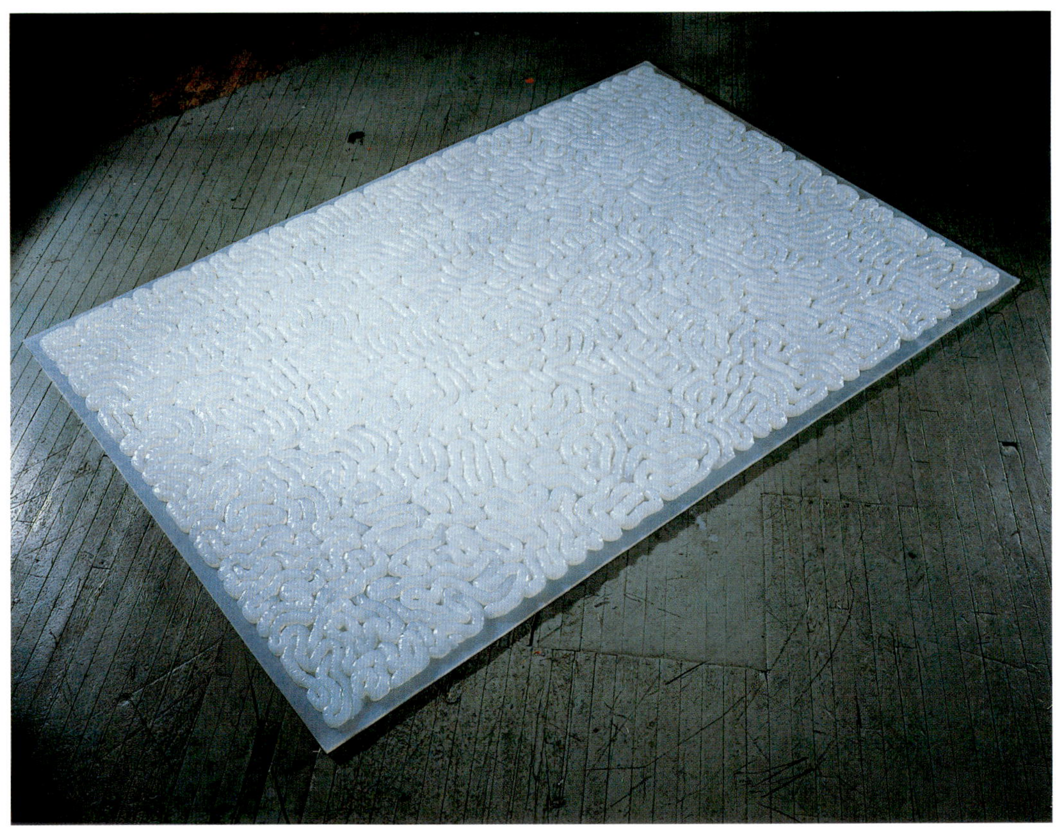

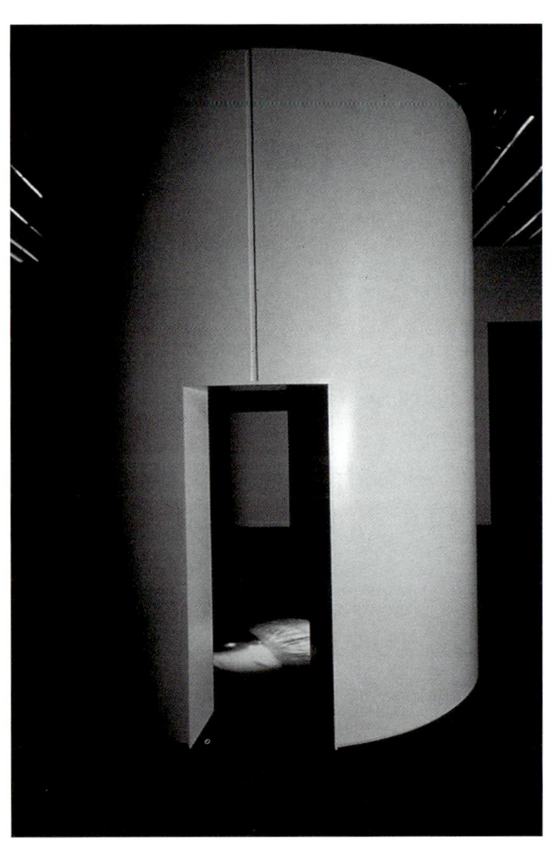

Entrails Carpet, 1995, cat. no. 11.

Fig. 23. *Corps étranger* (Foreign Body), 1994.

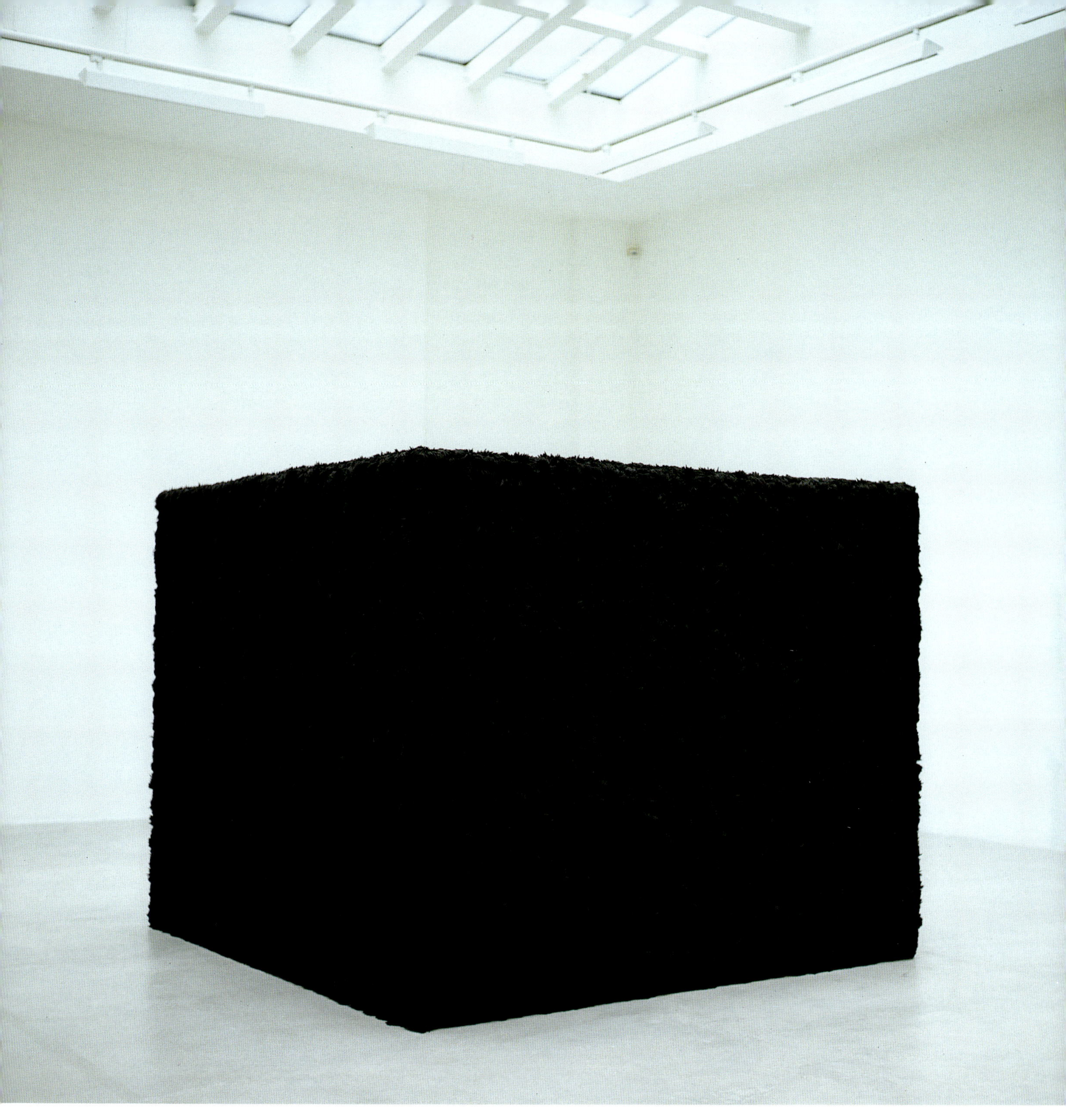

Socle du Monde
(Pedestal of the World),
1992 (refabricated 1996),
cat. no. 10.

are startling in their consistency and powerful impact. In each, Hatoum has employed metal and light to create inaccessible spaces. As in her earlier performances, which often included tables and chairs, these new sculptures show bed frames and bedsprings stripped down and manipulated to suggest themes of separation rather than repose, tension rather than rest. Hatoum's ease in moving from her highly personalized form of performance and video to sculpture, and her dexterity with materials, recall a similar shift in the work of Bruce Nauman a decade earlier. Like Nauman, Hatoum has evolved from making works featuring her own body to sculptural environments fraught with tension and activated by the engagement of the viewer.

This is not to say that Hatoum's evolution away from her own body as a subject and from videotape images has been absolute. One remarkable exception is *Corps étranger* (Foreign Body), 1994 (fig. 23, p. 52), a video installation made for an exhibition of Hatoum's work at the Musée National d'Art Moderne, Paris, in 1994. In this, Hatoum created a small, shell-like tubular environment inside which only a few people may stand. Projected on the floor is a videotape that Hatoum made of her own skin and hair that also delves inside her body with the aid of endoscopy and coloscopy, medical procedures employing fiber optics to film the digestive system and the colon and intestines, respectively. As the camera moves relentlessly through the artist's body, the sound of a heartbeat reverberates emphatically, magnifying the effect exponentially. The work stands in contrast to Hatoum's earlier performances in which she effectively politicized her body, and to contemporaneous pieces by Matthew Barney, which plumb the internal workings of the body in a fantastic manner. Hatoum's images are clinical, yet the fever pitch of her explorations of her body ultimately yields an installation of disconcerting power.

For all its relentless, probing intensity, *Corps étranger* is nonetheless exceptional in Hatoum's work of the 1990s. The degree to which Hatoum has modified her position and the direction of her art in recent years is perhaps best seen in the sculpture *Socle du Monde* (Pedestal of the World), 1992 (refabricated 1996; cat no. 10, p. 53). The sculpture refers directly to a landmark work of the same title made by Piero Manzoni thirty years earlier. Manzoni's legacy centers on his critique of the nature of art and the identity of the artist, an activity that exalted the artist's breath or excrement as art or resulted in sculpture pedestals on which the artist, or a member of the public, might stand. Manzoni's *Socle du Monde*, 1961, is an iron cube installed in a Danish park. The French-language inscription "Socle du Monde, socle magic n. 3 de Piero Manzoni—1961 Hommage à Galileo" is inverted on the base, effectively enshrining the earth as the sculpture. The reference to Galileo—the sixteenth-century astronomer and physicist who proved the Copernican theory holding that the planets revolve around the sun—underscores the fallacy of glorifying art or separating it from more pressing realities.

Although Hatoum's *Socle du Monde* is an homage to Manzoni and also made of iron, her version is instead composed of iron filings held in place by magnets mounted within. The surface of her cube—the ultimate in self-evident modernist sculptural forms—is articulated with an endless pattern resembling entrails. The sculpture is thus deceptively rich in its references, extending from Hatoum's interest in Minimalism while a student, her performances of the early and mid-1980s with their allusions to blood and internal organs, to the scatological works of Manzoni and the articulated cubic sculptures of Eva Hesse.

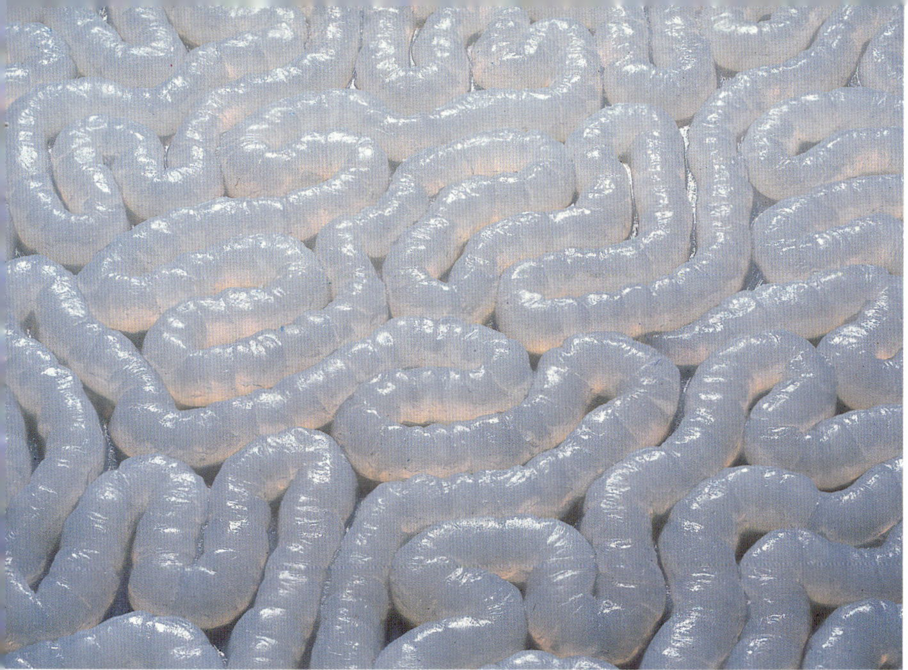

Entrails Carpet, 1995, detail, cat. no. 11.

When Hatoum first exhibited *Socle du Monde* in 1992, she published a statement in which she noted Manzoni's achievement and also related it to the 1990s:

> *Thirty years later, the plinth, which always denotes the separate and inanimate character of what is placed upon it, has itself lost its homogeneity and stability and taken on the appearance of a decaying unstable structure. ... Today, the idea of a pedestal for the earth fixing it at the center of the universe may suggest a revival of anachronistic ideas and blind beliefs which are becoming more and more apparent in every part of the planet.*[7]

Hatoum has taken up the idea of "anachronistic ideas and blind beliefs" in two recent works, *Entrails Carpet* (cat. no. 11, p. 52 and above) and *Prayer Mat*, both 1995. Just as she transformed the plinth metaphorically, from an object providing support for art into a decaying structure, Hatoum here destabilizes the carpet and the prayer mat—objects that have long been central to the export trade of the Middle East and its predominant religion, respectively. For *Entrails Carpet*, Hatoum applied the same meandering organic pattern to a beautifully translucent surface of molded silicone rubber. In the case of *Prayer Mat* the surface is composed quite literally of hundreds of thousands of brass pins, pressed through the weave of the backing to create a seemingly solid surface. In the center of the carpet she inset a brass compass, an obvious reference to the practice of worshipers, who several times daily align themselves toward Mecca in preparing to pray. Just as Hatoum deconstructed the modernist cube in *Socle du Monde*, in the two carpets she forces a reconsideration of this quintessential Middle Eastern object.

In a recent statement, Hatoum emphasized the viewer's two-step process of perception: an initial impression of sensuality is followed by a recoil once the deep-seated implications of the work are understood. She has emphasized that "there is no single or precise meaning in the works; both function on a subtle phenomenological level to create a feeling of not necessarily nameable or explainable unease."[8] Hatoum's recent work indicates that while her engagement with the issues that have long concerned her has in no way lessened, she has come to employ materials metaphorically and expansively. In her ability and her willingness to make art without naming and explaining reside the maturity and expressive depth of her work.

Notes

1. Anastasia Aukeman, "The Body Politic," *World Art* 3 (1995): 32.
2. Hatoum, conversation with author, New York, January 20, 1996. See also Lynn Zelevansky, *Sense and Sensibility: Women Artists and Minimalism* (New York: Museum of Modern Art, 1994), 14–18.
3. Quoted in Sara Diamond, "An Interview with Mona Hatoum," *Fuse* 10, no. 5 (1987): 49.
4. Ibid., 47.
5. Hatoum, conversation with author, New York, January 20, 1996.
6. Quoted in *The British Art Show 1990* (London: South Bank Centre, 1990), 62.
7. *Pour la Suite du Monde* (Montreal: Musée d'Art Contemporain de Montreal, 1992), 7.
8. Hatoum to author, January 9, 1996.

OLGA M. VISO

Mike Kelley
Failure and Sublimation

I like to think that I make my work primarily for those who dislike it. I get pleasure from that idea. But the desire to undermine things is not so interesting in itself—I think that's the basic definition of art. What's interesting is how it's done.[1]

—Mike Kelley, 1992

Mike Kelley's art has been repeatedly characterized as an "aesthetic of failure."[2] Working with a variety of media over twenty years, he has explored human propensities, perversions, and insufficiencies on numerous levels. Rather than critique the individual, Kelley reveals human idiosyncracies as failures in regard to unattainable ideals of perfection promulgated by the culture at large. Focusing on what is most repressed and taboo in American culture, he uses failure and sublimation as the rich materials of his art.

Kelley's keen interest in these themes may be traced to his earliest performances of the 1970s and early 1980s, such as *Confusion*, 1982, constructed around failed systems of logic. Through complex word and object associations, the artist cunningly led even the most discerning of viewers into improbable conclusions and absurd assumptions, which seemed rational by the highly structured flow of the performances. Kelley's large-scale multimedia projects of the 1980s and early 1990s explored similar clashes in opposing ideologies. Taking on authority—religion, government, corporate America, and the family—Kelley has tended to develop his projects around broad and varied themes. *Pay for Your Pleasure*, 1987–88, perhaps one of the artist's most controversial and well-known large-scale projects, linked artistic genius with criminality and focused on the cultural fascination with violence, finally commenting on its perverse romanticization. Kelley's widely popular installations of soiled homespun toys made from 1987 to 1991, mixed notions of "high" art with "low" craft to express failed childhood at the hands of adult expectations.

Throughout his career, Kelley has often chosen to work with unconventional materials, opting for a style and an aesthetic in keeping with that of mainstream American culture and the diverse subcultures it propagates. His aesthetic may be defined by the kitsch and the familiar, as well as the base and the profane. From the colorful felt banners popularized in the 1960s by the artist-nun Sister Mary Corita, and church-bazaar craft dolls, to erotica and tattooed renderings on the bodies of miscreant youth, Kelley's visual language has delighted in the vernacular—often a form of co-opted modernism. His drawing style, generic and cartoonlike, has also tended to the commonplace, recalling dictionary illustration. Interested in the places where high culture meets low, Kelley has nonetheless often eschewed the high/low distinction commonly associated with his work, preferring instead the terms "allowable" and "repressed."[3] His choice of terminology is important and reveals his interest in processes of enculturation, the adoption of traits and values of one cultural group by another. The socialization of adolescents has been a particular focus of his thinking. As Kelley explains, his primary concern regarding the subject lies in "the point at which it becomes glaringly obvious that we are unnatural and that normalcy is an acquired state."[4] In Kelley's most recent work, he has observed that the same fluid standards of normalcy apply to the practice of art, a field also driven by the current style or dominating tradition. If art is seen as an ideological system, Kelley argues that it, too, invites investment of belief, creating ideals and expectations, in which failure is inherent for those who work outside the "allowable."

Kelley's most recent multimedia project, "Missing Time," takes that position as he turns his scrutinizing eye on himself and his educational past. Examining his own fictive state as an artist, Kelley tackles the authority of his formalist art training. Tracing his early influences, he deconstructs the dominant modes of thinking that informed his education, linking it to dysfunction and types of abuse. In dismantling his own art history, Kelley weaves in the current psychological and legal debates over "false" and "repressed memory syndrome,"[5] as well as his interest in methods of memory-recall therapy used in incidences of alien and satanic abduction. As part of the ongoing project, he has created three distinct groups of related paintings, a selection of which has been assembled for "Distemper." An exhibition of his work consisting solely of recent paintings may seem odd, particularly if one considers that in 1976 the artist gave up painting as an independent medium for a more conceptual mode of working. Kelley's renewed interest in conventional painting, however, has become critical to his current thinking and seems relevant to examine here, particularly in the context of this exhibition, which posits a return by many contemporary artists to more traditional forms of artmaking but in less conventional ways. By bringing together the related series, Kelley's installation at the Hirshhorn marks the first examination of a body of work in progress that is resonant on its own terms.

Kelley's foray into personal biography may also seem curious for an artist who typically dons characters and personas often at odds with his own identity. Over the years, Kelley has taken on the mind-set of a woman, a child, a punk rocker, a janitor, and a member of a teen gang to create his work. He explains:

> *I'm often working "in-character," so if there is a psychology, it's a fractured, schizophrenic one. The heroic individual is replaced by a kind of multi-individual. I'm there but I'm trying to make it difficult to tell who this person is. It's important for those looking at the work to remember that it is art—it's about posturing.*[6]

This multidimensional approach has allowed Kelley to maintain a certain remove in his oeuvre. "Missing Time," however, suggests that he is not exempt from his

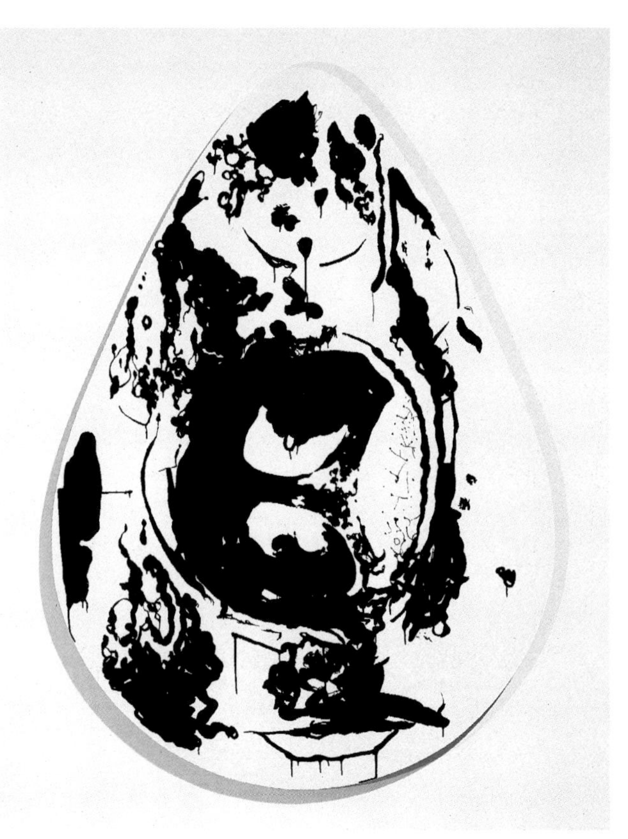

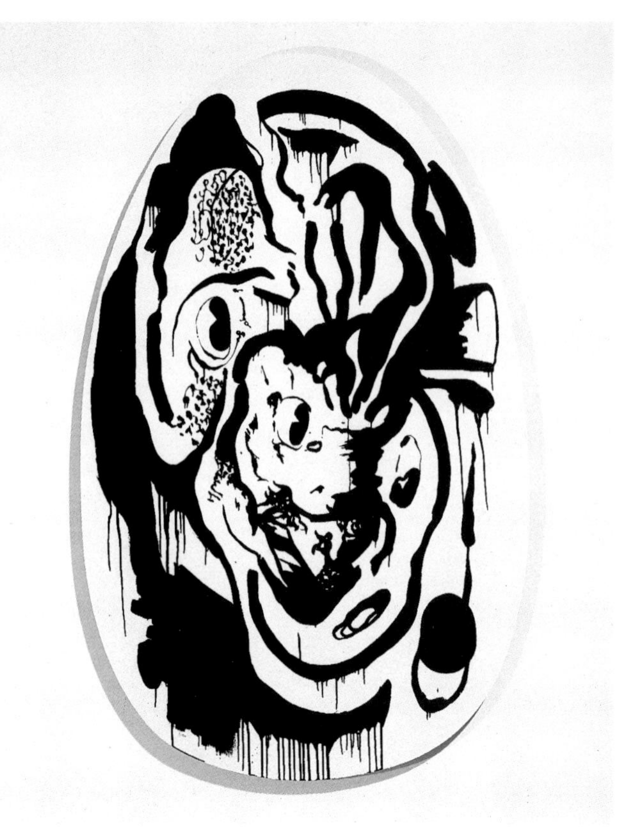

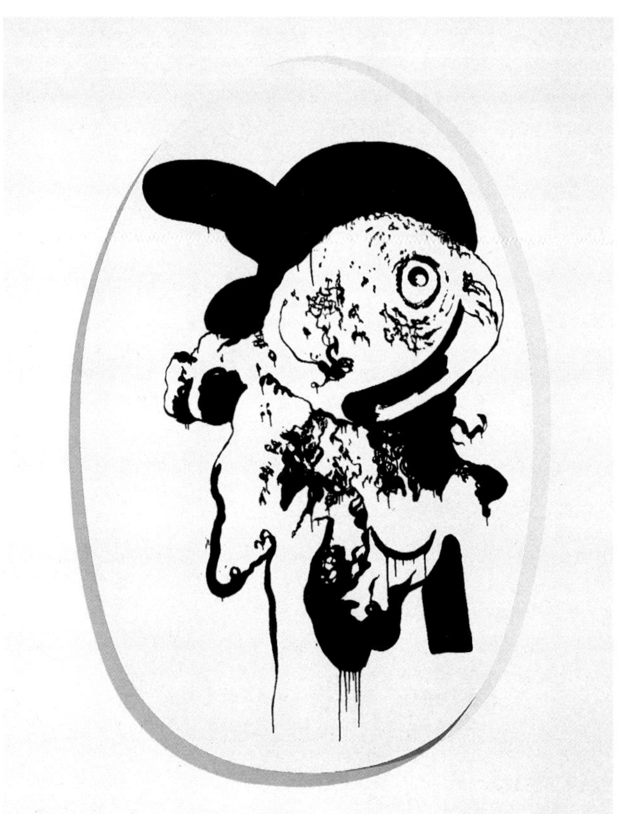

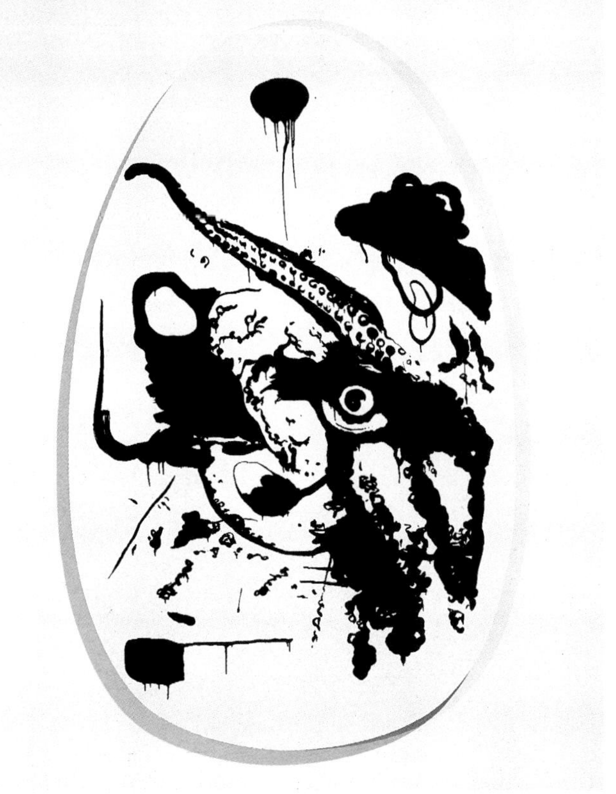

Untitled #2, 1994, cat. no. 12.

Untitled #3, 1994, cat. no. 13.

Untitled #7, 1994, cat. no. 15.

Untitled #9, 1994, cat. no. 16.

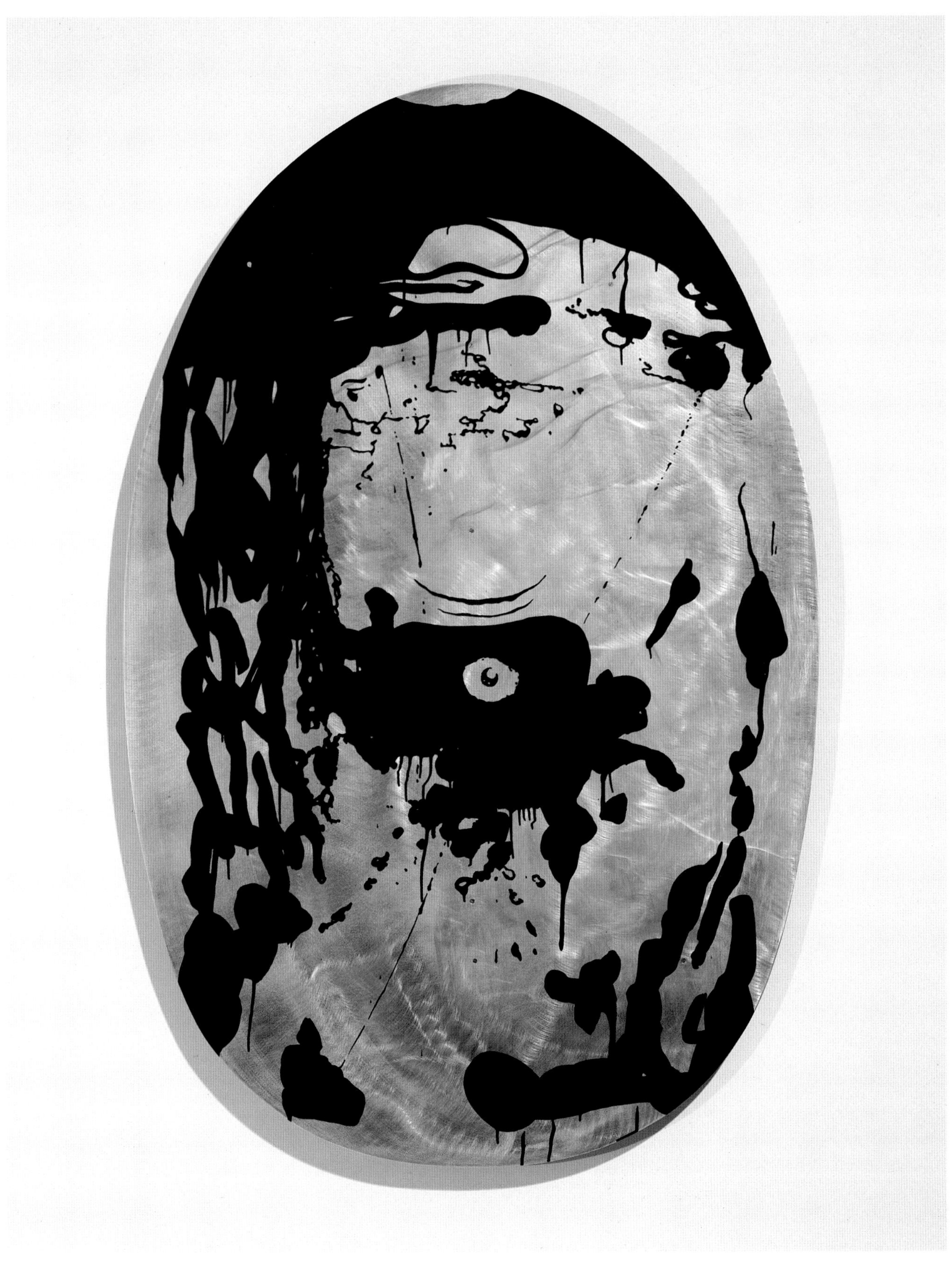

Untitled #5, 1994, cat. no. 14.

own piercing mode of examination that reveals the complexities and underlying strategies that control our lives.

Kelley began working on "Missing Time" while preparing for a midcareer retrospective organized by the Whitney Museum of American Art in 1993. That exhibition followed the wide success of his sculptures and installations of 1987 to 1991 created from abject toys. Kelley was fascinated by the focus of popular and critical response to his stuffed-animal work, in particular to the audience's emphasis on themes of child abuse. For him, the reaction seemed symptomatic of a larger cultural phenomenon, which he began to explore. After being historically positioned in late twentieth-century art by the Whitney retrospective and analyzed by that viewing audience, Kelley realized that he had become a "fictive" character. He explains, "Following the retrospective, people began to construct a psychology of me based on my work as an artist. It became clear that they wanted me to be an abused child."[7] Struck by the fact that institutional abuse had not been proposed as a cause for the strangeness of his artistic output, he began to use the curious psychology the audience had ascribed to him as a springboard in "Missing Time." Operating on the presumption that his work must have been affected in some way by his early education, despite his conscious rebellion against it, Kelley concluded that "the 'symptoms' of my recent work must be the by-product of elements of my training that I repressed. And, the repression proves, this training must have been traumatic—it must have been a form of abuse."[8]

Kelley's assessment of his educational past as a form of abuse is perhaps extreme but decidedly in keeping with the way he typically structures his projects. His guiding premise functions as an overarching construct in which to explore broader cultural issues. The aspect of personal biography may, on some level, represent his own poignant response to conflicted feelings following his retrospective. As an artist who has always "bucked" the system, Kelley's "acceptance" by the system no doubt led to serious reflection.

In establishing the framework, Kelley began by reexamining the drawings, paintings, and collages he made as a young undergraduate studying art at the University of Michigan, Ann Arbor, from 1972 to 1976. He recounts, "I chose to confront my old works to consciously relearn the rules under which I produced them, in order to perhaps understand my abuse and to more consciously deal with it in future art works." In doing so Kelley evaluated his training at Michigan as staunchly academic. The dominant influence at the time was a gestural abstract formalism in the manner of Hans Hofmann. As Kelley recalls:

> *That was "serious" painting. Painting arguments were still caught up in questions of composition and had not really gotten past the shock offered by Pop Art and Color Field Painting—the horrible realization that composition could be as easy as centralized iconic placement or all-over monochrome dispersion.*[9]

Coming out of this milieu, Kelley's early works reveal a strange fusion of both modes, a gestural form of Pop typified by the paintings of the popular art school gurus Robert Rauschenberg and Larry Rivers. Reacting against those giants, Kelley infused the style with the seeds of what would become resonant in subsequent work—low, fringe aesthetics and images of subcultural figures, including Sun Ra, Jimi Hendrix, and Patty Hearst. Many of the collages contain visual references to second-rate comic books, grade-B science-fiction movies, erotica, seasonal childhood kitsch, and logos of political underground groups such as the Symbionese Liberation Army.

The first series of paintings in "Missing Time" consists of ten untitled works, which were exhibited in the early fall of 1994 at Rosamund Felsen Gallery in Los Angeles. Roughly basing them on the shape of an egg, Kelley cut out ovoid sheets of thick aluminum, then painted the forms with enamel in a reserved palette of black and white. Drippy biomorphic blobs inhabit the pristine white surfaces. Inspired by American sci-fi lore and extensive research into popular accounts of UFO sitings and encounters from the 1940s to the present, the paintings reflect Kelley's interest in "exploring tropes of picturing the unpicturable."[10] He became particularly intrigued by the propensity of American sci-fi subgenre to characterize aliens, unidentified formless matter fallen from the sky, and the earth's "primordial soup" as oozing, organic, and bloblike. That stereotypical rendering in film, literature, video, and published accounts is manifested in his series. Beady disembodied eyes (see cat. nos. 12–16, pp. 58–59) peer out from the panel surfaces as if an alien creature had been splattered between two slides under a microscope.

The blobs recall Kelley's *Incorrect Sexual Models*, 1987, in their graphic simplicity and biomorphic deformity, and they bear a relationship to the undifferentiated, "odorless lumps" of 1991 and the various "Garbage Drawings," 1988, in which Kelley created lurid abstractions based on the clouds of dirt that forever consumed the army private of *Sad Sack* comics. Viewing the recent paintings as an extension of his interest in depicting formlessness, Kelley does not consider them to be formalist at all, although he refers to its modes and measures; the untitled paintings, rather, challenge that aesthetic. The graphic tension between the clean industrial surfaces and the messy quality of the painted blobs belies the formalist and gestural modes of Kelley's art training, first touched on in the student work. The duality becomes even more apparent in the series that followed, which are the result of a more consciously "regressive"[11] mode of thinking.

In "The Thirteen Seasons (Heavy on the Winter)," 1994, Kelley regularized the varying oval shapes of the aluminum panels into that of cameos, drawing on the cameo's association as a carrier of memory. Rendered on wood, the thirteen panels in the series were first exhibited at the Jablonka Galerie, Cologne, in 1995, together with reworked paintings and drawings of the 1970s.[12] Exploring the darker side of Santa Claus, Halloween, Charlie Brown, and the Mighty Morphin Power Rangers, "The Thirteen Seasons" explodes the system of values underlying the material culture of post-1950 American childhood. Evil villains, scary monsters, religious icons, and kitschy holiday fare excavated from his past and referencing the student works are served up with the most gruesome of consorts. In *#1, The Birth of the New Year* (cat. no. 17, p. 62), the red Power Ranger is apotheosized with various multicultural Santas, which are arranged together in a nasty phallic trinity. In *#7, The Descent* (cat. no. 19, p. 63), Halloween motifs layered over with stamped candy canes and Christmas ornaments take on outrageous proportions as Kelley elevates the scene to a moment from Christ's Passion. Everywhere in the series, childhood stuff is blended in with grotesque religiosity and adulthood perversions in typical inflammatory Kelley style. If we apply Kelley's psychotherapeutic terminology, the sublimations of the student are confronted and resolutely challenged by the abused adult.

In *#11, The Giving Old Man* (cat. no. 20, p. 63), Kelley blatantly refers to his Hofmannesque training in the rectangular patches of color that dominate the bare panel. Equating the modern master with

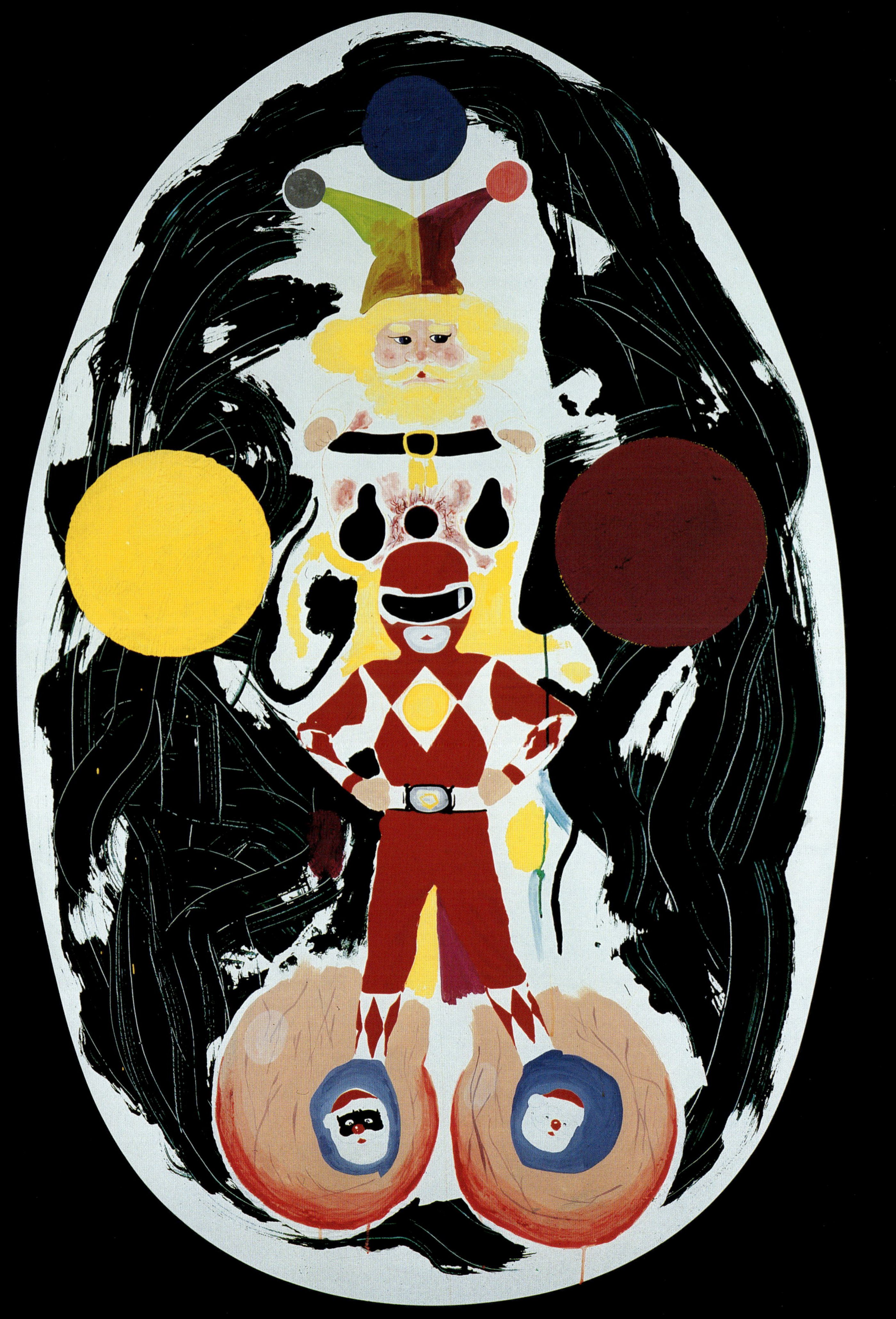

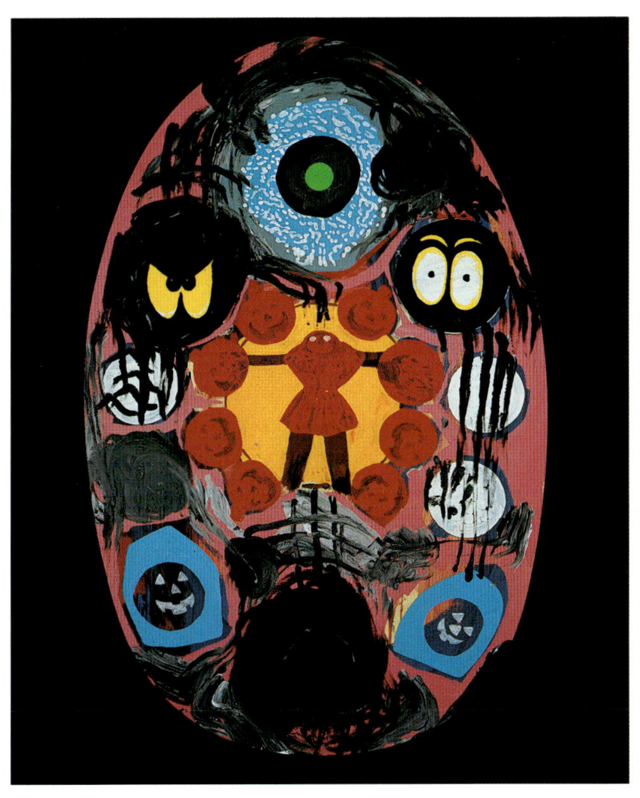

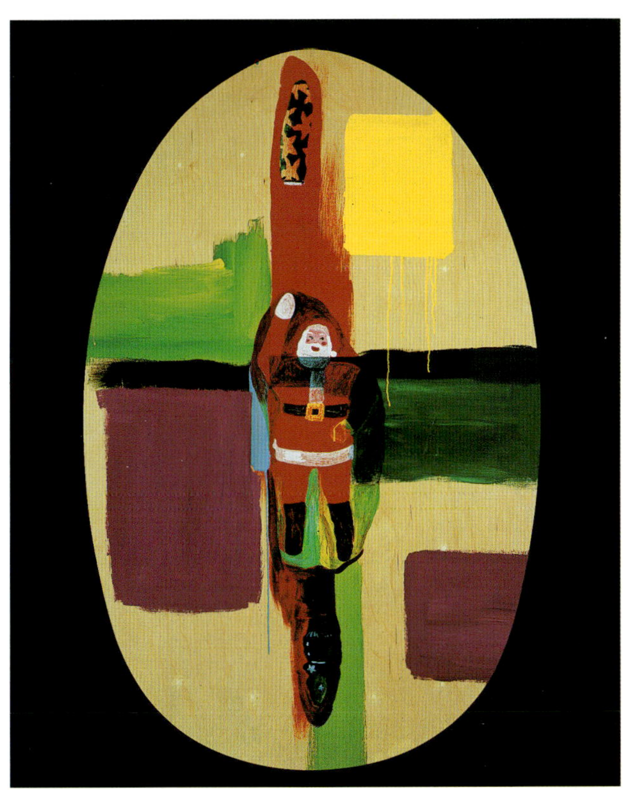

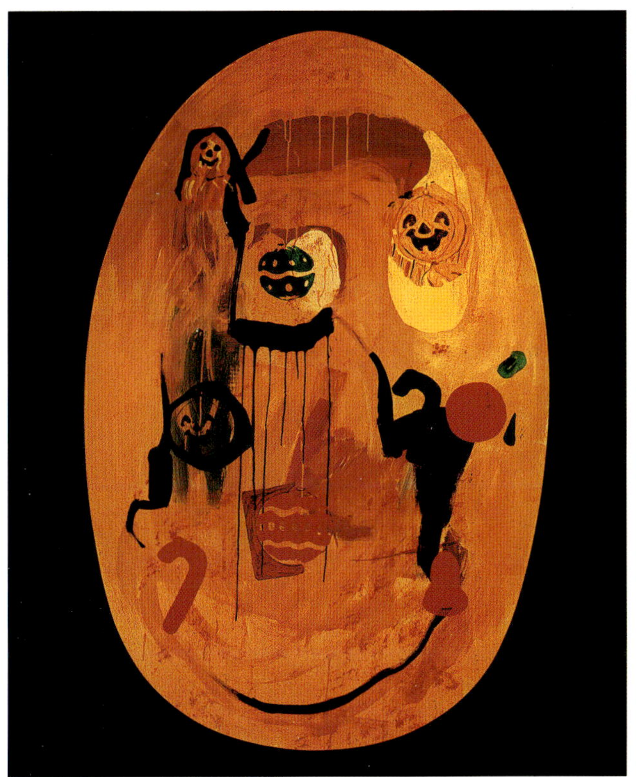

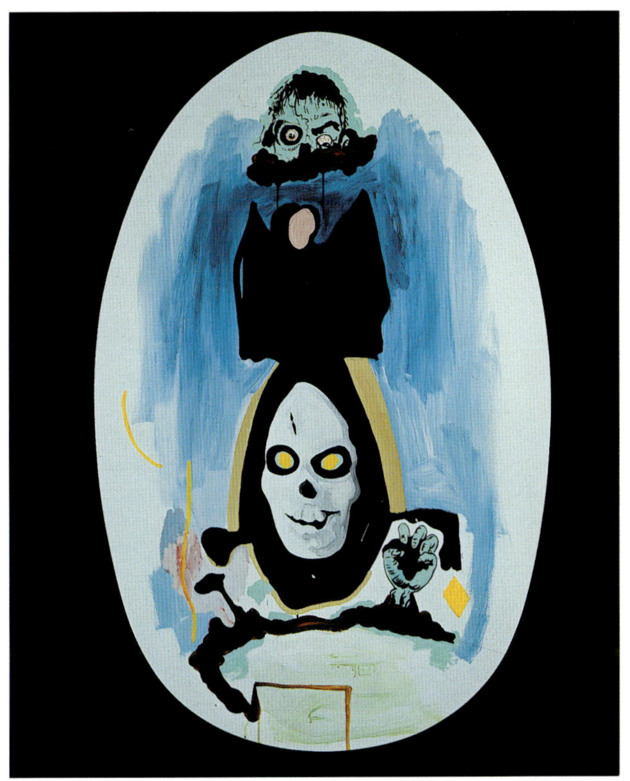

Opposite: #1, *The Birth of the New Year*, 1994, cat. no. 17.

#6, *The Fall*, 1994, cat. no. 18.

#7, *The Descent*, 1994, cat. no. 19.

#11, *The Giving Old Man*, 1994, cat. no. 20.

#12, *Death*, 1994, cat. no. 21.

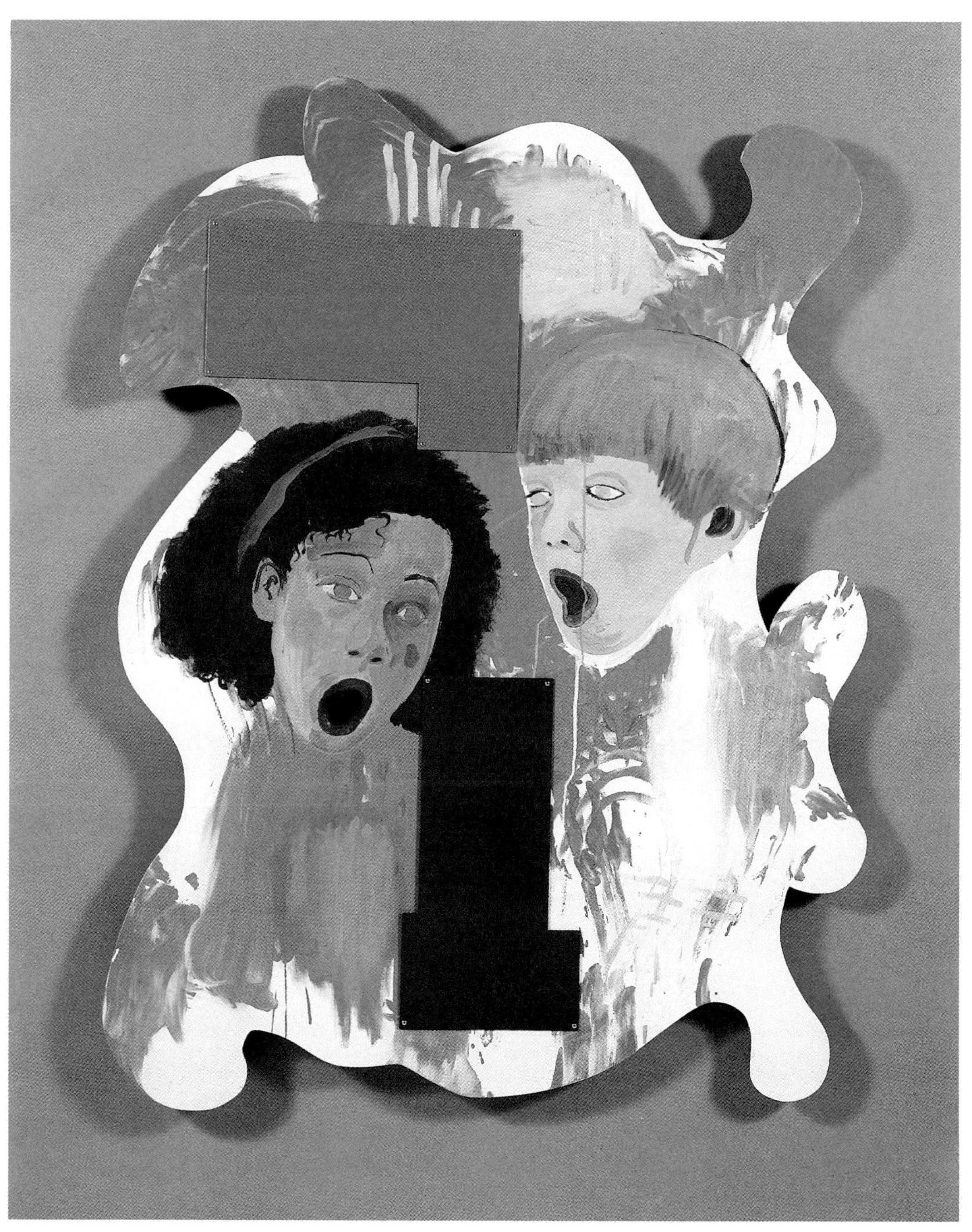

Prenatal Mutual Recognition of Betty + Barney Hill, 1995, cat. no. 24.

the childhood icon Santa Claus, Kelley contends that the subject of one's idealization and reverence is eventually exposed. The Hofmann reference became a recurring motif in Kelley's subsequent exhibition, "Towards a Utopian Art Complex" at Metro Pictures, New York, in the fall of 1995. Here, entire gaps in his formative memory were wryly given prominence in the architectural models of his home and the various schools he attended (see *Educational Complex*, 1995, p. iv). Constructed out of foam core, the gaps (or repressed memories, Kelley would suggest) manifest themselves as undefined, rectangular-shaped spaces in the final structures. Left open, they reflect Kelley's inability to recall entire floors and wings of buildings he inhabited day after day. The spaces are mirrored in related paintings, including *Liberal Paganism*, 1995 (cat. no. 23, not illus.), and *Prenatal Mutual Recognition of Betty + Barney Hill*, 1995, (cat. no. 24, p. 64), as patches of color bolted on the panels's surface, suggesting the Hofmann influence as the cause of his repression. The artist's interest in occult psychology and memory-recall therapy is further explored in various elements of the installation, including related works on paper, photographic collages, and sculptural constructions. *Prenatal Mutual Recognition of Betty + Barney Hill* refers to the first documented case of alien abduction from the 1960s, in which hypnosis was used to recover "missing time."

Kelley has been criticized for his harsh assessment of his educational past and, in general, for the confrontational, moralizing stance of his art. The quote by Kelley that opens this essay suggests that inciting such reaction is part of his intent. Indeed, he takes pleasure in nagging and in obfuscating whatever we think we understand, including our feelings about him. In this context, the "Missing Time" project both reinforces and reveals Kelley's blunt, rhetorical character. Analyzing the ideological function of art as a true satirist, one could also argue that for the first time, Kelley gives us a tiny glimpse of Mike Kelley the person, letting us know, even for an instant, that he, like the rest of us, is a product of a culture and its failures and a person unwittingly of his time.

Notes

1. Quoted in interview by Julie Sylvester, "Talking Failure: Mike Kelley and Julie Sylvester," *Parkett*, no. 31 (1992): 101.

2. In her catalog introduction to Kelley's midcareer survey at the Whitney Museum of American Art, New York, Elisabeth Sussman described Kelley's work in terms of failure [Sussman, et al., *Mike Kelley: Catholic Tastes* (New York: Harry N. Abrams, 1993), 15]. Julie Sylvester made failure the topic of discussion in an interview with Kelley, "Talking Failure," 100–103.

3. Quoted in Sylvester, "Talking Failure," 103.

4. Ibid., 100.

5. "Repressed memory syndrome" is a psychotherapeutic term used to describe the unconscious blocking of memory owing to traumatic experiences, particularly in childhood sexual abuse cases. Recent changes in the law have now made it possible for victims of childhood abuse to bring charges against their abusers long after occurrences of abuse, if memory of those events is newly recalled in therapy. The detractors of repressed memory syndrome question the verifiability of such memories and refer to it as "false memory syndrome."

6. Quoted in Sylvester, "Talking Failure," 101.

7. Kelley, telephone conversation with author, December 19, 1995.

8. Mike Kelley, "Missing Time: Works on Paper 1974–76, Reconsidered," *Missing Time* (Hanover: Kestner Gesellschaft, 1995), 32.

9. Ibid.

10. Sussman, *Mike Kelley: Catholic Tastes*, 29.

11. Kelley, telephone conversation with author, December 19, 1995.

12. Later in 1995, Kelley's reworked drawings became the subject of a solo exhibition at the Kestner Gesellschaft, Hanover.

OLGA M. VISO

Guillermo Kuitca
Connection and Contradiction

The contrast of being on the inside or on the outside part of the "world" or withdrawn from it is the metaphor of my work itself.[1]
—Guillermo Kuitca, 1994

Guillermo Kuitca's paintings of architecture and topography are psychologically charged, and redolent with dualities, tensions, and contradictions. His variations of house plans, city maps, genealogical charts, prison cells, cemetery plots, and theaters blur distinctions between absence and presence, the past and present, fiction and reality, and they consider with great subtlety and power the volatile places where the exceedingly private and intensely public nature of human existence clash and converge. A keen observer of the human condition, Kuitca is fascinated by how we are often circumstantial neighbors unknowingly linked to one another—by bloodline, coincidence, socially determined situations, or occurrences as inconsequential as the proximity of one name to another in a telephone-book listing.

Unlike many artists of the past decade who have investigated the body to understand the human condition, Kuitca has analyzed the spaces individuals occupy and inhabit to probe human nature. Looking to the mechanisms that have developed to define and organize the world, such as mapping and charting, and to the systems created to house, store, entertain, and contain humanity and its many physical and social processes, Kuitca has focused in particular on the spaces where individual and communal experience and personal and collective memory are exchanged. These tenuous points of intersection between the public and the private spheres of life and the many attendant contradictions are at the heart of his artistic endeavor.

Kuitca's compositions are often painted from viewing angles to which we are typically not privy or conscious, and they are punctuated by a profound sense of loss and dissonance. Achille Bonito Oliva has said about Kuitca's paintings that they are "intangible works of control, and at the same time of vertigo. The togetherness of the two

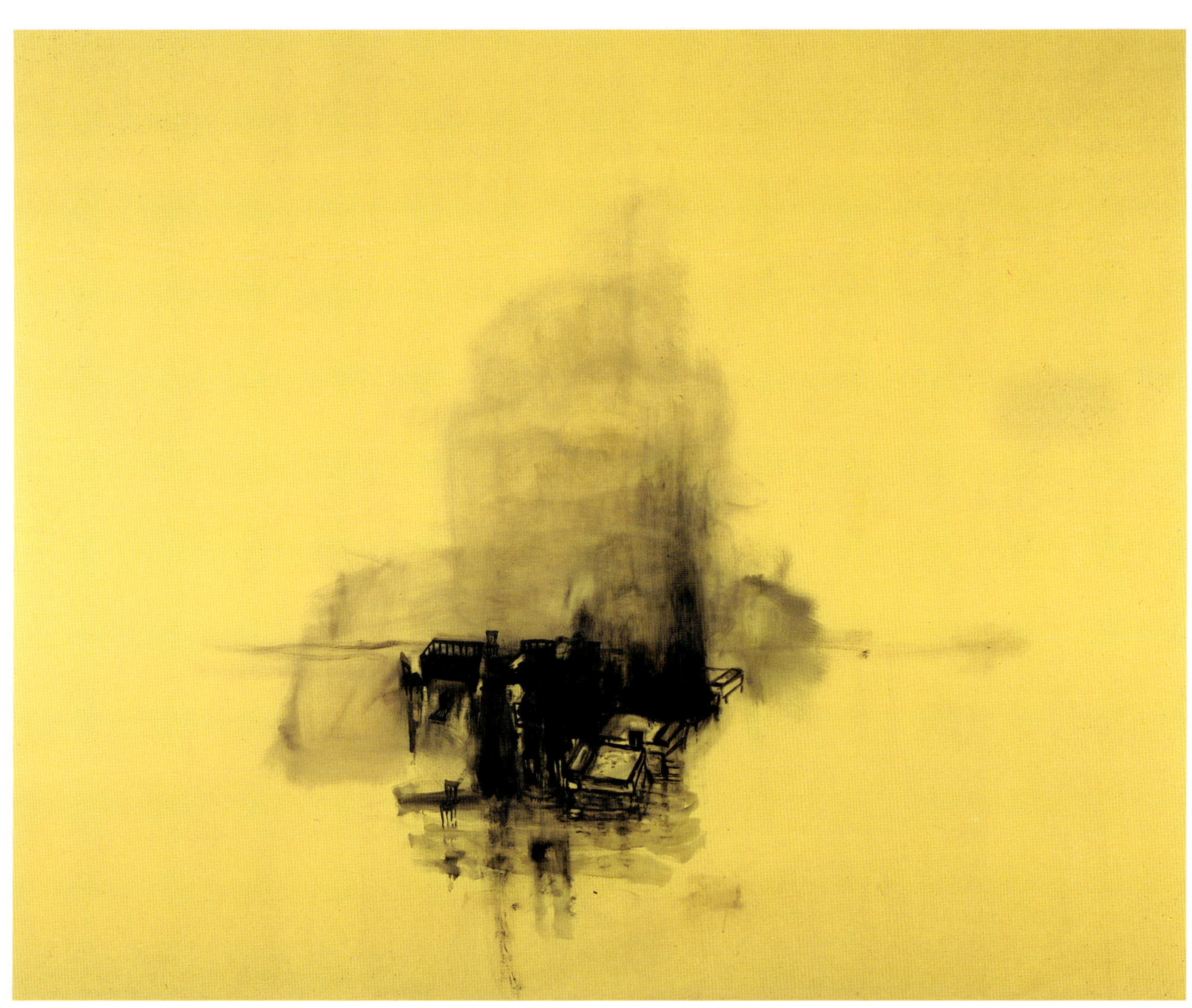

Untitled, 1994, cat. no. 27.

moments becomes the task of the artist."[2] Delighting in duality, Kuitca reinforces themes of connection and contradiction by conflicting the relationship between the spectator, the painting, and his own enigmatic presence as the maker of his art. An examination of Kuitca's oeuvre from the early 1980s to the present sheds light on the intriguing, evolving dynamic and reveals the fluid and evanescent disposition of the artist suggested by the puzzling quote that introduces this essay.

As a young painter in Argentina in the early 1980s, Kuitca began to receive significant attention for his paintings inspired by his experience working in the theater. Bearing titles drawn from plays, literature, and popular music, his paintings of bizarre interiors reminiscent of stage sets present tiny figures who act out mysterious and disturbing dramas, as in *Si Yo Fuera el Invierno Mismo* (If I Were Winter Itself), 1986 (fig. 24). Indeed, in many of the mise-en-scène paintings from 1982 to 1987 (and in more recent paintings such as *Untitled*, 1994 [cat. no. 27, p. 67], in which Kuitca revisits an earlier theme), the spectator enters the stage slightly off cue, having arrived moments before or after an uncertain event. Overturned chairs, sullied beds that appear to be on fire, and spotlit microphones abandoned by their performers imply traces of humanity. Our vantage point is generally somewhere above the picture plane. As we look upon his scenes, we sense that Kuitca, too, has left the premises. Quiet and still, time seems suspended; only the viewer's experience may activate the stage and complete the open narrative.

Dispensing with the human figure, subsequent paintings of the 1980s explored themes of estrangement by freely varying the floor plan of a three-room apartment. Here, too, access to the paintings was provided from a position far above ground. The typically aerial, overhead views of the architectural footprint were also complemented by axonometric renderings as in *Porgy and Bess*, 1988 (fig. 25). Providing a three-quarter elevation, the odd angle (also taken from above) exposes the inner quarters of private, personal spaces. Although the human figure

Fig. 24. *Si Yo Fuera el Invierno Mismo* (If I Were Winter Itself), 1986.

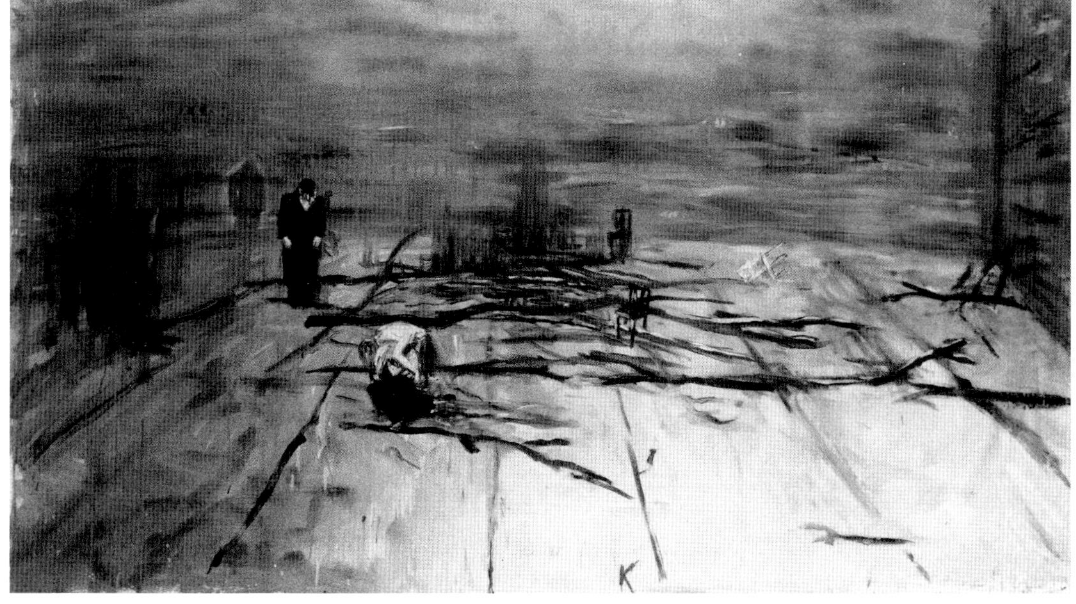

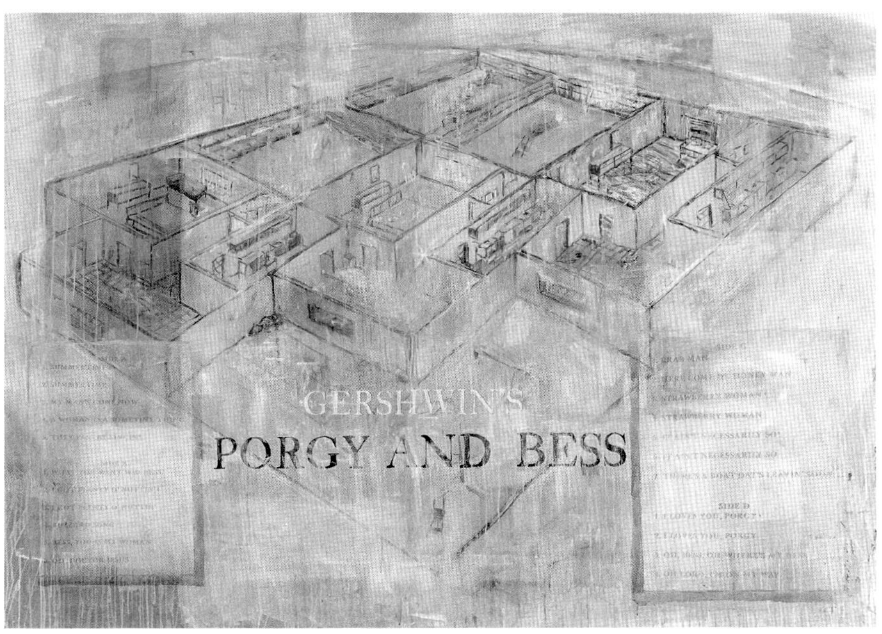

Fig. 25. *Porgy and Bess*, 1988.

is absent from the structures, the intimate lives of the inhabitants are totally eviscerated. Kuitca's intrusive vision makes the viewer both the voyeur and the violated, for the familiar spaces, the walls, and the living that occurs between them are too close to our personal experience not to afford some level of discomfort.

In 1987, Kuitca began to paint street maps on canvases, and he eventually rendered them atop mattresses hung on the wall and on small, child-size beds that he assembled into sculptural installations (see *Untitled*, 1993, p. iii). His fascination with mapping, like housing, was an outgrowth of his interest in the "silent theaters of human interaction."[3] Employing standardized maps drawn from as far afield as Canberra, Hanover, and Santiago de Compostela, Kuitca undermined their integrity by using them as abstract forms. He preferred to use maps that had no particular association or topical significance, and he often picked cities because he liked the way the words sounded or because they suggested remote locations.[4] Kuitca would often repeat the name of a single city along all the major arteries—creating unchartable territories that are dreamlike and evocative of the fluid notions of origin and place in a transient, global society. Symptomatic of his desire at the time to move from the introspective space of the home to a global arena, Kuitca described using maps as a material that "helped me to get closer, while I was getting further away."[5] Indeed, in Kuitca's hands, maps become intense psychological spaces that chart human experience far beyond topographical realities. Of the viewing angle in the map paintings, Kuitca has commented:

> *I like the idea of looking at maps from a distance. "Angle" is a good word because the maps, to a certain extent, are a representation of what could be seen as an exaggeration of the point of view that can be found in all of my work. The paintings have always been based on the angle from which I have approached things. For instance, do you realise that the angle from which I look at the maps is like seeing one angle look at another angle?*[6]

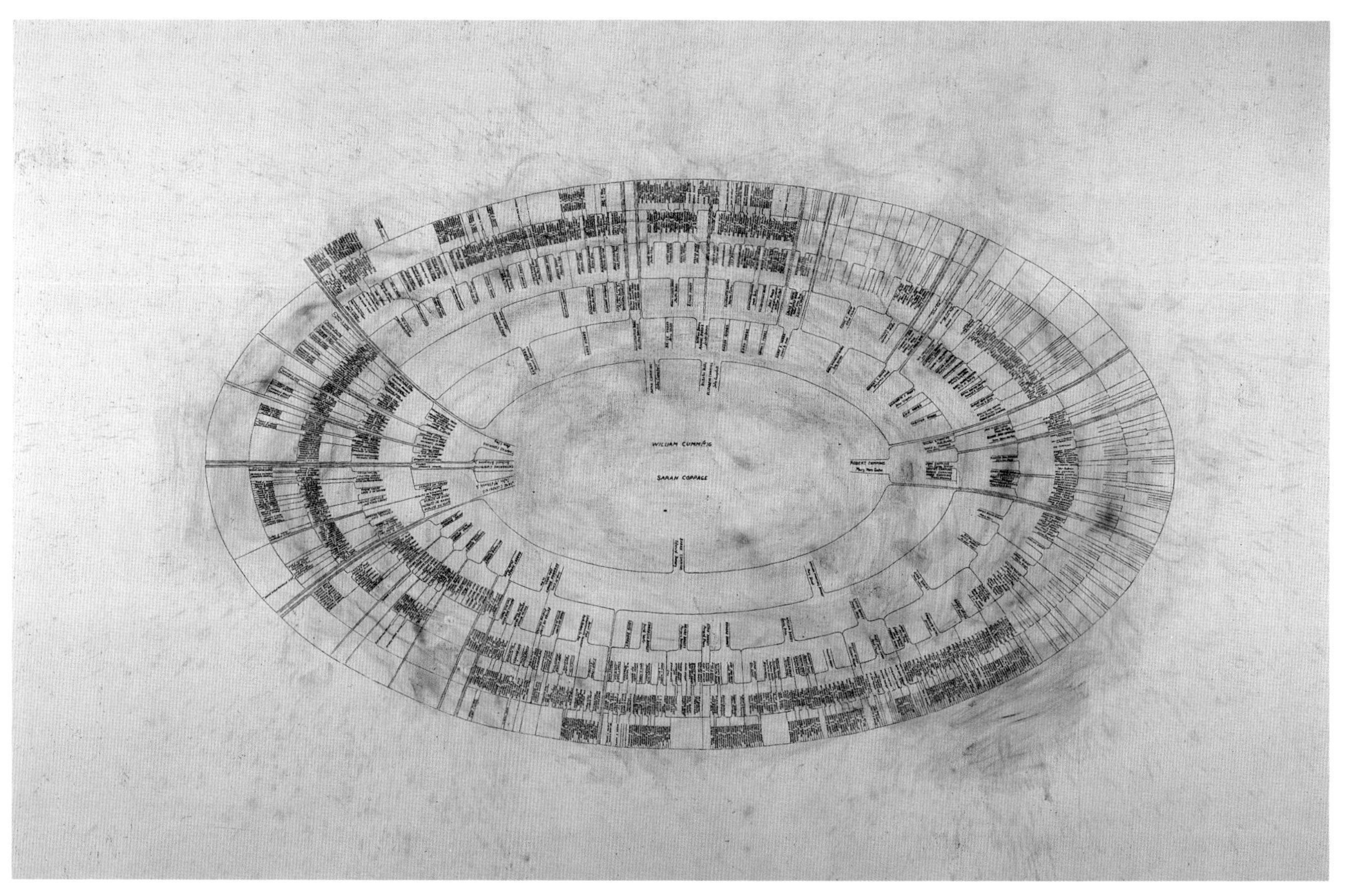

People on Fire, 1993,
cat. no. 26.

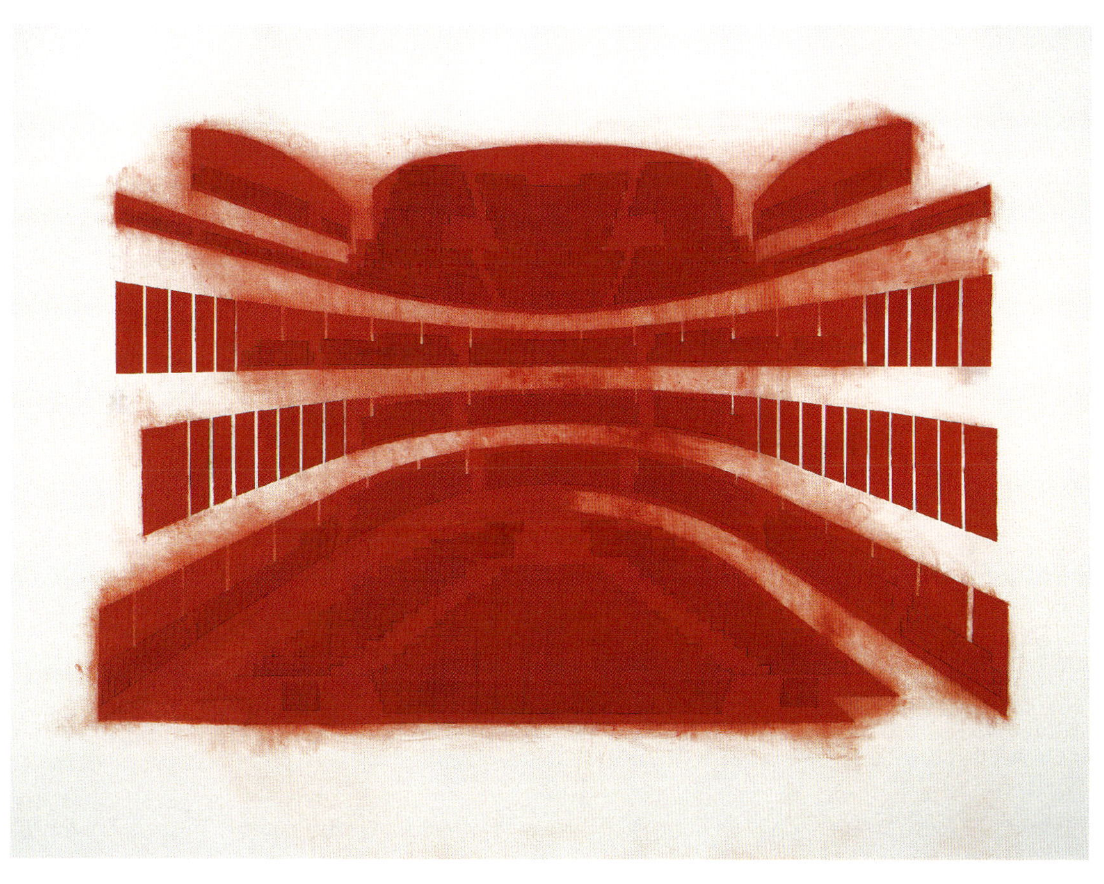

Mozart–da Ponte I, 1995,
cat. no. 28.

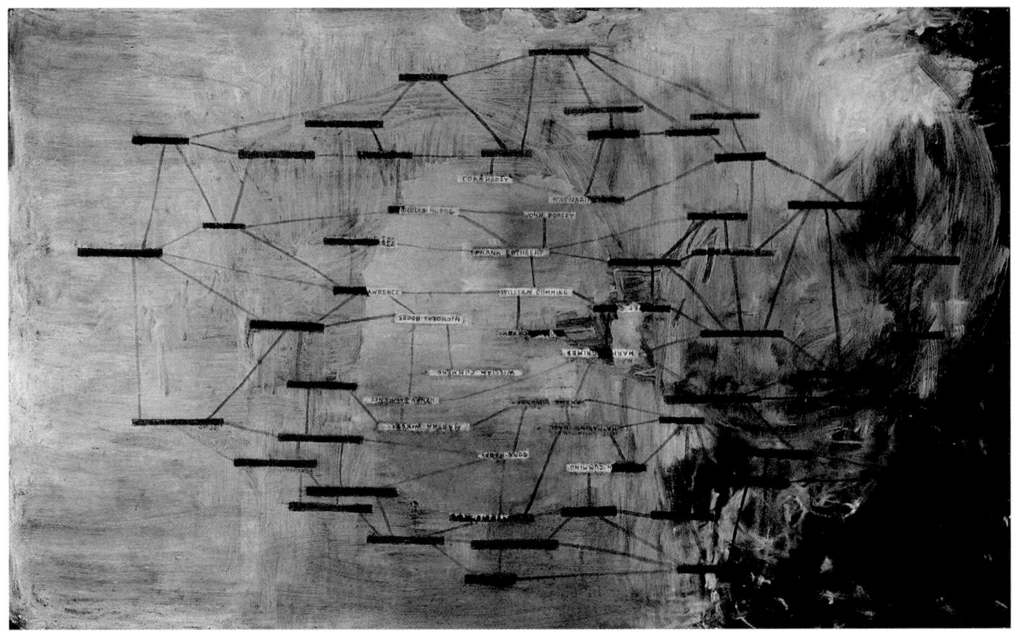

People on Fire, 1993, cat. no. 25.

The skewed and self-reflexive angle of viewing that seems to turn in on itself also characterizes "People on Fire," 1993 (cat. nos. 25 and 26, p. 70 and above), a group of thematically related paintings of the same title made from 1991 to 1993 that use genealogical charts to map the architecture of human relationships. Representative of a "chain reaction,"[7] the charts trace human drives, longings, and ambitions. Using them as the material for his art, Kuitca selects family trees of anonymous individuals who have no personal significance: "Because I can manipulate the sensation, I am able to work with what I consider to be very valuable material, but to which I personally cannot give any specific value."[8] The distance Kuitca imposed between himself and his work in these paintings also characterizes the stance he imposes on the viewer. Sharing his detached position, we remain removed from the images apart from the sensations and associations we may bring to them. As with the stage sets, the ability to activate a possible narrative is in our hands.

In 1991–92, Kuitca painted "The Tablada Suite," a series of ten canvases named after a Jewish cemetery in a Buenos Aires suburb that renders the plan of the cemetery, as well as other institutional plans of theaters, a convention center, a hotel, a hospital, and a prison. Despite their quiet, monochromatic intensity and the soft smearing of graphite that reveals the artist's hand, Kuitca's detachment from the plans is perhaps even more pronounced than in earlier paintings. The mark of his presence stands as a curious foil to the impersonality of the anonymous spaces and the meticulous manner in which they have been rendered; every seat, bed, cell, and plot are carefully delineated to diagram master plans of human interaction and activity. As abstractions of ideas, the institutional plans, like the earlier map paintings, represent a whole body of understanding concerning our society.[9] They also chart places where individuals relinquish control to others and lose, to some extent, their individuality as personal encounters are exchanged for mass experience.[10]

As a watchful observer, Kuitca ponders the powerlessness of the individual and typically separates himself from the arena. In the large, horizontal *People on Fire,* 1993 (cat. no. 26, p. 70), however, Kuitca manipulates the sensation and takes an active role. The artist recalls the process of painting the monumental canvas that inscribes a family tree into the architectural plan of a coliseum as highly physical. He referred to himself as almost "messianic" in the control he exerted over the fate of entire family branches.[11] Straddled across the painting's surface, Kuitca drew the plan from the center out, allowing his body to smear the canvas freely and erase complete lineages. This work marks Kuitca's deeper engagement with the physical possibilities of painting.

Among Kuitca's most "physical" canvases to date are those from a recent body of work, "Puro Teatro," 1995, that returns to the theater as a subject and further radicalizes the relationship between the viewer, the artist, and his work. The word "physical" is not used here to describe virtuoso handling or the process of painting as in "People on Fire"; it is used, rather, to delineate the aggressive displacement of the viewer afforded by the installation of the painting and the angle of vision upon which we gain access to the picture. In the Hirshhorn's *Mozart–da Ponte I,* 1995 (cat. no. 28, p. 71), the large and imposing view of an acclaimed European theatrical space has been simplified and somewhat abstracted, although the seats have been carefully plotted as in works from "The Tablada Suite." Kuitca has hung the painting low to the ground, inviting us, figuratively, to walk on stage. Through that simple process, he has cleverly thrust us into the painting's narrative. Placed at center stage, we are no longer the anonymous, complicit spectator at the artist's side; we are now the actors in an uncertain drama and subject to the scrutiny of others. Alone in the blood-red theater, the audience is implied solely by the expectation of their arrival, or the "skin" that remains via the sequence of numbers that delimit their seats.

According to the artist, the strange inversion that occurs as we experience the painting has the effect of making one "more accused";[12] in other words, we are made to feel more responsible for the actions and narrative that ensues. As a participant in what Kuitca refers to as the "phenomenon of the text," we take part in an experience based on tradition and ritualized artifice, where both the audience and the actor control the text through their familiarity with the plot and accompanying lines.[13] The irony of this experience lies in the suspension of reality that happens during the performance; fiction becomes reality for the actor who assumes a prescribed role, as well for the viewer who engages in the possibility of the story's truth to escape his or her own reality even for a brief moment. In "Puro Teatro," Kuitca likens the ritualized artificiality of the theater to human experience. Rather than engage in a poetic yet predictable performance, *Mozart–da Ponte I* invites us to take a more self-determined position.

The suggestion of a greater responsibility on the part of the viewer presents an intriguing development in Kuitca's oeuvre in the direction of social response and responsibility. Although the artist has eschewed sociopolitical interpretations of his paintings in the past, he admits that he comes closer to dealing with social content in "Puro Teatro" than in previous work.[14] In a number of related paintings from the series, for example, Kuitca color-coded sections of the theaters to delineate their varying sales prices, thus implying the inscription of a class structure in the skeletons of the buildings. Although they have been rendered abstractly by the artist, we sense that the structures exist in real time. Again, Kuitca remains curiously

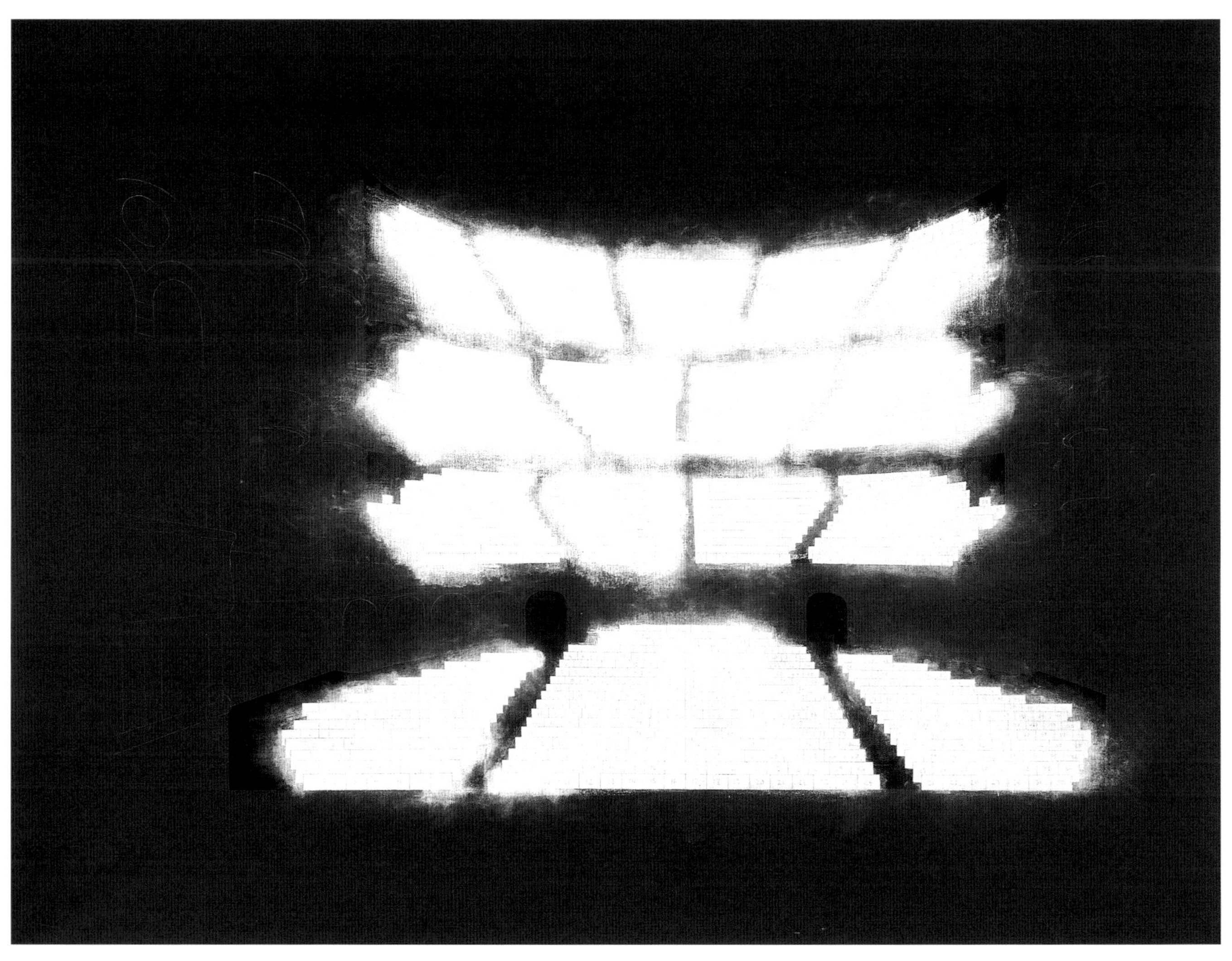

Untitled, 1995, cat. no. 30.

Untitled, 1995, cat. no. 29.

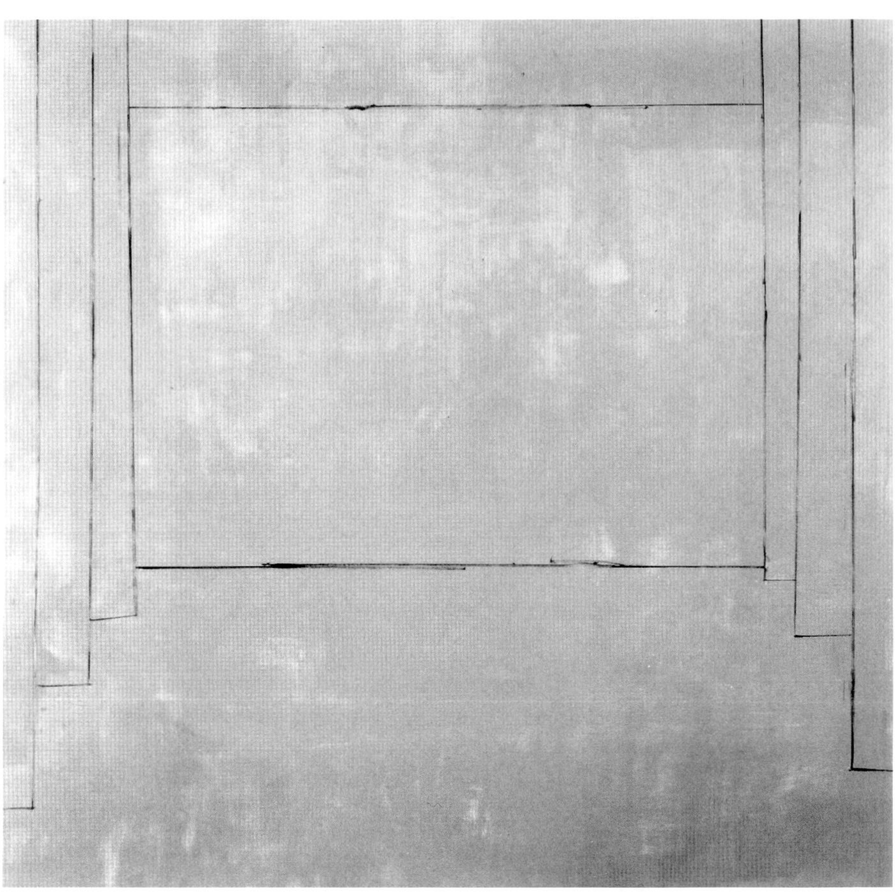

Fig. 26. *Untitled*, 1995.

both inside and outside of the work, as well as removed from the experience.

The reserved control with which the artist observes humanity and allows it to direct itself willfully into unknowing fate suggests his position as that of an omniscient being. Rather than all-knowing, Kuitca has characterized his fluid and everchanging angle of vision as "panoptic," that is, comprising all views in one, permitting everything to be seen at once.[15] He has also explained his viewpoint in terms of a mirror, qualifying that it does not reflect reality per se; it acts, rather, as a fracturing prism that suggests numerous other realities that are made visible yet remain impenetrable.[16] The duality of the mirror and its fracturing nature typify *Untitled*, 1995 (cat. no. 29, p. 75), also from "Puro Teatro," which Kuitca describes as the outcome of a chain reaction. Beginning with a cluster of chairs and beds, he expanded the nucleus of objects exponentially to cover the entire canvas, thus creating a confused network of mirror images made possible by his panoptic vision. Kuitca's ability to zoom in on microscopic detail or soar upward to gain an encompassing aerial perspective further defines the panopticon, an optical instrument that combines a telescope and a microscope. Filled with contradiction, the panopticon also constitutes a prison that is built radially to afford a single guard complete surveillance of his prisoners. Seated in a central position, the guard becomes ironically imprisoned by the unrelenting eyes of those he watches.

In an effort to understand the aspect of dislocation and inversion in the artist's work, Lydia Dona considers Kuitca's position as that of a "meta-identity"—an identity "that is removed from place or site, that is more Other and Elsewhere."[17] In the following excerpt of an interview with the artist, Dona characterized the dislocation as "almost like an aspiration of the physical dislocation of your own body removed from your painting, inventing that Other, which itself almost disappears. Then, you reappear."[18] Kuitca's vanishing presence is perhaps nowhere more apparent than in *Untitled*, 1995 (fig. 26), one of the last installments of "Puro Teatro." The gray stage outlined by a simple calligraphic suggestion sits empty and abandoned. Bearing no illumination, the work serves as a striking contrast to *Untitled*, 1995 (cat. no. 30, p. 74), the ethereal blue theater, the explosive luminescence of which appears to emanate from within. With no audience, actors, or the slightest suggestion of human presence past or present, Kuitca has displaced even himself from the silent, anxious space of the empty theater and joins us quietly on the outside, just before he vanishes.

Notes

1. Quoted in Anne Horton, "Kuitca at Sperone Westwater," *Art and Auction* 16, no. 10 (May 1994): 84.
2. Achille Bonito Oliva, *Guillermo Kuitca* (New York: Annina Nosei Gallery, 1991), 5.
3. Jorge Luis Borges, *El hacedor (The creator)* (Buenos Aires: De maker, Barber van der Pol, 1960), quoted in Rina Carvajal, "Mapping Out the Self: The Work of Guillermo Kuitca," *Guillermo Kuitca* (Rotterdam: Witte de With Center for Contemporary Art, 1990), 7.
4. Quoted in interview by Ed Shaw, "Mapping the Interstates of the Mind," *Art from Argentina 1920–1994*, ed. David Elliott (Oxford: Museum of Modern Art, 1994), 125.
5. Ibid.
6. Ibid., 124.
7. Quoted in interview by Lynne Cooke, "Iterations," in *Guillermo Kuitca: Burning Beds, A Survey 1982–1994* (Amsterdam: Contemporary Art Foundation, 1994), 17.
8. Quoted in Shaw, *Art from Argentina 1920–1994*, 127.
9. Ibid., 125.
10. Matthew Weinstein, statement in *Guillermo Kuitca: Burning Beds*, 56.
11. Conversation with author, New York, October 21, 1995.
12. Ibid.
13. Ibid.
14. Ibid.
15. Quoted in Cooke, "Iterations," *Guillermo Kuitca: Burning Beds*, 19.
16. Conversation with author, New York, October 21, 1995.
17. Lydia Dona, "Guillermo Kuitca Interview," *Journal of Contemporary Art* 6, no. 1 (Summer 1993): 57.
18. Ibid., 58.

Charles Ray
Abstract Sculpture and Lived Reality

I haven't been able to figure out how to make abstract sculpture that has a contemporary meaning to it.[1]

—Charles Ray, 1995

Charles Ray's desire to create an abstract sculpture may seem an odd goal for an artist who has made predominantly figural works since 1990. Inspired by mannequins of the commercial world, he has adopted their form to render figures that disturb and disrupt the senses in their skewed, exaggerated proportions and their often startling specificity. Producing tension and anxiety in the viewer, Ray's mannequin sculptures such as *Family Romance*, 1993 (illus. p. ix), register hallucinogenic moments that provide a glimpse into our own neuroses, challenging us to reconsider our relationships with others. Direct and deadpan, his works have been described as absolute in their "affectless self-sufficiency."[2] Spare and essential, his work provides everything you need to know to respond to it—nothing more, nothing less. One must only focus.

Tracing Ray's development as a sculptor sheds light on his desire to make a wholly abstract sculpture. Such an examination reveals that a reductivist sensibility has always guided him and continues to punctuate even his most representational works. Arguably, Ray has been contemporizing notions of abstract sculpture since the early 1970s, when he used his body as a formal element, pinning himself between a plank of wood and a wall (fig. 28, p. 80). Trained in a formalist tradition, Ray's early works of the 1970s bear the influence of Anthony Caro and modern British sculpture as transmitted by instructor Roland Brenner (a former student of Caro's) at the University of Iowa, 1971–75. There Ray began to weld, and he made abstract, painted steel sculptures inspired by the weightless character of Caro's cantilevered, planar forms in space. The young sculptor also shared an interest in the work of Mark di Suvero, Robert Morris, and the Minimalist Donald Judd. The precariousness of Richard Serra's severe propped and stacked lead forms based on weight and

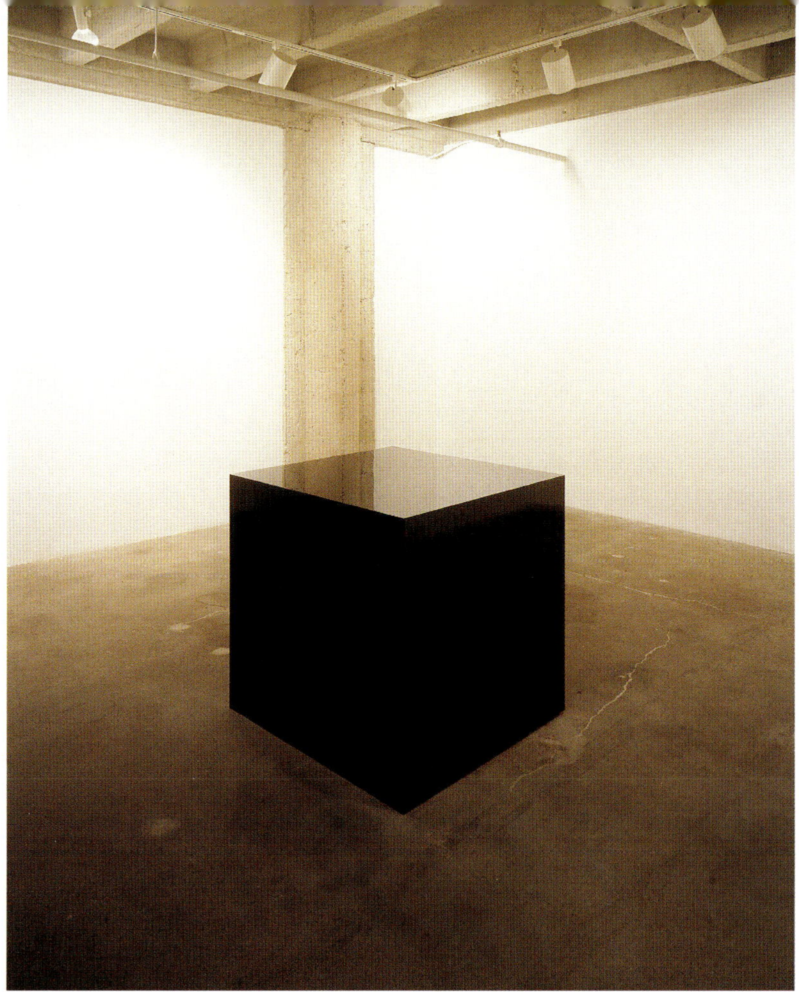

Fig. 27. *Ink Box*, 1986.

measure struck Ray the most. He also began to focus on balance and tension. Using weight and compression to keep blocks of stone and concrete from toppling over, he eventually dispensed with structural welds and bolts. Delicately poised or wedged, his works, like Serra's, held what he considered to be the "notion of event,"[3] simultaneously registering the physical process of their making and an inherent volatility. For Ray, the projection of an imaginary chain of events—of dropping or shattering—involved the spectator in a new way that challenged the stability of Minimalist form. The implication of an event gave the work a certain "presentness."[4]

Inspired by the increasing engagement of many artists with the body, Ray created a hybrid form of performance and sculpture in *Plank Piece I–II*, 1973 (fig. 28, p. 80). Like many artists of the 1970s, including Dennis Oppenheim, Vito Acconci, and Chris Burden, Ray strove to dematerialize the art object. He used his body as sculptural material and gleaned from performance its eventful aspect. Yet, dissatisfied with the medium's theatricality and its bodily associations, he turned away temporarily from that direction. In 1976 he made a group of sculptures that further dematerialized form while projecting action. The most successful was *Stairway*, 1976 (destroyed), a staircase made entirely of glass and suspended seven inches above actual steps. Establishing a "dialectic between event and sculpture,"[5] the function of the staircase was sublimated by the work's powerful, rhythmic sense of form and its utter fragility. Subsequently, as a graduate student at Rutgers University from 1977 to 1979, Ray reinserted his body into sculpture, still searching for a better solution to the equation between the language of formalism and the notion of event.

After a difficult period following the death of his brother, Ray moved to Los Angeles in 1981 to accept a position at the University of California, Los Angeles, where he still teaches. In an effort to commemorate his late brother and also the recently assassinated Egyptian president Anwar Sadat,

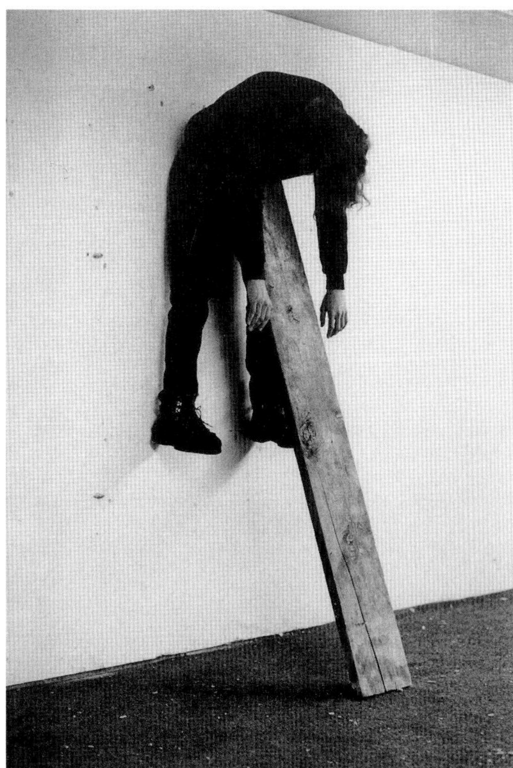
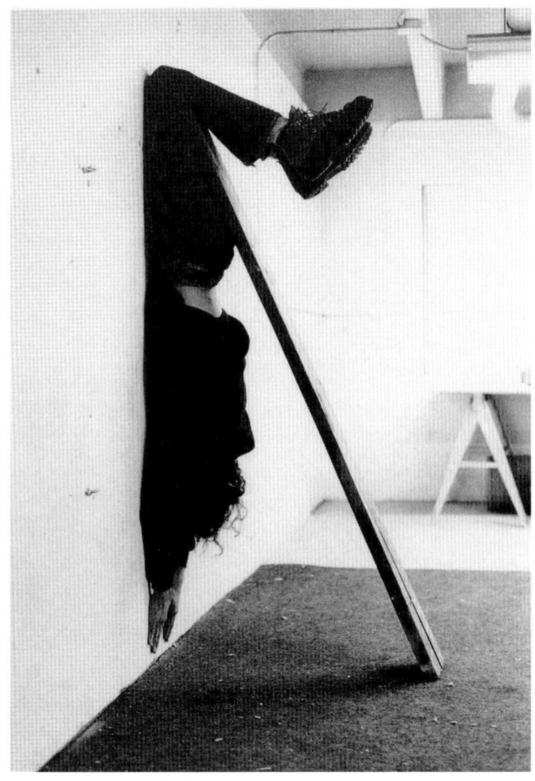

Fig. 28. *Plank Piece I–II*, 1973.

he returned to the "plank pieces" of the 1970s. For *In Memory of Sadat*, 1981, Ray entombed himself in a hollow geometric form, instilling a tension between the body as object and persona that would characterize a group of untitled sculptures from 1981 to 1985, presented as ephemeral, motionless "performances" in alternative spaces throughout Los Angeles. By treating the body "in a very formal Caro-esque way," Ray distinguished himself from other artists of the time who used the body as a field to act upon.[6] He discussed the work in purely formalist terms: "There's really no room to formalize them any more, to rearrange them, they're honed down into simple, aesthetic formal structures.... But there's a person in there! I think that's ludicrous or awful."[7]

The aspect of the absurd and the formal self-sufficiency central to this work have become hallmarks of Ray's style. Their characteristic "presentness" and immediacy struck critics, including John Miller, who described the experience of viewing the sculptures in terms of collapsing metaphors, or associations that disintegrate by their sheer realness and absurdity.[8] The notion of collapse, of a fragile balance between the familiar and unfamiliar, the abstract and the identifiable, typifies a number of works Ray created after 1986, including *Rotating Circle*, 1988, a large cut-out spot in the wall that literally spun in place. Ray recalls "trying to make something that was so abstract it became real and so real that it became abstract. You go in so far you come out on the other side."[9] Drawing on audience perception and expectations of the proverbial and the accepted, Ray's works since 1986 capture the equation between both moments and focus on the potential for their undoing. They are fragile, perfect moments, in which collapse—both physically and conceptually—is inherent.

In *Ink Box*, 1986 (fig. 27), what appeared to be a spare, solid metal structure proved to be a hollow container filled to the brim with black printer's ink. Critics noted the refreshing directness of this and other of Ray's cube sculptures that subverted Minimalist form, remarking on their ability to throw awry the anticipatory feelings induced by Minimalism.[10] In other works, Ray created subtle perceptual and psychic disruptions that further engaged the viewer. His thin black line that ran from floor to ceiling (*Ink Line*, 1989) revealed the accuracy of the title; the sculpture consisted of a steadily flowing stream of ink operated by a hidden system of pumps. A wooden table set up like a still life presented a static arrangement of banal household objects. Intense focus and scrutiny, however, suggested the possibility of movement; in reality the objects on *Tabletop*, 1989, were rotating in place at nearly imperceptible speeds. Drawing on the sense of security induced by generic forms, Ray set up the viewer for what art critic Lane Relyea aptly described as the "onslaught of unfolding experience."[11] By forcing the viewer to ponder objects that are so familiar they are ignored, Ray induces a psychic double take that plumbs the unconscious. Cultural critic Brian Wallis describes this experience in terms of the "uncanny," which he defines as "a disruptive repetition, a return to the familiar and the unfamiliar, some manifestation of repressed material that returns in ways that disrupt unitary identity, aesthetic norms, and social order."[12]

A keen observer of contemporary life, Ray draws on popular culture and the most basic aspects of human experience as source material for his art. Rather than appropriate pop culture out of a desire to satirize and demonize, he accepts contemporary life and even finds its forms and manifestations beautiful. He considers shopping malls and movies to be barometers of our time, and he contends that fashion pictures and objects such as shopwindow mannequins are our popular art forms, bearing serious consideration for what they say about the values of our society. He claims that his mannequin-inspired sculptures of the early 1990s developed out of an interest in mannequins as a type of contemporary figuration. For him, they provided a way of making nonacademic figurative sculpture that connected human experience.[13]

In *Self-Portrait*, 1990, Ray's first mannequin sculpture, the artist inscribed the features of his own face onto the generalized body of a store-bought mannequin. Revealing the spare sensibility of his early work, this and subsequent sculptures challenge the viewer's expectation with a greater psychological intensity. *Family Romance*, 1993 (illus. p. ix), for example, presents an intriguing group portrait of a family of four. Standing in a row holding hands, their naked bodies seem odd in mannequin form. What is so startling about the figures (cast in fiberglass) is not their individualized features but their skewed, equalizing proportions despite their varying ages. Giving three-dimensional form to the Freudian concept of "family romance," Ray articulates the most sinister of childhood psychological desires.

In *Oh! Charley, Charley, Charley...*, 1992, the sculptor cast his own naked body eight times in various states of sexual arousal and systematically arranged the casts in an autoerotic encounter. Discussed in terms of Freudian psychology, gender politics, the commodification of contemporary life, the artist's sexual orientation, and the impact of AIDS on our culture, the sculpture has generated wide commentary. When confronted with the homoerotic suggestions and the strong desire to complicate his sculptures, Ray replies with a disarming innocence and candor. While his response may at first seem flippant, the utter directness of his statement underscores the artist's keen ability to reduce issues to the most basic and fundamental. He explained in an interview, "I was getting divorced from my wife, I was involved with different girlfriends and partners, you know. You realize at a certain point that you just—you just like sleeping with yourself."[14] His commentary sheds further light on his decision not to depict sexual intercourse. As the artist explains, that act would have undermined the formal integrity of the composition.[15] Indeed, such a relationship between component parts would have no doubt thrown the work off balance.

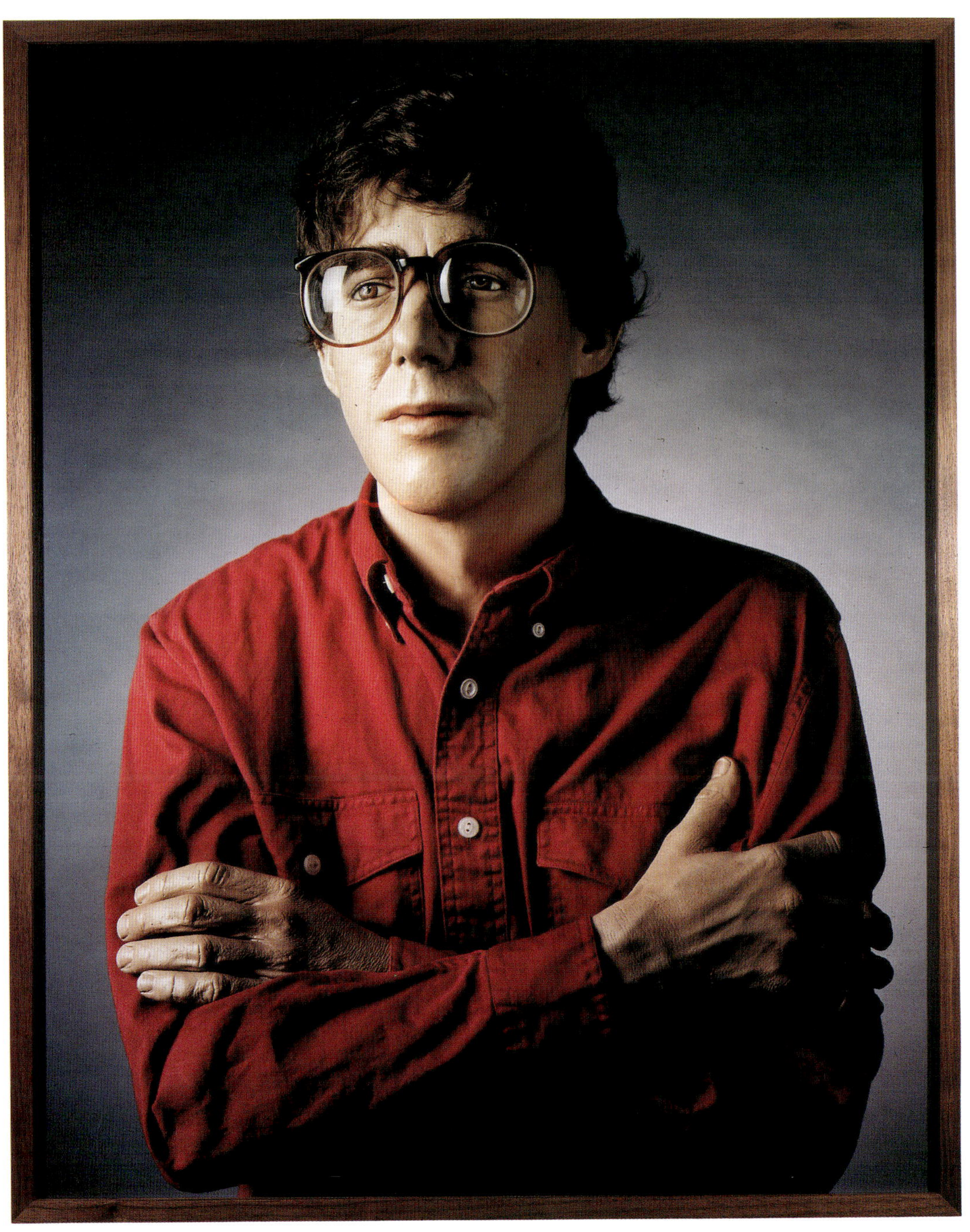

Fig. 29. *No*, 1992.

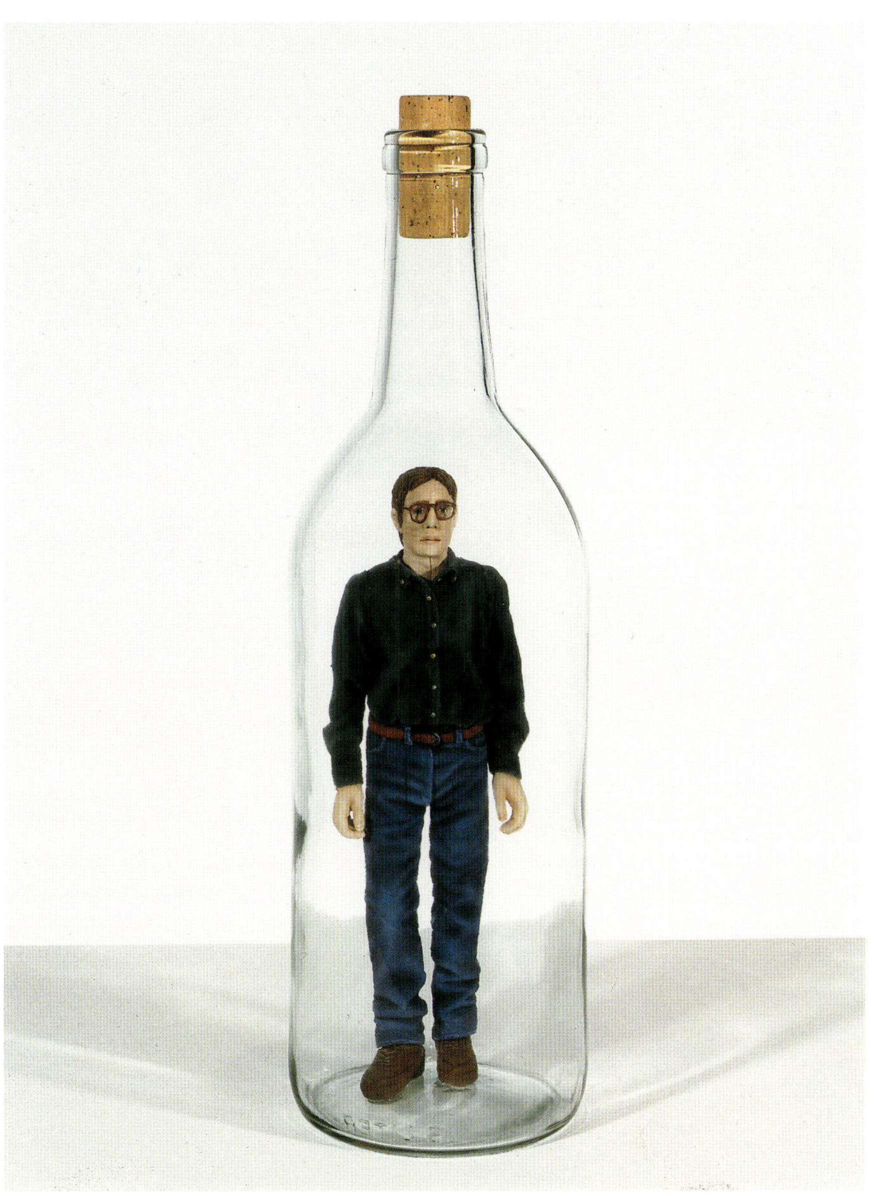

Fig. 30. *Puzzle Bottle*, 1995.

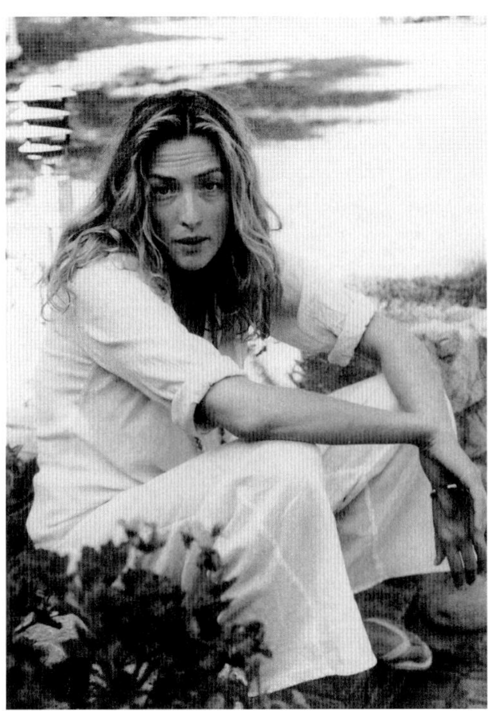

Fig. 31. *The Most Beautiful Woman in the World*, 1993.

Ray's two-pronged commentary aptly expounds upon what the artist has described as his struggle for equations.[16] Indeed, Ray's sculptures are a product of carefully postulated oppositions, between abstraction and representation, perceptions of the real and the ideal, static form and the implication of event, and what art critic Peter Schjeldahl has described as the equation between "self-sufficient sculpture and the greatest possible comprehension of lived reality."[17]

If Ray's oeuvre is viewed in these terms, it is not difficult to understand the artist's desire to create a wholly abstract sculpture that has contemporary meaning. His much admired *Puzzle Bottle*, 1995 (fig. 30, p. 83), was born of such an intent. Featuring a miniature self-portrait, the tiny sculpture (evocative of a ship-in-a-bottle) was pieced together inside a clear glass wine bottle from twenty-one individual parts. Rather than an exercise in self-portraiture or an expression of feelings of containment, the sculpture, he explains, was driven by his concern to understand the abstract space inside the bottle.[18]

Since making *Puzzle Bottle*, Ray has been shooting film sketches in 16 mm to trigger ideas for new works. Exploring a variety of subjects and areas of interest simultaneously is typical of his working process, and in the past he has immersed himself in certain subjects, including physics and phenomenology, as points of reference and departure. Recently he began to sew and research watch- and puzzle-making in a project in which he literally takes apart his clothes in an effort to understand their manufacture, then obsessively attempts to reassemble them out of new material.

Also of great interest to Ray at the moment are the paintings of the American realist Thomas Eakins (1844–1916). Although that influence may seem surprising, an examination of Eakins's paintings proves that the two artists are not unlikely companions; Eakins, indeed, shared many of Ray's concerns. An uncompromising realist, Eakins's obscure narratives also often take considerable effort to unravel, despite their seeming directness and simplicity. Rendering human experience with a frank honesty, Eakins's paintings have been described as absorbing in their psychological intensity. In that respect, Ray finds Eakins to be remarkably grand in his staunch Americanness and in his ability to transcend convention and mediocrity.[19] In the essay "Realism, Writing, and Disfiguration in Thomas Eakins's *The Gross Clinic*" (1987), Michael Fried describes the tension between the representational field in Eakins's painting and the artist's affirmation of the formal as a quality in the work that frustrates and disrupts the viewer.[20] Fried further contends that Eakins's subtle disfiguration of reality provides a new experience of the real.[21] One may argue that the same elements create dissonance in Ray's sculptures.

In *FASHIONS Spring 1996* (in progress at this writing), Ray creates a "living" sculpture in 16 mm film. The short film features a running sequence of shots of a woman dressed in makeshift clothes. Posed against a wall on a slowly rotating platform, she is motionless but for the revolving stand. It is not clear to the viewer if she is a sentient being or a mannequin. Her clothes are constructed out of an array of mismatched remnants acquired from a local fabric store. Ray has pieced together the fragments and variously taped, wrapped, and tied them around the woman's body to create a selection of outfits. Each time the figure completes a revolution on the turntable, the screen cuts to a new ensemble. In some instances the garments are more conventional, while at other times they are fanciful creations that fluctuate between the wearable and the sculptural—not unlike the latest in haute couture. In Ray's curious fashion display the wearer is not, however, a withering supermodel desired by men and women alike. She is, rather, a common woman—neither beautiful nor ugly, neither voluptuous nor overly thin. No matter how bland or revealing the dress, Ray's model, like her black shoes, umprimped hair, and distinctive arm tattoo, remains the same. She is neither romanticized nor idealized; her "beauty" remains unenhanced by the clothes or the alternate personalities the artist projects onto her body. She functions, in essence, like a mannequin, serving as a curious foil to Ray's three Amazonian mannequin sculptures, each titled *Fall 91*, 1992, who don various poses and outfits.

Ray has indicated that the new film emanates from his own thoughts about an ideal woman, a subject he touched on in a project for *Parkett* magazine, *The Most Beautiful Woman in the World*, 1993 (fig. 31). In the series of casual snapshots of supermodel Tatjana Patitz, Ray considers what happens to the ideal if removed from the surreal fashion context. Here, Patitz's beauty seems genuine, yet painfully real, as she looks into the artist's camera with indifference and even frustration. The desire to possess her or her beauty is shattered as we realize that her on-camera fashion persona is, as Ray would suggest, a mere hallucination.

The tensions between the real and the ideal, abstract form and the body, and lived and structured experience are at the heart of Charles Ray's art. The fragile balance between these moments is the source of dissonance in his work as well as its strength.

Notes

1. Quoted in Dodie Kanzanjian, "Ray Beyond Cool," *Vogue* 185, no. 9 (September 1995): 606.

2. Robert Storr, *Parkett*, no. 37 (1993): 29. In the same issue of *Parkett*, Peter Schjeldahl also characterized Ray's works in these terms (Peter Schjeldahl, "Ray's Tack," 18).

3. Quoted in interview by Joan Hugo, "Between Object and Persona: The Sculpture Events of Charles Ray," *High Performance* 8, no. 2 (1985): 27.

4. Ibid.

5. Ibid., 28.

6. Quoted in interview by Marc Selwyn, "New Art L.A.: Eight Young Artists Discuss Their Work," *Flash Art*, no. 141 (Summer 1988): 115.

7. Quoted in *High Performance*, 29.

8. Ibid.

9. Quoted in interview by Lucinda Barnes, "Interview with Charles Ray," *Charles Ray* (Newport Beach, Calif.: Newport Harbor Art Museum, 1990), 12.

10. Peter Schjeldahl, "Think Box," *Village Voice*, 5 March 1991, 77, and Lane Relyea, "Charles Ray: In the No," *Artforum* 31, no. 1 (September 1992): 64.

11. Relyea, *Artforum*, 64.

12. Brian Wallis, "Anxious Bodies," *PerForms* (Philadelphia: Institute of Contemporary Art, 1995), 12.

13. Quoted in interview by H. B. [Hudson] in *Charles Ray* (New York: Feature, 1992). Exhib. pamphlet.

14. Quoted in interview by Francesco Bonami, "Charles Ray: A Telephone Conversation," *Flash Art* 25, no. 165 (Summer 1992): 98.

15. Klaus Kertess, "Some Bodies," *Parkett*, no. 37 (1993): 39.

16. Schjeldahl, "Ray's Tack," 18.

17. Ibid.

18. Conversation with author, Los Angeles, July 12, 1995.

19. Ibid., Washington, D.C., December 1, 1995.

20. Michael Fried, "Realism, Writing and Disfiguration in Thomas Eakins's *The Gross Clinic*," *Realism Writing and Disfiguration: On Thomas Eakins and Stephen Crane* (Chicago: University of Chicago Press, 1987), 72–75.

21. Ibid., 64.

OLGA M. VISO

Doris Salcedo
The Dynamic of Violence

Violence belongs to all of us. It has its own dynamic greater than all of us.[1]
—Doris Salcedo, 1995

Exploring the dynamic of violence via objects potently charged with the residue of humanity is the mission of a sculptor whose artistic pursuit has become a fervent calling. Venturing into the Colombian countryside with representatives of human rights groups and churches, Doris Salcedo visits abandoned villages, sites of murders, and mass graves. She interviews both the perpetrators and the survivors of her country's mortal civil conflicts. By recovering the traces of abominable acts, Salcedo maps the experience of violence in her art. The artist recounts:

> *Every time I visit a place, there are traces of a violent event. Even two years after a massacre, there's a special feeling. I'd like to bring that feeling back through objects that have the aura of pain imprinted on their surfaces.*[2]

Salcedo's sculptures and installations fashioned from domestic furniture and found objects bear the memory and pain of suffering. Tattered and worn, they stand as monuments to a humanity that has been silenced and forgotten.

Violence in Colombia is a daily reality. With the highest murder rate in the world, it is estimated that two thousand people die annually as the result of civil and governmental conflicts.[3] Caught between battling political factions, paramilitary squads, guerrilla bands, drug traffickers, and other special interests, the poor, as Salcedo explains, often become the pawns of those who seek power. Since the mid-1980s tens of thousands of people have been abducted, tortured, and assassinated.[4] Known as *desaparecidos*, those who have been "made to disappear," they are, for all intents and purposes, erased from public record. Fleeing indiscriminate violence, another million Colombians have been displaced from their homes. Although Civil War has never been declared in the Republic, periods of prolonged conflict

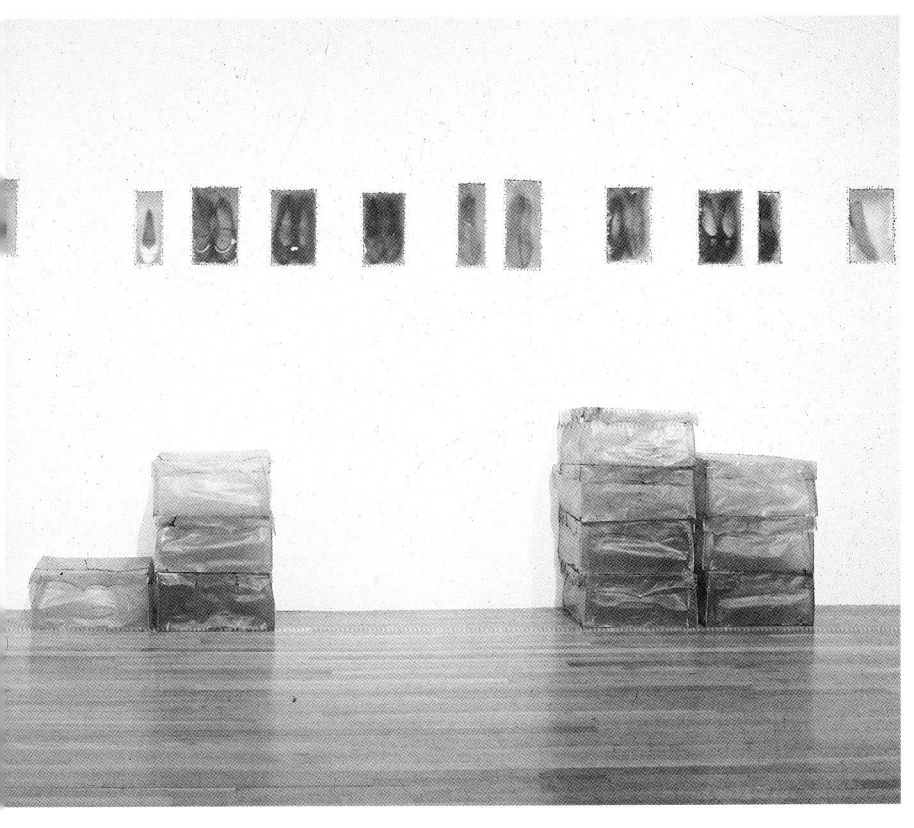

Fig. 32. *Atrabiliarios* ("Defiant"), 1992.

are ironically referred to in the third person as "La Violencia" (The Violence).[5]

For Salcedo, violence has always been an obvious and an unavoidable theme. As a graduate student at New York University in the early 1980s, she researched transcripts of therapy sessions with Vietnam veterans. Then as now, she chose to focus on the effects of extreme strife rather than on its spectacle. Having distanced herself from the situation in her homeland by going to New York, she returned to Bogotá following her graduation in 1985 to witness the beginning of one of the most intense periods of "La Violencia," inaugurated by the takeover of Bogotá's Palace of Justice by guerrilla forces.[6] Blocks from the site of the siege and the brutal massacre of guerrillas and civilians that ensued, Salcedo realized that she had no choice but to make that experience the subject of her art. Her works from 1985 to 1989 addressed themes of social sickness. Using latex, polyester resins, and later, discarded hospital furniture and animal fiber, she attempted to figuratively heal "wounded," abandoned objects by wrapping them in gauze and animal skin.[7]

In 1989, Salcedo became interested in a specific case of disappearance covered in the press. The story reported the poignant identification of a body by someone who recognized the description of a loved one's shoe in a list of "N.N." (No Name) individuals. Published in a Medellín paper, the "N.N." list provided a roster of unaccounted victims of homicide accompanied by physical descriptions of bodies as they were found. During the course of two years of research related to the case, Salcedo discovered that female *desparecidos*, unlike those who are male, are subjected to extended periods of capture and rape before they are executed. The artist thus made the plight of women her focus in the sculptural installation *Atrabiliarios* ("Defiant"), 1990–91 (fig. 32). Taking shoes (found on site during her visits or given to her by victims' families), she incorporated the mismatched personal effects into nichelike constructions set into the wall. Covering the openings with taut animal fiber, she sutured the edges, fastening the sheets onto the wall with surgical thread. Both eerie and ethereal, the shoes fade in and out of our focus of vision through the semitransparent skins. All the shoes are women's, with the exception of one that belonged to a man, referring to the original victim from the newspaper article.

Since creating *Atrabiliarios*, Salcedo has made investigative research a vital part of her process, and she pursues individual stories via the newspaper, word-of-mouth, and her own field research. Her untitled sculptures of plastered shirts from 1989 to 1993 (illus. p. vi) were inspired by the 1988 massacres at La Negra and La Honduras banana plantations. Stacked in varying heights and impaled with steel lances, the sculptures are grouped to suggest that the fluctuating price of bananas in

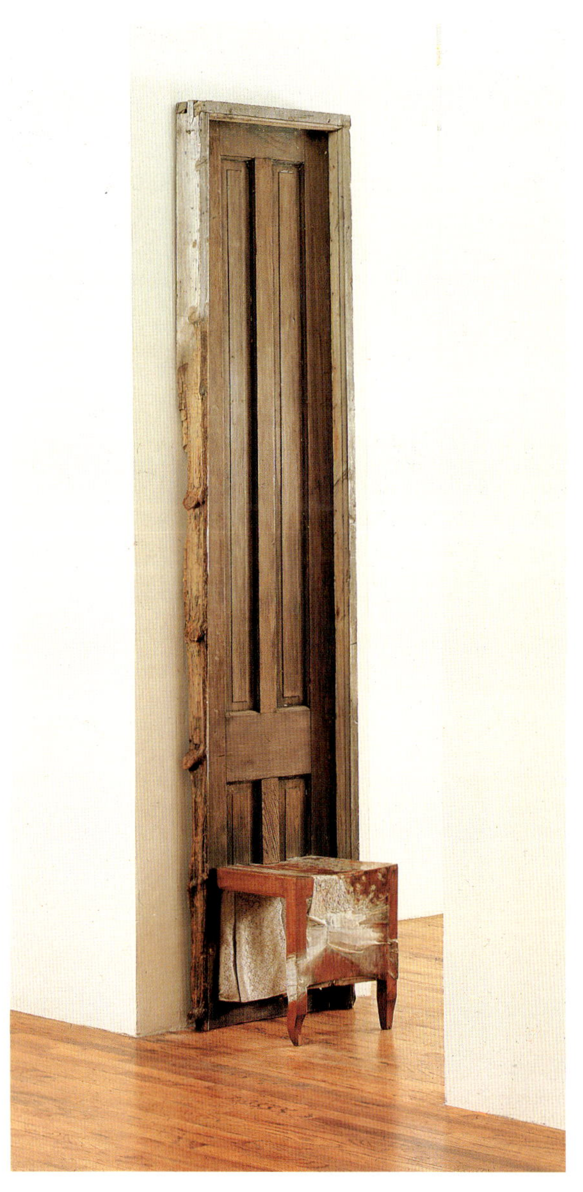

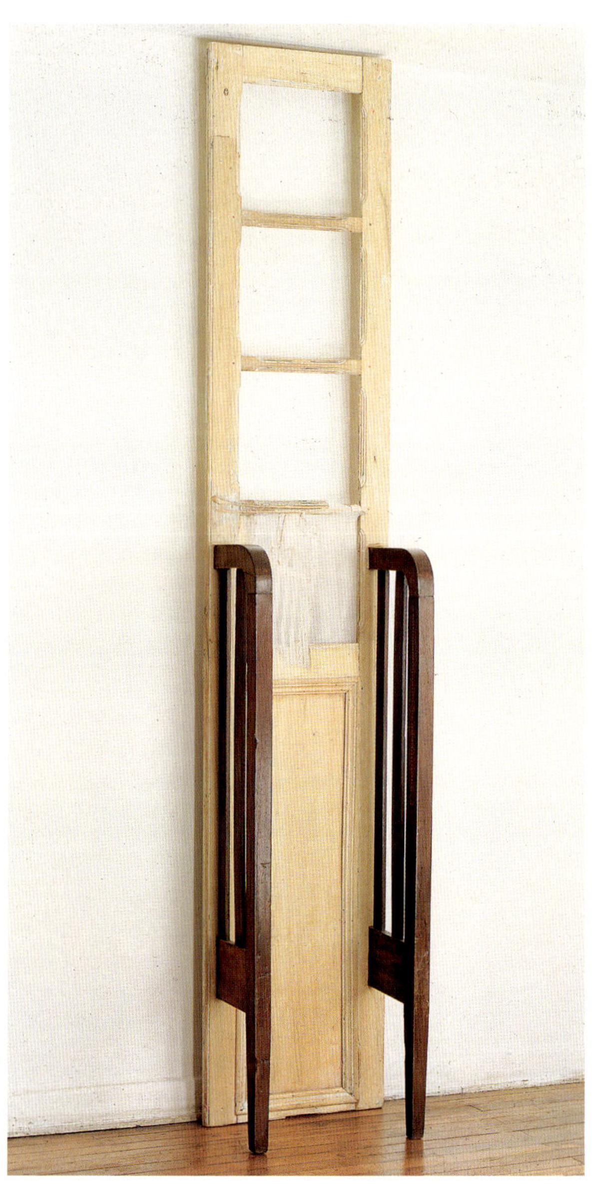

La Casa Viuda I
(The Widowed House I),
1992–94, cat. no. 32.

La Casa Viuda IV
(The Widowed House IV),
1994, cat. no. 33.

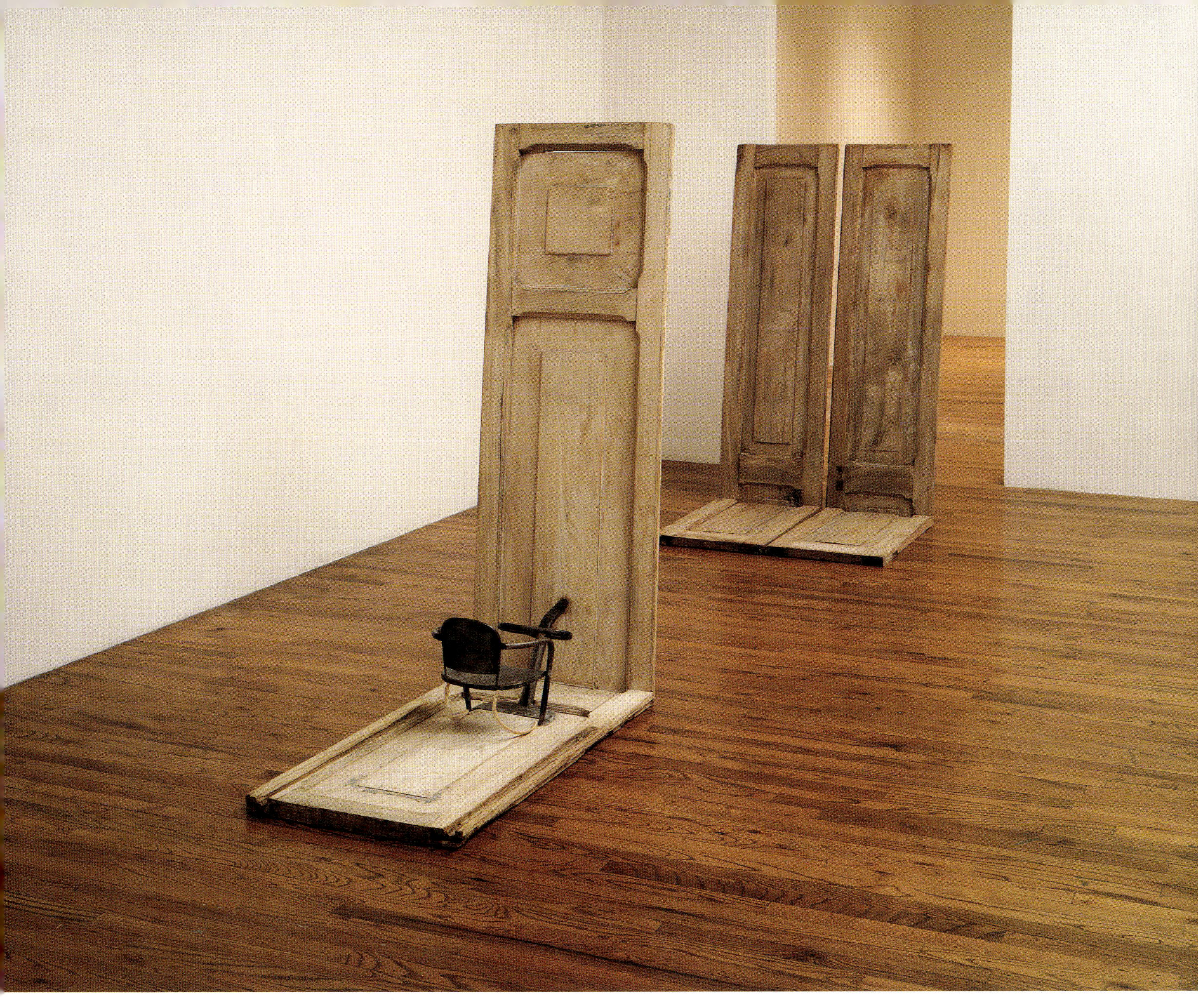

La Casa Viuda VI
(The Widowed House VI),
1995, cat. no. 34.

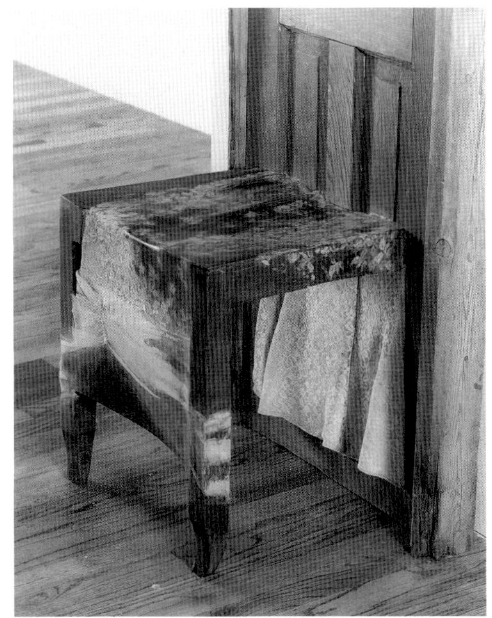

La Casa Viuda I (The Widowed House I), detail, 1992–94, cat. no. 32.

our supermarkets is often impacted by the number of deaths in the fields. The ongoing series of sculptures "La Casa Viuda" (The Widowed House), 1992–95 (cat. nos. 32–34, pp. 88–90), conveys the horrific experience of death squads that come for their victims in the night. Individuals are reportedly pulled out of bed and murdered in front of their families. The intensity of such moments is manifested through the violent conjunction of furniture and door fragments in Salcedo's sculptures. Zippers, kitchen utensils, and human bone are further grafted onto the figurative "widowed" houses whose objects "scream" of the hostile violence they have witnessed. As Salcedo explains, the home contains objects that give voice to an individual's absence.[8] A bureau, a chair, a stack of shirts in the closet, or the impressions left on a mattress by frequent use stand as potent, visceral reminders of those lost. Invoking these reminders, Salcedo displaces the pain of missing loved ones onto the surface of objects used in the practice of living.

In *La Casa Viuda I*, 1992–94 (cat. no. 32, p. 88 and above), the seat of a chair emerges from a stained wooden door panel, and pieces of lacy fabric appear to bleed from the wood. Typically situated in a space that interrupts the passage of the viewer, Salcedo's "La Casa Viuda" sculptures compel us to confront awful moments. The door panels used to construct *La Casa Viuda VI*, 1995 (cat. no. 34, p. 89), fold abruptly and bend upward; their disfigurement gives the impression of a jolting, momentous fall. Based on the story of a child who witnessed his father's execution after he disobediently opened the front door of his house, thereby allowing the assassins to enter, *La Casa Viuda VI* triggers the child's painful memory. We sense that the horrible moment, permanently inscribed in Salcedo's sculpture, is caught in a repetitive cycle that mirrors his own traumatic reliving of the events. Since making *La Casa Viuda VI*, Salcedo has become interested in how children deal with extreme loss, and she has followed the case of a group of orphans from a village near the Panamanian border, where the situation is particularly volatile. Despite the often painful specificity of her sculptures, the artist closely guards the individual narratives. Indeed, the stories are not essential to reading her work, which speaks to suffering on a universal level.

A number of contemporary artists have considered the subject of mass violence and the issues of power and control at work around the globe. French artist Christian Boltanski's "Monuments" of the 1980s commemorate victims of the Jewish Holocaust in silent, ritualistic installations composed of intricate wires of lit bulbs and photographic portraits of anonymous faces. Chilean artist Alfredo Jaar's illuminated lightboxes present images of marginalized peoples and consider the complex and often imbalanced relations between industrialized nations and countries of the Third World. Using photo-based imagery as the basis of their sculptural environments, Boltanski's and Jaar's works reconstitute memory, evoke loss, and reveal the exploitation of others. Although Salcedo may share their approach conceptually, her work differs dramatically from these and other artists. Liberated of the image, the photographic record of the individual or crisis, Salcedo's "monuments" transcend

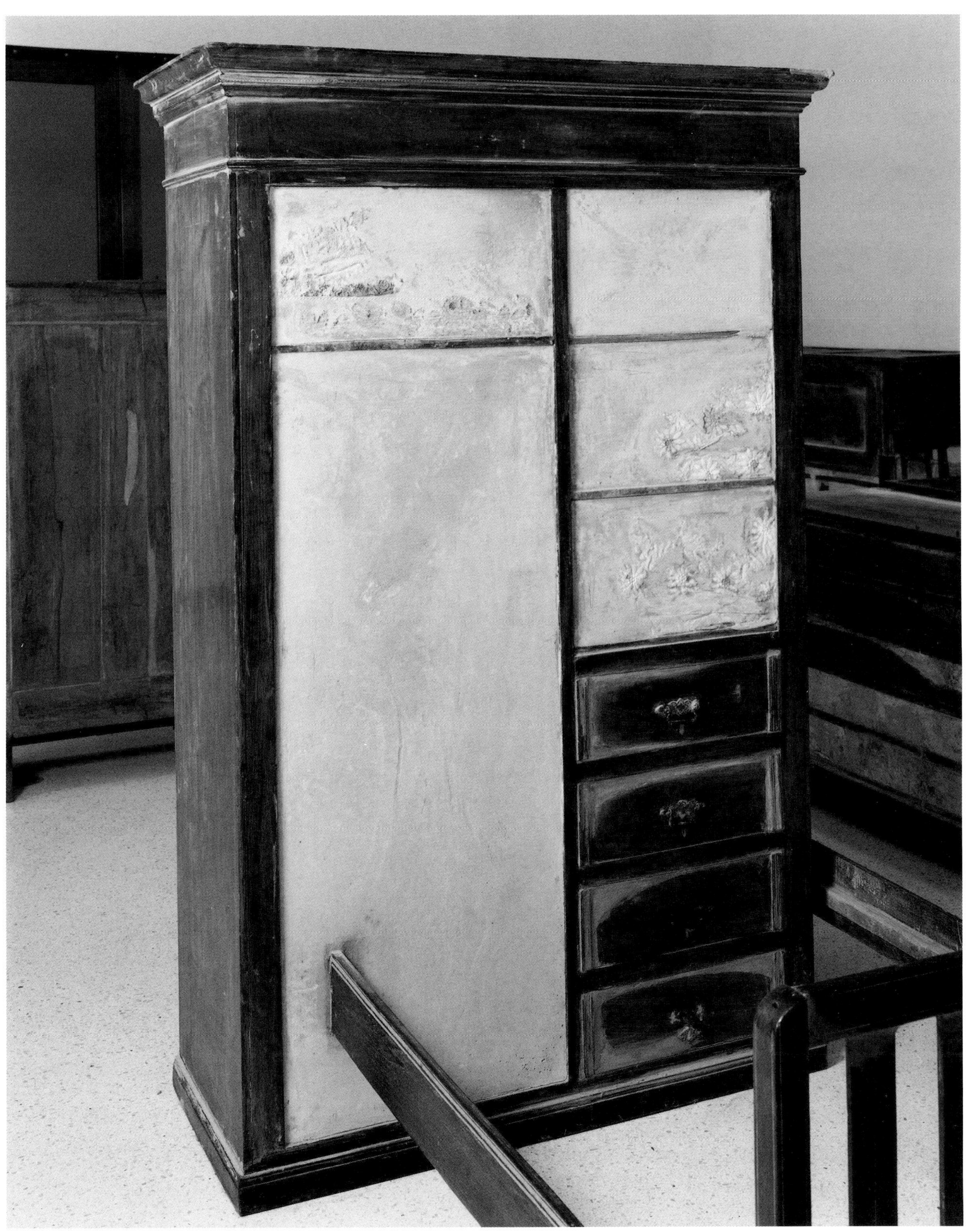

Fig. 33. *Untitled*,
detail, 1995.

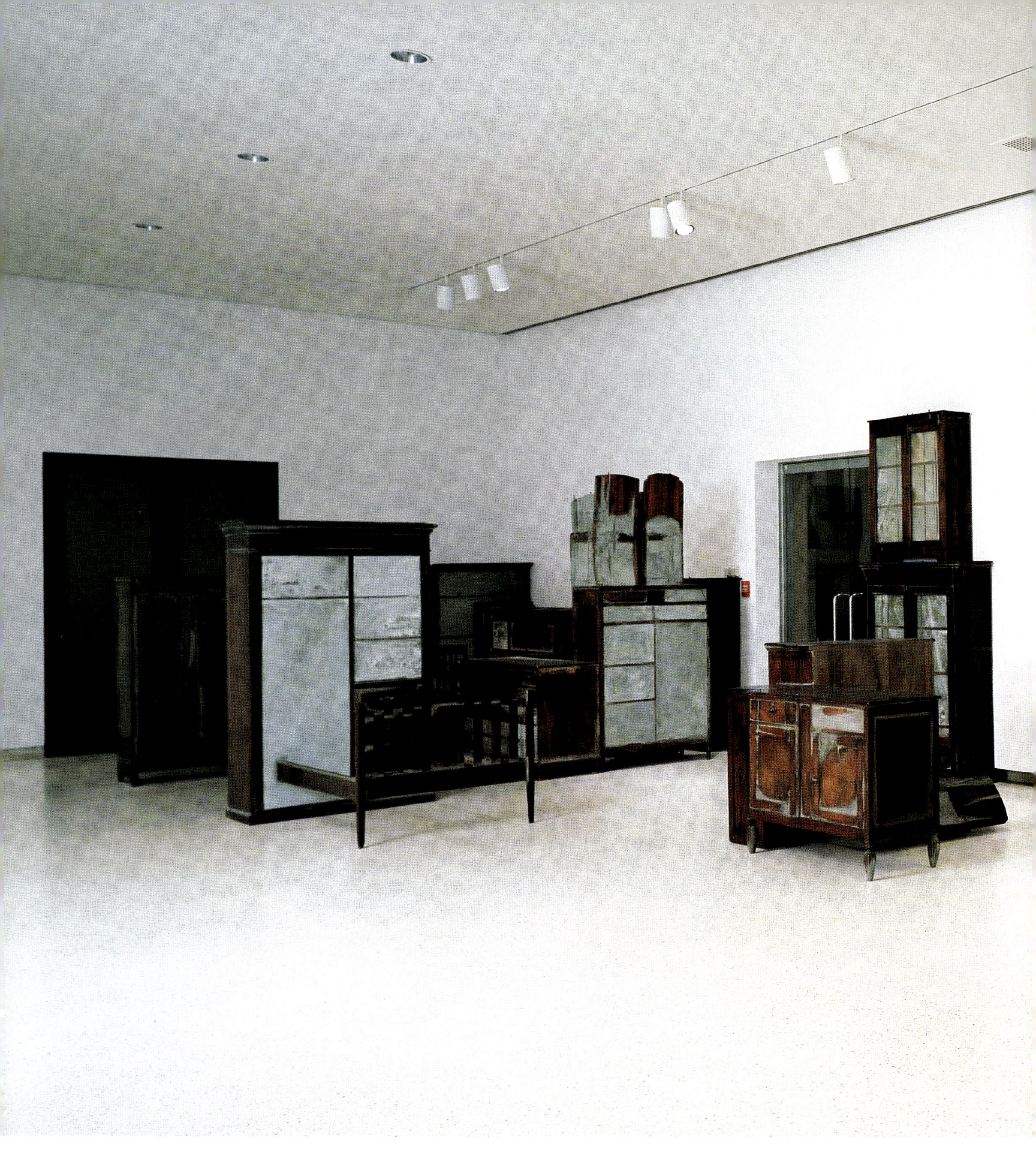

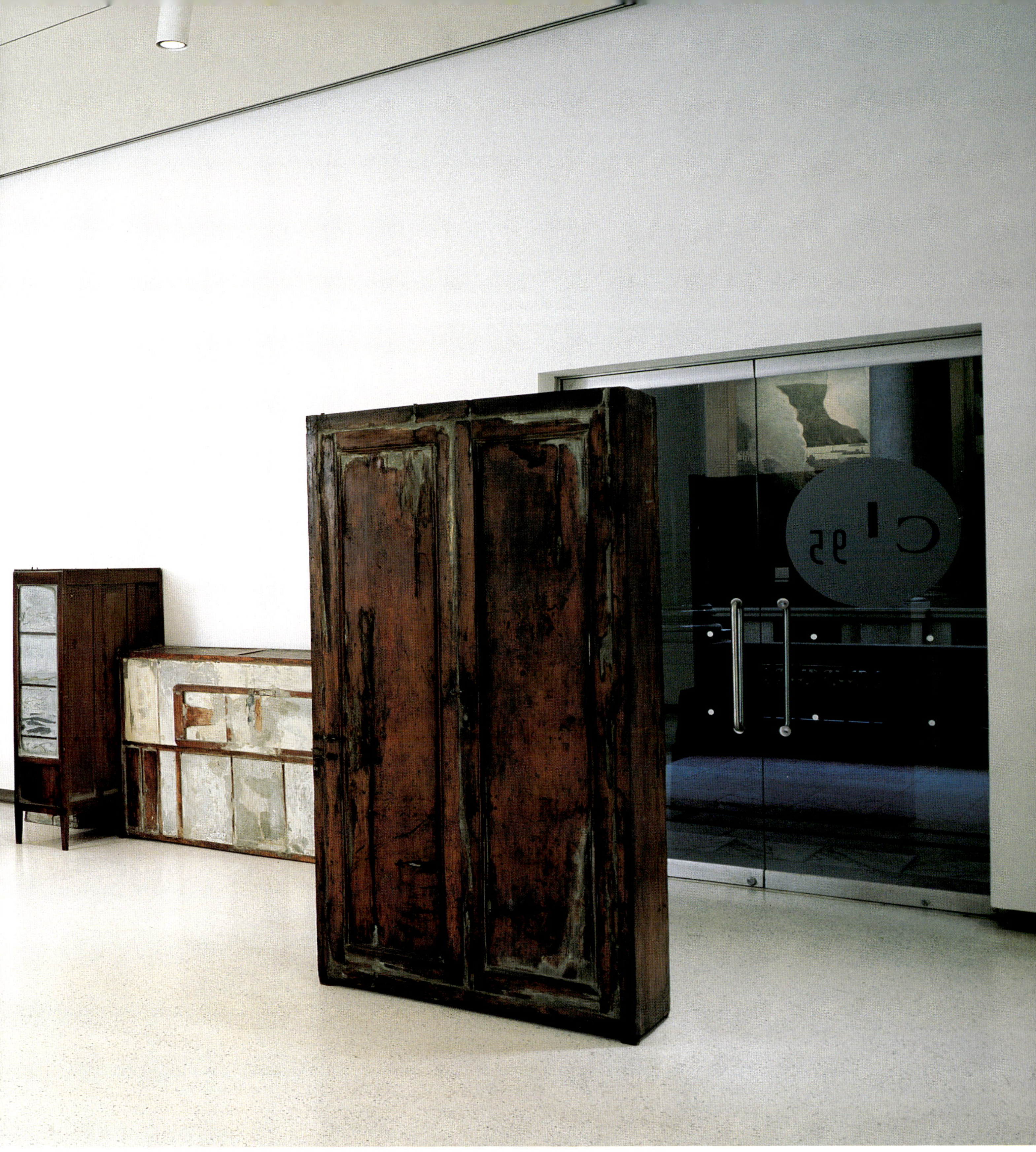

Fig. 34. Installation,
Carnegie International 1995,
The Carnegie Museum of Art,
Pittsburgh.

the sensational and the more didactic approach of an artist such as Jaar. Salcedo's oeuvre underscores a theme in this catalog's introduction, that artists are responding to the social realities of our time in new ways. Creating a different type of political art, Salcedo and her colleagues represented in "Distemper" seek to connect with humanity rather than assign blame.

Salcedo considers that being an artist is relevant to society on many levels, and she describes her role in this context in specific terms: to delay death and to ritualize life.[9] The notion of delay is indeed central to her art, and one of the intriguing characteristics of her sculptures is the manner in which they record a rupture in time. Registering suspended moments, time is simultaneously arrested and accelerated as the past and the present violently collide. According to Salcedo, this collision is symptomatic of violence, which confuses time and "crushes things into moments."[10] The temporal rift, of seeing one's life flash before one's eyes in the face of death, is evocative of Jorge Luis Borges's *Secret Miracle*, 1978. The story of a Jewish writer sentenced to death during the Nazi era has a particular resonance for Salcedo. Just before he is executed, the writer in the story asks God to grant him a secret miracle, to allow him to finish his final book. Granted the wish, the author rewrites the entire book in his mind. Time is slowed down and imminent death is effectively delayed. Invoking Borges, Salcedo affirms: "This is the gift art can give us, the delay. This is how art is important to society."[11]

Coupled with her desire to delay death is Salcedo's need to silence what she has described as the "screaming" nature of domestic objects. An entire body of work has emanated from this intent, and, since 1989, the artist has buried furniture in concrete for this express purpose. Working with self-leveling concrete, Salcedo pours the material into the surfaces and voids of bureaus, armoires, and chairs. Metal rods pierce the structures like spines, supporting the voluminous weight. For all their mass, the objects are punctuated by a shocking fragility afforded by their worn, weathered surfaces, cracked panes of glass, and the imprint of delicate fabrics enmeshed in the concrete (see *Untitled*, 1995, fig. 33, p. 91). Using a subtractive method, Salcedo treats the sculptures with chemicals that change the surface and reveal the fragments of clothes and belongings embedded within. Unlike scraping or carving, this method allows her to eliminate the traces of her own hand and underscores a distance she likes to maintain in her work. Reinforcing that distance, Salcedo claims that her sculptures are collaborations in which she allows the victim to occupy her mind and body. She often makes the distinction that she speaks *with* victims rather than *for* them.[12]

For her installation at the Carnegie International 1995 in Pittsburgh (fig. 34, pp. 92–93), Salcedo stacked and clustered more than twenty individual furniture sculptures throughout the expansive space, creating an eerie, dusty environment reminiscent of an abandoned warehouse. Their disquieting nature rendered viewers silent as they walked amid the "tortured" objects, metaphoric victims of an unspeakable sequence of events. The surfaces of the furniture, at once gritty and elegant, invited deep engagement, while the alternately spare and clustered groupings disturbed and repelled with a claustrophobic intensity. Comprising new and existing works, Salcedo's installation at the Carnegie represented the realization of an idea conceived many years earlier. In that powerful installation, Salcedo commemorated for the first time on a truly monumental scale those, who in her country, have been silenced. For the survivors, who have been dispossessed of any form of recourse, public acknowledgment, or avenues for collective mourning, the artist provided a rich space of ritual and reclamation.

For Salcedo, the aspect of ritual is critical to contemporary society, particularly in a time when ritual is considered a suspect and even meaningless practice in certain parts of the world. By bringing aspects of ritual to her work—ceremony, commemoration, observance, reenactment, and the invocation of the dead—she provides a secular setting in which loss is communally acknowledged, accepted, and observed. It is her fervent belief that art must recover the aspects of ritual to deal with violence and thus initiate the process of healing. These goals link Salcedo's art to that of Joseph Beuys, an early formative influence for Salcedo and an acknowledged inspiration to many of the artists represented in "Distemper." Salcedo also credits Robert Smithson's concept of "nonsites" as an important resource. Just as Smithson would relocate shards of earth and stone from the environment into the gallery to contain the earth's process of erosion, Salcedo arrests death by transferring sites of intimacy and violation into the public space of the museum. As a neutral site, the museum is an institutional entity pregnant with its own ritual and cultural associations. It is a place where history and commemoration are aptly at the core of its existence.

Providing an alternative to conventional forms of commemoration, Salcedo's sculptures are not unlike Maya Lin's Vietnam Veterans Memorial in Washington. Challenging in form and in their powerful, quiet subtlety, Salcedo's sculptures provide a place where ritual is possible rather than imposed. James Lingwood has used the term "reluctant monuments" to describe the work of a number of contemporary sculptors, including Stephan Balkenhol, whose public works "express no desire to dominate public space" or "speak the conventional script of public sculpture."[13] These monuments proclaim no victory or virtue, only "silent, resilient humanity."[14] The term seems applicable to the work of Doris Salcedo, who commemorates silent, resilient humanity in the face of extreme adversity. By ritualizing life through the intimate and the familiar, Salcedo recovers an erased history and brings the necessarily private spectacle of mourning to the public sphere—a space of refuge prohibited in her native land and a conflicted space of indifference in the world at large.

Notes

1. Salcedo, in her lecture at the Museum of Contemporary Art, San Diego, July 7, 1995.
2. Bill Stamets, "If the Shoe Fits," *In These Times* (Chicago), 3 April 1995, 10.
3. Figures reported by the Center for Investigations and Popular Research as quoted in Ken Dermota, "Colombian Protests Violence with Sculpture," *Christian Science Monitor*, 16 August 1995, 14.
4. Ibid.
5. The years between 1948 and 1958 marked the first wave of "La Violencia." The death toll during that decade has been estimated at two hundred thousand. The second wave of extreme violence began in 1985 (Salcedo, telephone conversation with author, December 12, 1995).
6. Ibid.
7. Ibid.
8. Salcedo, in her lecture, San Diego, July 7, 1995.
9. Ibid.
10. Ibid.
11. Ibid.
12. Ibid.
13. *Stephan Balkenhol: Über Menschen und Skulpturen/About Men and Sculpture* (Stuttgart: Edition Cantz, 1992), 60.
14. Ibid.

NEAL BENEZRA

Thomas Schütte
A Path toward That Goal

Utopia means a goal, and in our time a path toward that goal.[1]
—Thomas Schütte, 1994

Thomas Schütte's work and approach to art fall outside the range and scope of mainstream contemporary art. Employing a wide variety of media, Schütte composes a dialog between men and women and their environment, and he insinuates art and its larger possibilities into the conversation. Paradoxically, he merges an expansive vision of art's possibilities with a profound skepticism borne of the failures of our century and, in his view, of most modern art.

Schütte's first important experience of art came at the age of eighteen, in 1972, when he attended Documenta V in Kassel.[2] There, he was particularly impressed with artists whose work was nontraditional, including Joesph Beuys who, in addition to setting in motion the *7,000 Oaks* project, also set up an office of the Organization for Direct Democracy and spent one hundred days interacting with visitors to the exhibition. Schütte was also enamored of artists such as Daniel Buren and Bruce Nauman, both of whom were reconsidering the articulation and psychological implications of architectural forms. The following year, Schütte entered the Düsseldorf Kunstakademie, where he studied under Fritz Schwegler and Gerhard Richter. The school was the liveliest in Europe at that time, and among Schütte's colleagues were Ludger Gerdes, Harald Klingelhöller, Reinhard Mucha, Thomas Ruff, and Thomas Struth. The mid- and late-1970s were challenging years in which to attend art school in Düsseldorf, but they were rich with possibilities. Although Beuys was no longer teaching at the academy, his activist example and charismatic personality still dominated the city's art world. Younger artists, Schütte among them, were struggling to establish an idealistic position, one that might be distinct from the cult of personality that still surrounded Beuys. They were reacting, as well, to the growing commercialism that accompanied the renewal of painting under Neo-

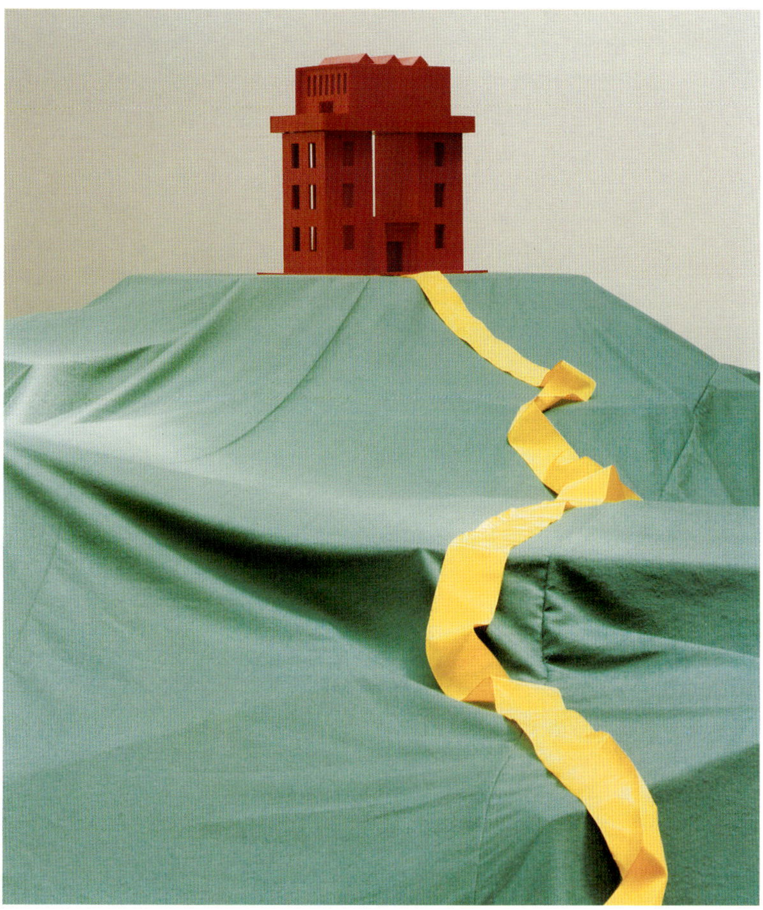

Fig. 35. *Studio II in den Bergen* (Studio II in the Mountains), detail, 1984.

Expressionism in the late 1970s. From the outset of their careers, they were suspicious of the seductions of the art market. Schütte and Mucha, in particular, maintained an equivocal stance in relation to the art world, and the work that they made often existed outside that context. Theirs was an imagination in the service of the mind, in which works often took the form of objectified thoughts.

Although Schütte was a student of one of Germany's leading painters, Gerhard Richter, he never identified himself with the medium. As he once said, "I paint but I am not a painter—if there's no green I'll use blue."[3] What Richter offered his students was an antidote to what they believed to be the excesses of Neo-Expressionism; here was a brilliant but dispassionate painter who possessed the methodology of a conceptualist and whose example encouraged a multiplicity of possibilities. For Schütte, a number of additional influences proved crucial. From a formal standpoint, Schütte has noted his debt to Minimalism: "It was this generation that established the grammar, the training and the language. They address the fundamental problems of lighting, material, meaning, and space."[4] And yet, for Schütte, as for Mucha, Klingelhöller, and the others, formal accomplishment was never an end in itself. Schütte's early works, from the late 1970s and early 1980s, represented a fundamental rethinking of the role of the artist. In 1977 he made pieces such as *Mauer* (Walls), in which panels were painted to resemble bricks and then mounted on a wall. In other works he stacked painted monochrome panels, mounted rings, or applied a scalloped design motif to a wall. These first explorations were exercises in confronting a particular architectural space and determining the possible role of art in that setting. In the process, Schütte was seeking to exceed Minimalism with its systemic approach to the articulation of a space. "What I was attempting to do ... was to work without a mechanical system, without grids, or rectangles; to create a free form, discrete decoration."[5] Finally, these were early postulations about the role of art outside the gallery or museum and the manner in which an artist might intervene in a nontraditional setting.

The principal vehicle for Schütte's ideas in the early 1980s was the model.[6] Schütte's can be distinguished from those of architects; rather than presentation pieces, his models are paradigmatic constructs for public and private interaction.

> *I used a model because this is something everyone understands, it was an easy way to make a standard sculpture. It's very accessible to a variety of readings. You can imagine it as the prototype for something bigger, or as something seen from a child's point of view.*[7]

In the early 1980s, Schütte conceived two types of models. One addressed and analyzed the role of art in large public settings.

For example, for the exhibition "Westkunst," a major international exhibition held in 1981 in Cologne, Schütte designed an elevated podium, a stepped quasi-architectural ramp that allowed the visitor to ascend and gain some visual and psychological perspective of the exhibition. Although the sculpture was realized only at small scale, conceptually the idea invited artists to consider, in the words of Schütte's friend and colleague Ludger Gerdes, "shaping the place of his work, instead of merely supplying finished products."[8] While unusual in the contemporary period, Schütte's pursuit recalls the idealism of integrated display embodied in Ludwig Mies van der Rohe's Barcelona Pavilion of 1928–29, or the many exhibition designs undertaken by El Lissitzky in the late 1920s.

Schütte developed a second type of model in the early 1980s. More fully architectural in concept, these were idealized residences and studios for artists, as well as various types of public institutions such as museums and theaters. The geometric simplicity of the highly symbolic and at times fantastic designs recalls the work of the late eighteenth-century visionary architects L. E. Boullée and C. N. Ledoux. Some, such as *Modell für ein Museum* (Model for a Museum), 1982, are bleak and even funerary in overtone; others like *Studio II in den Bergen* (Studio II in the Mountains), 1984 (fig. 35, p. 97), are perhaps more whimsical. Schütte's idiosyncratic utopianism is here more fully formed and apparent, and he has professed interest in Vladimir Tatlin—for example, his *Monument to the Third International*, 1919—and in institutions such as the Bauhaus, whose architects, designers, and artists proposed to reshape human interaction on the basis of a reconceived environment.[9] While these revolutionaries possessed a missionary zeal and an impassioned optimism, their faith was decimated by fascism and war. For Schütte, "the pictures of the war, of Auschwitz and Hiroshima,"[10] have rendered any such idealized faith unimaginable in our own time. As a result, the character of his architectural models and designs of the 1980s swing wildly between cynical, depopulated, de Chiricoesque cityscapes, and fanciful watercolor evocations of public spaces reminiscent of the work of Claes Oldenburg.

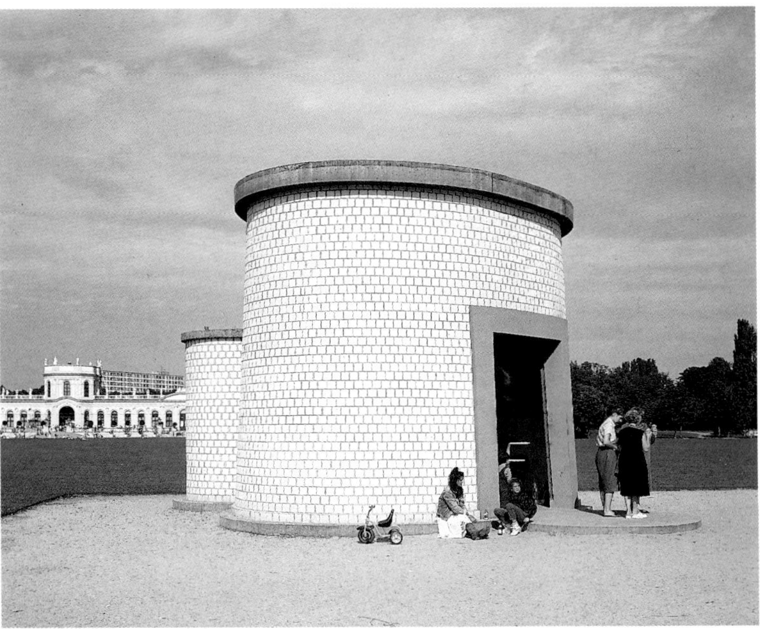

Fig. 36. *Eis* (Ice Cream), 1987.

This seemingly paradoxical discrepancy is most readily apparent in several public sculptures that Schütte completed from 1985 to 1987. On the one hand, Schütte made works such as *Tisch* (Table), 1985, a commissioned homage to Hamburg's resistance composed of an oversized and quite stern granite table with twelve chairs, and *Schutzraum* (Shelter), 1986, for the Sonsbeek sculpture exhibition in Arnhem of that year. The latter took the form of a cylindrical concrete aboveground bunker without doors or windows. The serious if paradoxical nature of the work—reminiscent of that of several of Bruce Nauman's sculptures—diverges from other public projects Schütte carried out in 1987: *Eis* (Ice Cream) 1987 (fig. 36), a functioning ice-cream parlor erected near the Orangerie in Kassel as part of Documenta VIII, and *Kirschensäule* (Column of Cherries), a monumental and altogether whimsical pair of Oldenburgesque cherries, mounted atop a huge base and sited in a Münster parking lot as part of "Skulptur Projekte Münster," also in 1987.

A marked change in Schütte's work occurred in the following year. Although characteristically enigmatic, *Mohr's Life*, 1988 (fig. 38, p. 100), reveals his redirection. First exhibited at the Galerie Philip Nelson in Lyon, the installation consists of a figurine wrapped in a human-sized shirt standing before a steel drying rack. One-hundred-thirty of Schütte's old socks hang from this full-size rack, which is set before an actual heater in the gallery. Nearby, another similarly garbed figure stands before four miniature easels, each of which bears an impastoed painting of a torrential rainstorm. Although Schütte had included figures in his work previously, they had most often been props used to create discordant architectural scale in his models. Here, they are grotesque caricatures modeled from children's clay. The figure bound in rope before the easel clearly recalls Nauman's *Bound to Fail*, 1967, a surrogate self-portrait in the form of a back bound in rope and cast in wax, in which the artist's title becomes both literally and figuratively true. Although Schütte's work is but a metaphorical self-portrait, *Mohr's Life* does reveal the artist struggling with the real and illusory demands of his life and career and questioning the purposes of his work.

Fig. 37. *Die Fremden* (The Strangers), 1992.

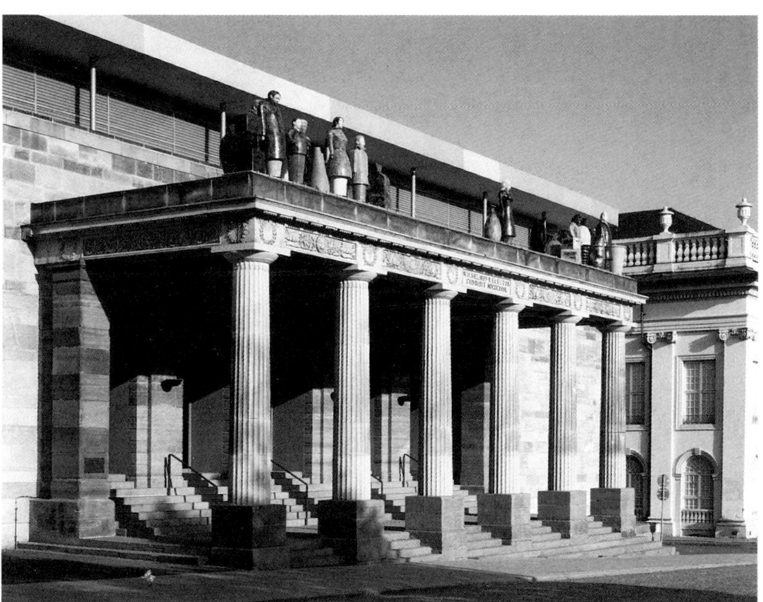

From this point, the figure became Schütte's principal subject. The following year, 1989, the artist developed *Monument for a Lost Sailor*, a proposed memorial to Alain Colas, a celebrated French sailor lost at sea during a solo transatlantic crossing in 1978. Intended for installation in the river port of Colas's hometown of Clamecy, Schütte's sculpture called for a large figure to be mounted directly in the water. According to changes in water level, the figure, with its horror-struck facial expression, would be visible in varying degrees above the surface of the water.

The marked change in Schütte's work became more dramatically self-evident in Documenta IX in 1992. *Eis*, Schütte's work for the 1987 exhibition—in which visitors were served ice cream just as they were plied with art—had good-naturedly commented on the spectacle of large international art exhibitions. Five years later, Schütte's *Die Fremden* (The Strangers), 1992 (fig. 37), took an altogether different tone. For this, Schütte installed a series of polychrome ceramic figures above the Neoclassical portico of the Roten Palais in the center of Kassel and directly overlooking the spectacle of Documenta. Positioned as a type of projecting pedimental sculptural group, the series most resembles a gathering of mourners; modeled in clay and colorfully glazed, each head has downcast or closed eyes. They are strangely self-contained, recalling chessmen or, perhaps more accurately, Etruscan funerary urns in which the ashes of the deceased are housed within the vessel that supports the bust. Indebted to tradition in the breadth of their reference and ennobling architectural placement, and yet utterly contemporary in their restraint, Schütte's *Die Fremden* showed the artist moving beyond paradigmatic public art and fully into the public sphere.

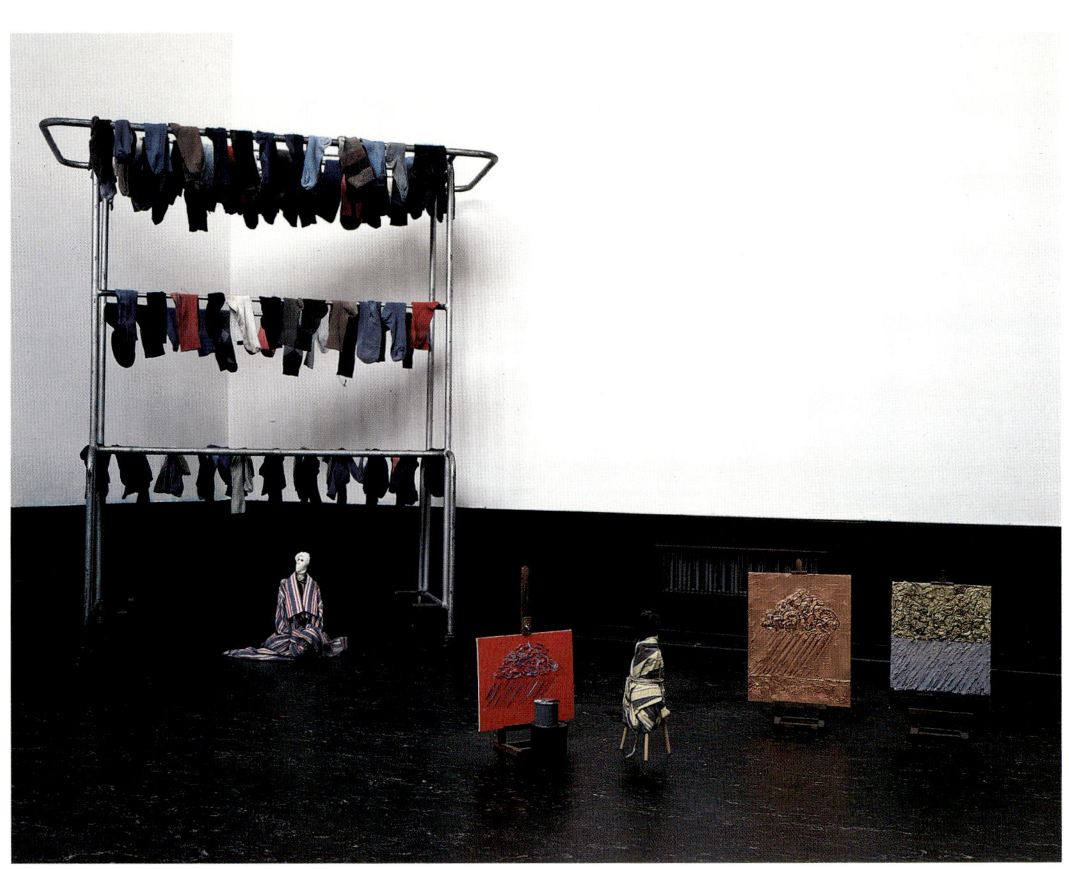

Fig. 38. *Mohr's Life,* 1988.

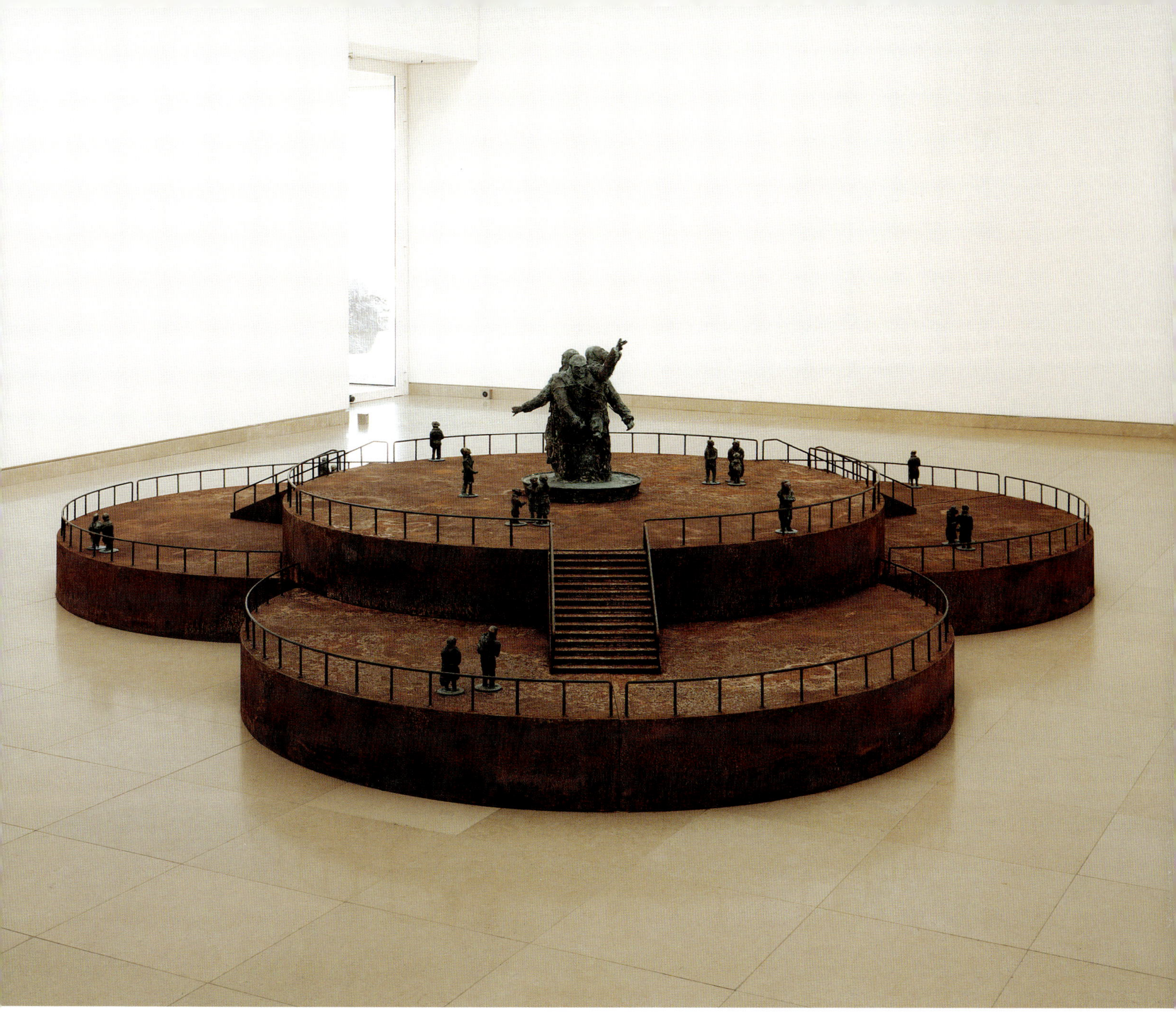

Grosser Respekt
(Large Respect),
1993–94, cat. no. 35.

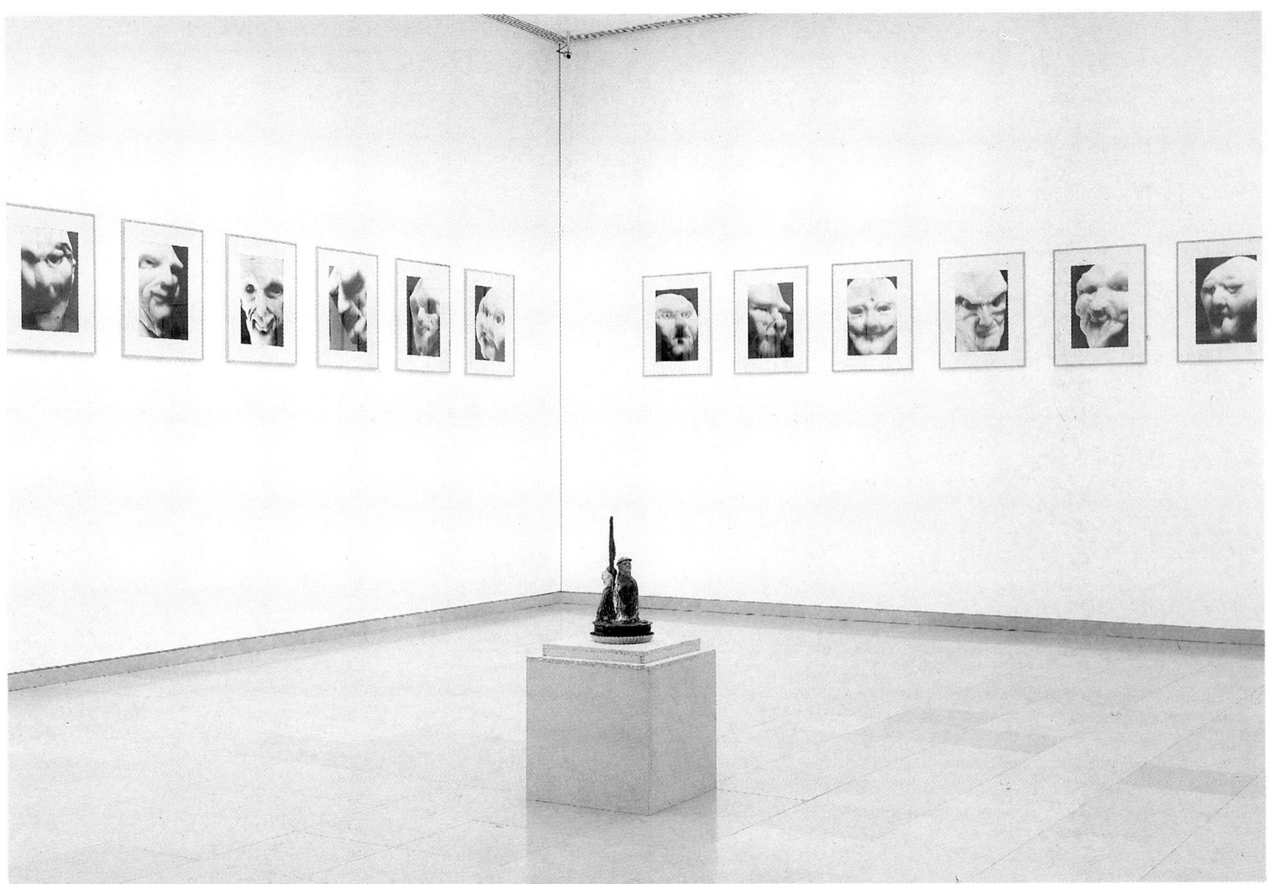

No Respekt (No Respect), detail, 1994, cat. no. 37.

Without calling undue attention to themselves, nor resorting to narrative pathos or self-conscious display, Schütte's ensemble cast a thoughtful, solemn mood over the exhibition.

Since 1992, Schütte has concentrated extensively on two bodies of work. One is a series of sculptures and related photographs titled "United Enemies," 1993–94. As in *Mohr's Life*, the clay figurines in the new series are dressed in old clothes and bound in rope, but now they are paired together. Their expressions are discomfortingly grotesque, recalling both the character masks of the eighteenth-century sculptor Franz Xavier Messerschmidt and, by virtue of their small scale, Honoré Daumier's biting satires in bronze of the mid-nineteenth century. Mounted on tall narrow bases and enclosed in bell-shaped glass vitrines, they resemble museological examples of a failed human species.

The other series has been called the "Respekt" trilogy.[11] Like "United Enemies," its pieces derive from earlier works, in this case *Mann im Matsch* (Man in the Mud), 1982–83, and *Zwei Männer im Matsch* (Two Men in the Mud), 1985. In those small models, Schütte placed one or two figures (one holding a flag) on four raised circular platforms arranged in an intersecting cloverleaf pattern. The inclusion of stairs linking the platforms clearly revealed them to be paradigms for public sculptures. And yet, in each case, the figures are stuck in the mud—literally and figuratively—and effectively rendered anti-monuments.

The "Respekt" series, *Grosser Respekt* (Large Respect), *Kleiner Respekt* (Small Respect), and *No Respekt* (No Respect), 1993–94 (cat. nos. 35–37, pp. 101–3 and x), demonstrates a shift in Schütte's work over the course of a decade. The works feature figures bound together in the manner of "United Enemies." The latter two are relatively small: *No Respekt* is a diminutive, motorized sculpture that rotates on a stationary base; the equally sized figures of *Kleiner Respekt* are mounted atop a tall vertical plinth. Whereas both can clearly be described as models, in which Schütte proposes alternative bases, *Grosser Respekt* implies nothing less than a full-blown public square. The piece measures sixteen feet in diameter and is composed of the same tripartite series of raised intersecting circular platforms bearing figures that is seen in *Mann im Matsch* and *Zwei Männer im Matsch*. Now, however, the stage is large and many of the actors (cast in bronze and numbering twenty-one) are engaged in heated dialog. Larger than the rest are three central figures, each of whom gesticulates wildly but ineffectually. They are also bound in rope, and in the unorthodox nature of their composition and their relationship, the trio recalls Auguste Rodin's monumental *Burghers of Calais*, 1884–89.

Although an idealized work, *Grosser Respekt* marks the growth of Schütte's engagement with figurative sculpture. From the alternately barren and playful architectural models of the 1980s, Schütte has found a way to renew public figurative sculpture in a completely contemporary manner. Like his peers Stephan Balkenhol and Juan Muñoz, Schütte works with the figure without a trace of self-consciousness or anecdotal pathos. His new figures address us with an insistence and an assurance that betoken an interest in an art of public purpose and a commitment to the still limitless potential of the figure in the sculpture in the 1990s.

Notes

1. Quoted in interview by Heinz-Norbert Jocks, "Gespräche mit Künstlern: Thomas Schütte," *Kunstforum International*, no. 128 (October-December 1994), 249.

2. Ibid., 244.

3. Quoted in interview by Iwona Blazwick and Andrea Schlieker, "Thomas Schütte," *Possible Worlds: Sculpture from Europe* (London: Institute of Contemporary Art and Serpentine Gallery, 1990), 71.

4. Ibid., 70.

5. Ibid.

6. For a discussion of Schütte's models, as well as related work by Ludger Gerdes, Harald Klingelhöller, and others, see Stephan Schmidt-Wulfen, "Models," *Flash Art*, no. 122 (March 1985): 70–73.

7. Quoted in Blazwick and Schlieker, *Possible Worlds*, 70.

8. Ludger Gerdes, "About the 'Model' in the Work of Thomas Schütte", *Thomas Schütte* (Bern: Kunsthalle Bern, 1990), 101.

9. See Schütte's comments in Jocks, "Gespräche mit Künstlern," 247, 249; Blazwick and Schlieker, *Possible Worlds*, 72; and Martin Hentschel, "Inside Out: Thomas Schütte in Conversation with Martin Hentschel," *Thomas Schütte*, 82.

10. Quoted in "Conversation Between Stephan Balkenhol and Thomas Schütte," in *Über Menschen und Skulpturen/About Men and Sculpture* (Stuttgart: Edition Cantz, 1992), 7.

11. Anne Rochette and Wade Saunders, "Figures of Estrangement," *Art in America* 83, no. 5 (May 1995): 104–5.

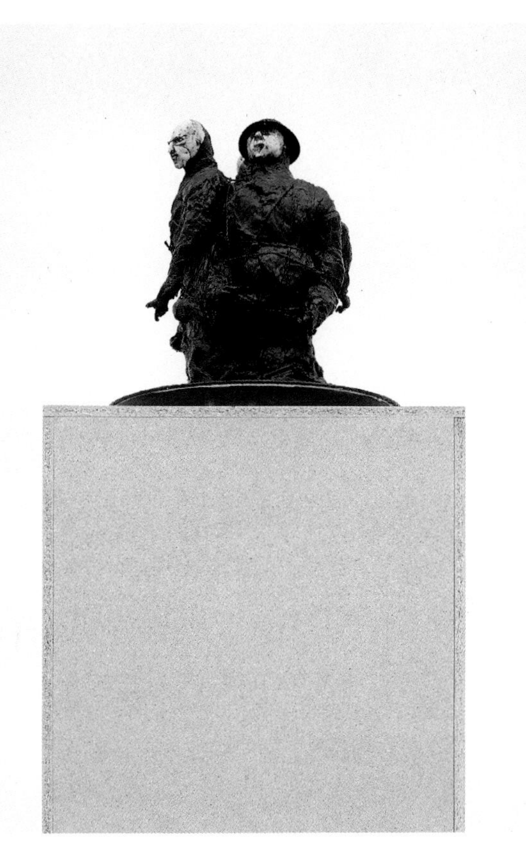

Kleiner Respekt (Small Respect), detail, 1994, cat. no. 36.

Rachel Whiteread
A Sense of Silence

I'm a socialist—it's very much part of my life. You can't help it, living somewhere like London where you're seeing things crumble around you and you're seemingly helpless to do anything.... But I'm a sculptor, not a politician. I am involved in the making of sculpture, of exploring formal questions about how a work sits on the floor, or about the space surrounding it.[1]
—Rachel Whiteread, 1992

Since her earliest exhibitions in London in the late 1980s, Rachel Whiteread has cast familiar objects of daily use. Working initially in plaster, then in rubber, and most recently in resin, she has methodically explored the theme of domestic life, evoking memory through simple materials and subjects. While Whiteread's work is formally assured, even authoritative, her pursuit is balanced between issues of sentiment and social engagement, between formal invention and the reinvigoration of cast sculpture.

Born in 1963, Whiteread has lived virtually her entire life in London. The youngest of three daughters, she grew up in Ilford, a suburb near London. Influenced by her mother, an artist, Whiteread studied painting at Brighton Polytechnic from 1982 to 1985, after which she returned to London to concentrate on sculpture at the Slade School until 1987. During those years she began to explore unusual ways in which to allude to the human figure. One of her early pieces consisted of a shirt hung on a hanger, with a hot-water bottle suspended inside and visible at the bottom. It was at this time that the London sculptor Edward Allington taught her to cast objects in wax and plaster. Of the latter, which particularly intrigued her, she would later comment: "It [is] a dead material, but the surface is very sensitive, it picks up details ... and embalms them, leaving mummified space and a sense of silence."[2] Initially, Whiteread gravitated toward objects she knew well, common items, she said, that fulfilled "an autobiographical impulse, using something familiar, to do with my childhood."[3] But rather than cast the object itself—taking an impression of the exterior surface as sculptors have done for centuries—Whiteread instead chose to make sculptures "constructed from negative spaces ... using a direct casting technique to reveal the negative, manipulating apparently mundane domestic items to produce

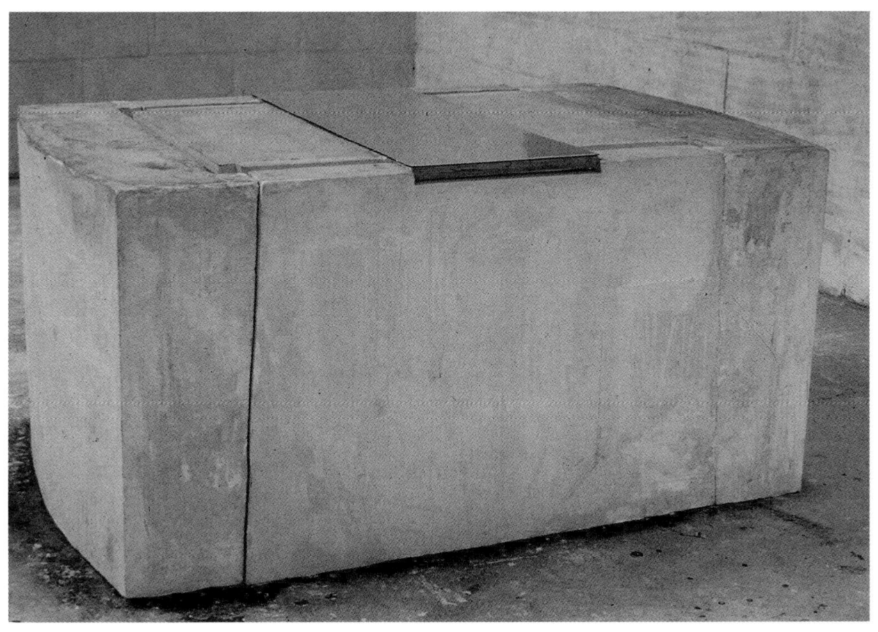

Fig. 39. *Yellow Leaf,* 1989.

pieces that surpass their original identity."[4]

Whiteread's first cast plaster sculpture was *Closet,* 1988. An upright plaster box covered in black felt and bearing the marks of moldings, shelving, and a door, the sculpture owes its theme, Whiteread says, to "a particular childhood memory: sitting inside wardrobes, the space and blackness, and of being in a completely dark room, the sense of a furry black space."[5] Whiteread's synthesis of memory and method—casting the interior meant rummaging around in the close quarters of a small bedroom closet to extract direct impressions of every indentation—implied an activity that was laden with sentiment but also eminently physical in nature.

Closet was shown in Whiteread's first solo exhibition at the Carlile Gallery in London in 1988, together with other plaster sculptures such as *Mantle,* 1988, a work shaped like a sideboard or a desk resting solidly on the floor. Whereas *Closet* turned a space inside out, *Mantle* was one of the first instances in which Whiteread cast the underside of a form. The sculpture reveals a Constructivist formal sense, in which the planar geometry of the object is balanced in an interlocking geometric composition and presented in a forthright manner directly on the floor. Conceptually, the idea recalls the work of Bruce Nauman, who in the late 1960s cast the space beneath or between objects in making several sculptures. While Whiteread's work is unquestionably indebted to Nauman and to formalist aesthetics, hers is perhaps a more allusive type of abstraction, for the subjects she chooses, her working processes, and the surface textures that result are all imbued with a quiet restraint. While Whiteread credits Carl Andre with providing her with the "confidence to place a white block in the middle of the floor and let it be simply a white block,"[6] she is equally inspired by Louise Bourgeois, Eva Hesse, and Richard Serra for the manner in which they personalized Minimalism.[7] A final piece in Whiteread's formative puzzle is London's bustling sculpture scene in the 1980s, when Tony Cragg, Richard Deacon, and Bill Woodrow, among others, were transforming Minimalist aesthetics through the revitalization of cast-off materials, labor-intensive methods of construction, and informal approaches to installation.

In 1989, Whiteread made a series of works based on tables and desks. These sculptures, with titles such as *Yellow Leaf, Fort,* and *Ledger,* took on a solid, cubic form. With their plaster stoniness and airless mass, they suggest sarcophagi, a reference that Whiteread acknowledged at the time.

> *I am making objects that are, I think, very much like tombs, the ways things are incarcerated, how you know there is something inside but you never actually see what it is. It wasn't until I made* Yellow Leaf *that the sarcophagus reference became apparent.*[8]

Whiteread's experience as a youth working on the maintenance staff in Highgate Cemetery in North London exposed her to old, decrepit, sometimes open crypts. "I had a sense of something being inside," she said. "Although I didn't want to look, I was curious. Peering through the cracks was, and remains, so compelling."[9]

Fig. 40. *Ghost*, 1990.

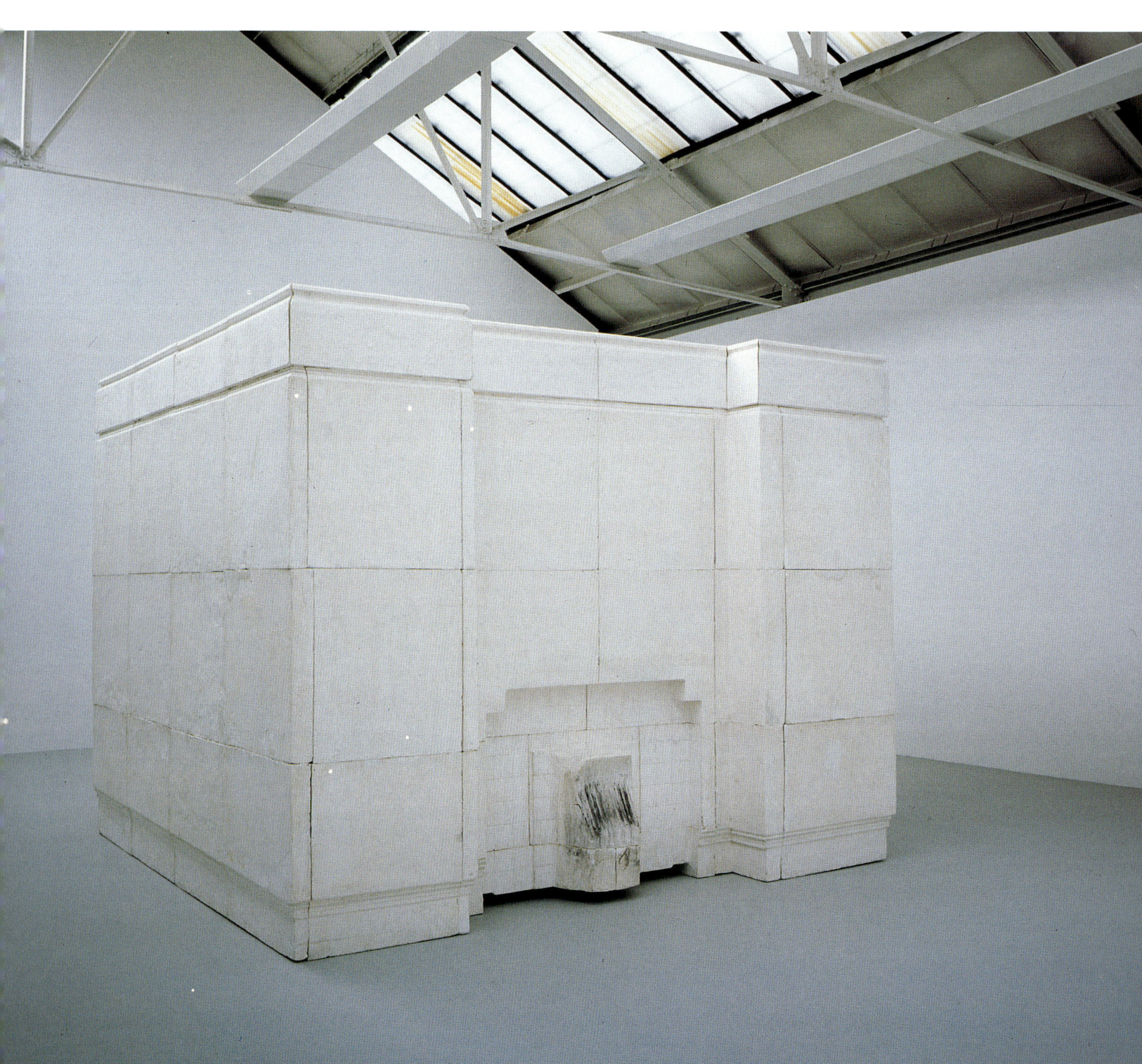

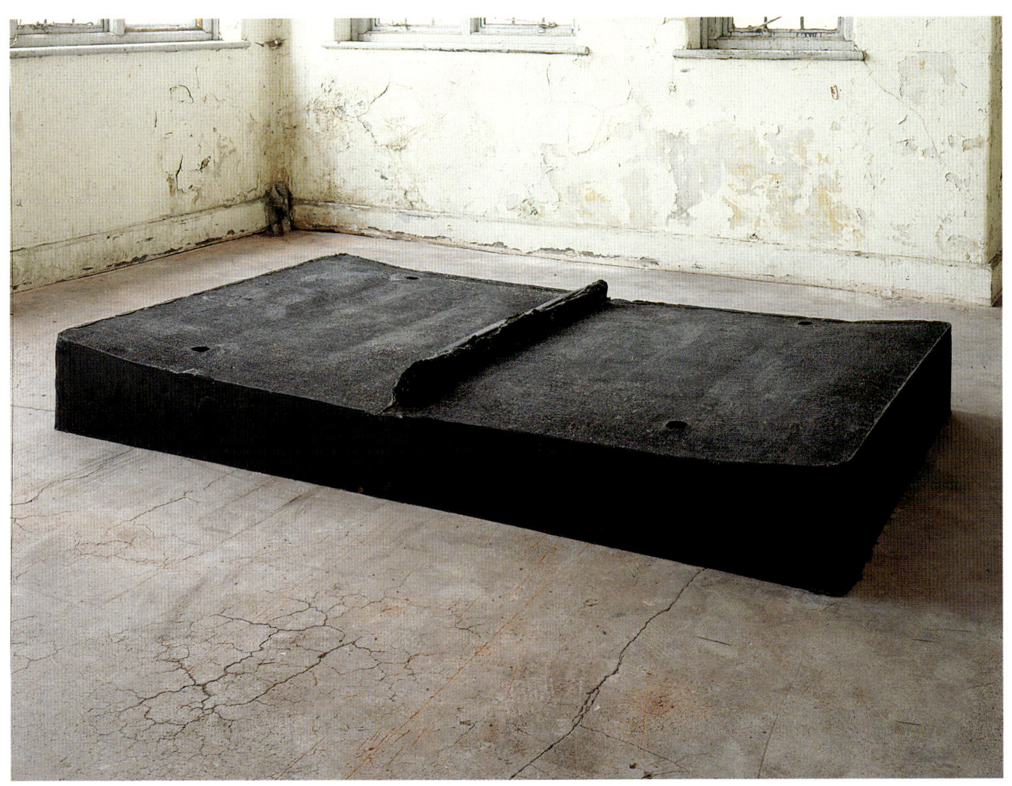

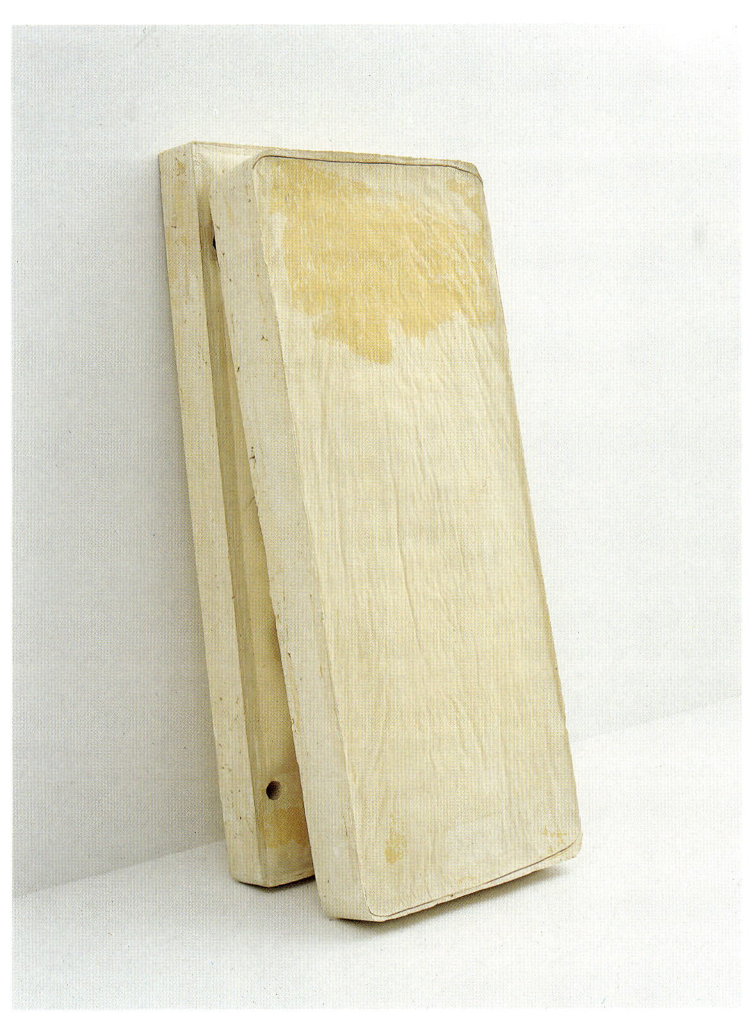

Untitled (Black Bed),
1991, cat. no. 38.

Untitled
(Yellow Bed, Two Parts),
1991, cat. no. 39.

The following year, Whiteread made *Ghost* (fig. 40, p. 106), her largest and most ambitious piece to that date. From casting discrete domestic objects, she was now taking on an interior environment itself, in this case an abandoned Victorian row house in North London. Painstakingly, she covered the room in plaster, eventually casting every inch of the parlor in five-inch-thick segments. When assembled for exhibition, the piece at first glance resembled an enormous tomb. But on closer inspection, one realized that, although exceedingly small, the block represented a family's shared social space. The sculpture is disorientingly surreal. Imprints of architectural features are plainly visible, yet the viewer's experience is thwarted: one is ever conscious of being on the outside unable to look in. In this sense, *Ghost* can be contrasted with Joseph Beuys's *Plight*, 1986, the artist's last work, in which he lined the interior of the Anthony d'Offay Gallery in London with rolls of felt and placed objects inside. While Beuys eloquently articulated the inside of the tomb, Whiteread created its monolithic exterior. But if Whiteread here treats death, she also imbues the decaying residence with monumental authority, recording and preserving it, and, finally, dignifying the lives lived therein.

In 1990, Whiteread made three related sculptures—*Ether* (fig. 41), *Valley*, and *Untitled*—which, while smaller than *Ghost*, bear similar funerary overtones. All three derive from the underside of cast-iron baths and have an overtly massive character. As Whiteread noted:

> *I used cast iron baths because I wanted the rust to leave a trace on the plaster—like scum left in the bath; creating a sense of something having been in there. I carefully scraped away the surface of the bath, getting the paint off it to make a surface that would bleed into the plaster, leaving this trace behind.*[10]

In completing two of the bath pieces, *Valley* and *Untitled*, the artist added a sheet of glass to the top surface, encasing and effectively entombing the hollow space below. For the latter, Whiteread said, she

> *drilled holes through the plaster and the glass on top of it so there was an airflow like nostrils. I felt it was too claustrophobic, like suggesting my own death; there was something sinister about these works.*[11]

Whiteread has attached many references to this group of works, ranging from lead coffins discovered in Spitalfields Church, London, in which bodies had decomposed to liquid, to her experience of seeing Lenin's glass-enclosed tomb in Red Square. She has professed admiration for the work of Piero della Francesca, knowledge of which leads us to conjure images of the imposing tomb in his *Resurrection* of 1540.

While Whiteread was recasting objects as a way of summoning up figurative traces, she simultaneously sought to approach the figure more directly. "I wanted to make something figurative. It was a way of using the mattress, or the spaces beneath beds or whatever as a metaphor for people."[12] Whiteread had cast a bed as early as 1988, but by 1991 the bed had become her predominant subject. Typically she would purchase decrepit, secondhand mattresses at Salvation Army shops and haul them to her studio to cast them. Sweat- and urine-stained, they were thoroughly imbued with the essence of lives lived, precisely the quality that drew Whiteread to them. Most affecting perhaps was *Untitled (Yellow Bed, Two Parts)*, 1991 (cat. no. 39, p. 107), a cast of the underside of a child's mattress and box spring. Installed by simply leaning the two forms one in front of the other against a wall, the sculpture is utterly forlorn. Looking like the remnants left behind by a family in haste to depart a residence, it suggests

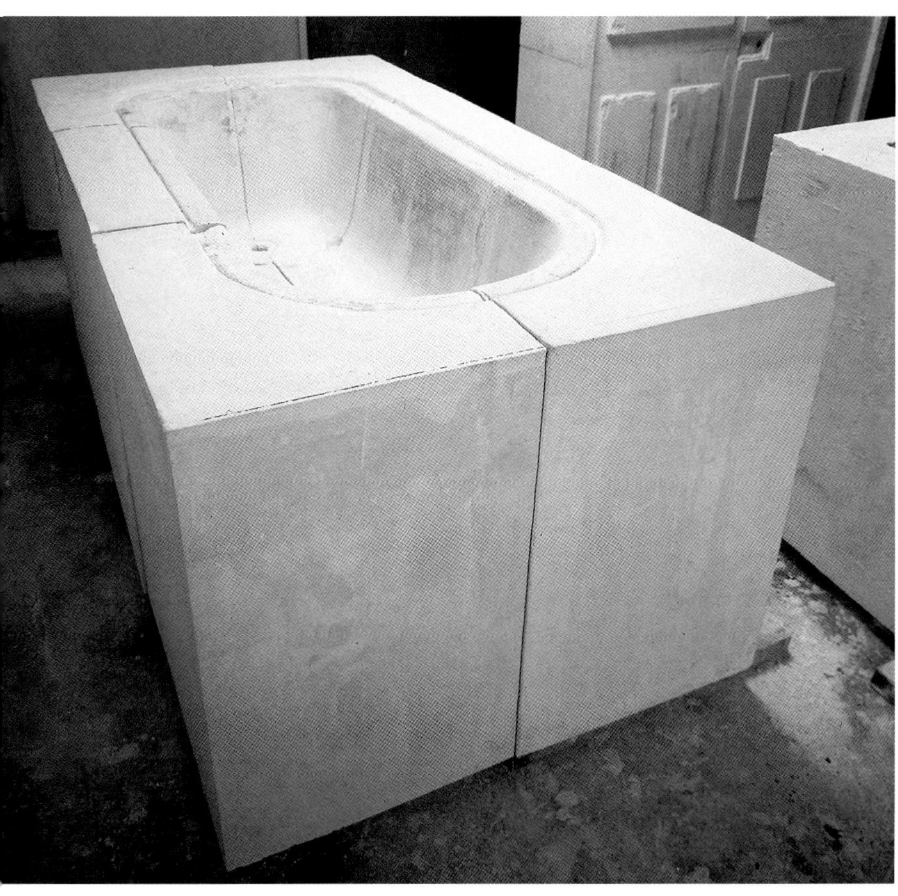

Fig. 41. *Ether*, 1990.

themes of loneliness and abandonment.

Whiteread's work with baths, mattresses, and especially, the full-blown domestic interior she adopted for *Ghost* had set her on a course of quiet social commentary. As she has noted, her politics have evolved from having "lived in London virtually all my life and ... seeing the deprivation, and seeing more and more homeless people everywhere."[13] And yet, Whiteread has continually balanced the social implications of her work with a clearheaded formalism. Heretofore, she had worked almost exclusively in plaster, a material that long since proved problematic from a practical standpoint. The artist habitually installed her sculptures squarely on the floor or leaned them against the wall, a practice that caused their edges continually to chip and crack. A turning point was reached with a new series of "mattresses" in 1991, for which she replaced plaster with a dense, amber colored rubber. Now when she leaned the sculptures against the wall they slumped plaintively. While these works in rubber—*Untitled (Amber Mattress)*, 1992 (cat. no. 40, p. 110), and *Untitled (Amber Bed)* and *Untitled (Double Amber Bed)*, both 1991—recall the early lead "prop" sculptures of Richard Serra, for Whiteread they were like "figures ... kind of forgotten about and left in the corner."[14] Although she would continue to make occasional pieces in plaster, rubber was now her predominant material.

Whiteread's change in direction proved to be of profound importance. Rubber offered her the practical advantage of greater durability as well as a wide range of colors, which lent her sculpture a new, sensuous character. In buttressing the social implications of her work with formal innovation, she was able to balance those elements and continue to grow as an artist.

Without question, the defining moment of Whiteread's still-brief career came on November 23, 1993, when jurors at the Tate Gallery voted her the winner of the 1993 Turner Prize. The award was emblematic of her status as Britain's outstanding artist of that year under the age of fifty. The same day, the Bow Neighborhood Council voted the demolition of *House*, 1993 (illus. pp. i and 114), a concrete cast of an entire row house in London's East End that was Whiteread's first outdoor sculpture.[15]

Following conceptually on *Ghost*, *House* was conceived in 1991. Whiteread's partner in the enterprise was James Lingwood, an independent curator and co-director of the Artangel Trust, a London foundation active in commissioning public art projects in Britain. Together, Whiteread and Lingwood searched for an appropriate, terraced house in North and East London, finally obtaining a temporary lease at 193 Grove Road. Whiteread took possession of the property and work was completed during the summer and fall of 1993.

Numerous artists have made existing architectural structures the subject of their work: Bernhard and Hilla Becher have photographed them, Christo has wrapped them,

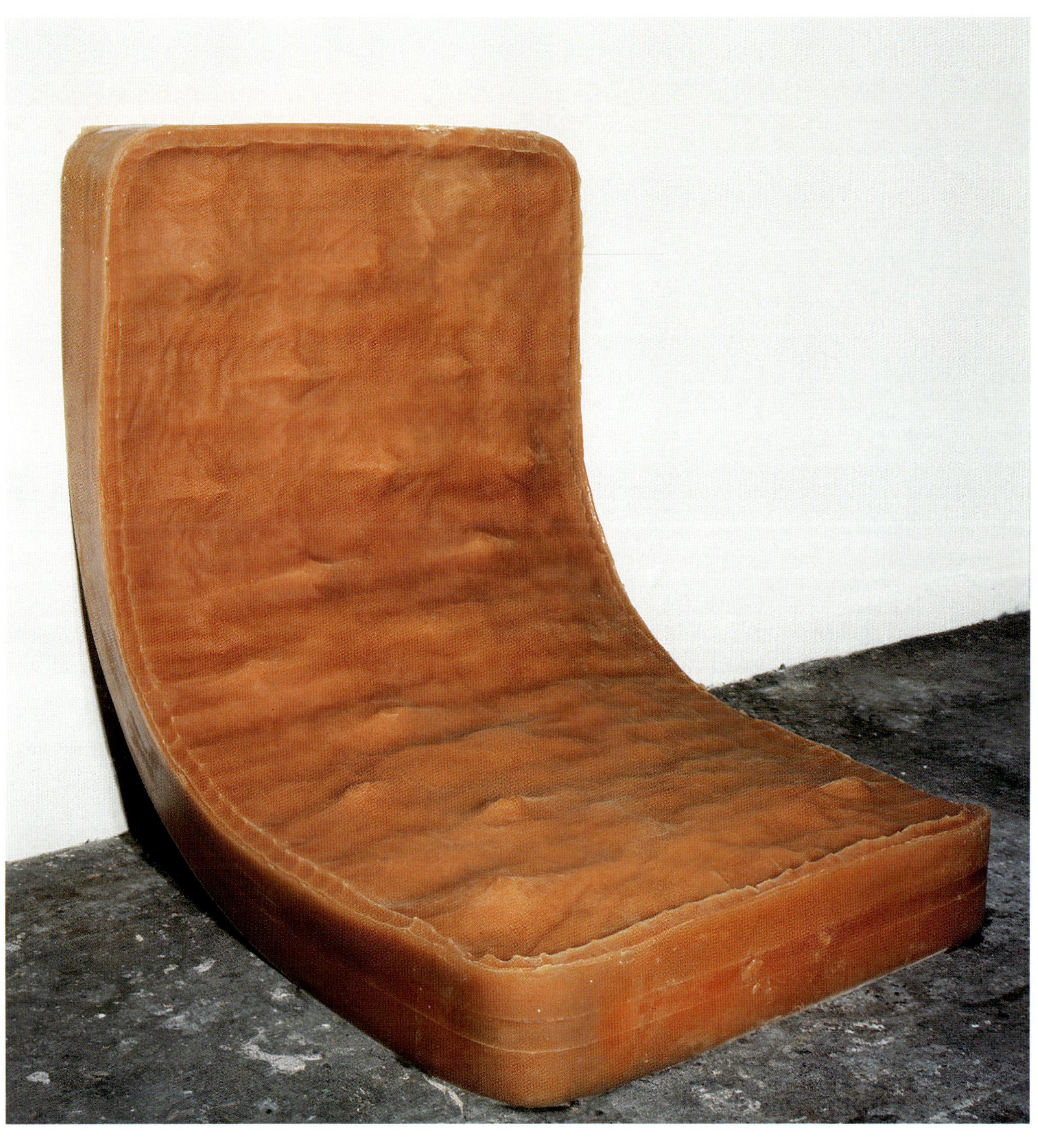

Untitled (Amber Mattress),
1992, cat. no. 40.

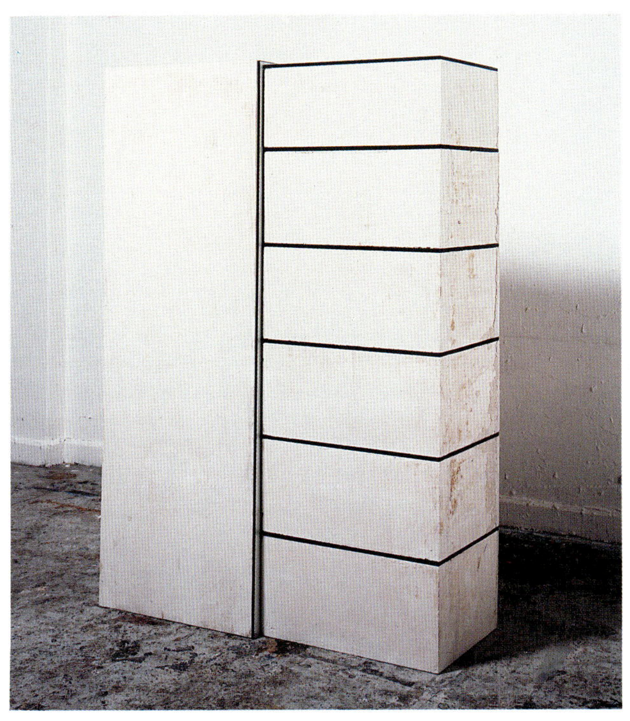

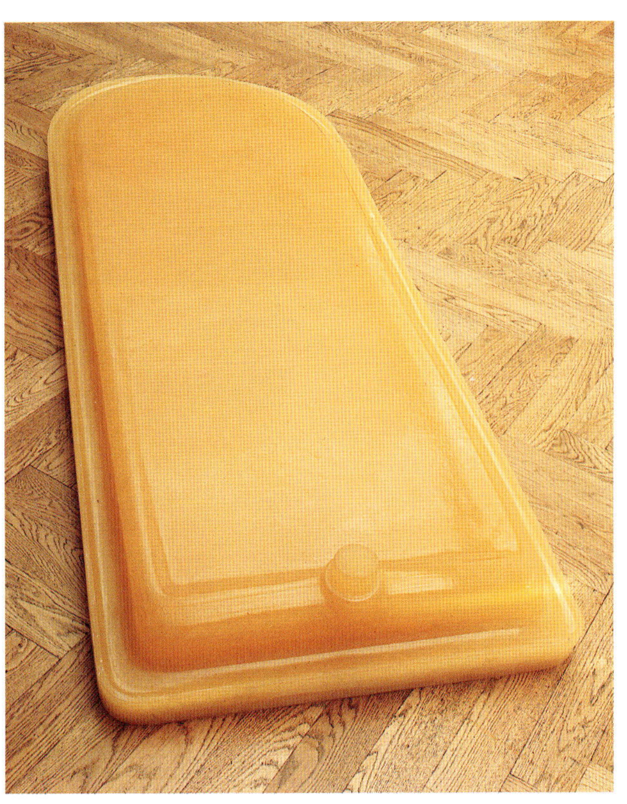

Untitled (Wardrobe),
1994–95, cat. no. 42.

Slab (Plug),
1994, cat. no. 41.

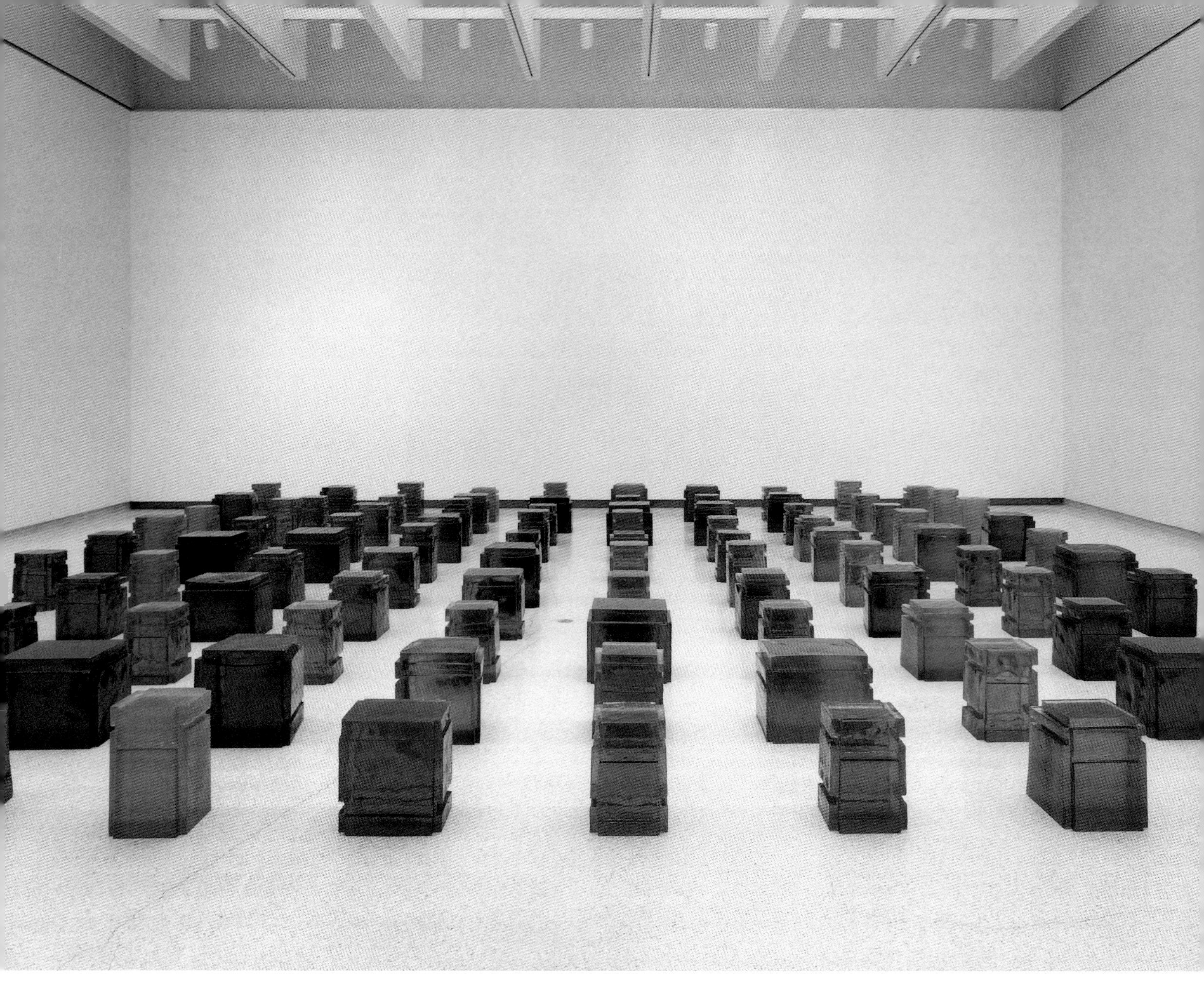

Fig. 42. *Untitled (One Hundred Spaces)*, 1995.

Dan Graham has critiqued them, and Gordon Matta-Clark has dismembered and deconstructed them. As she had done with *Ghost*, Whiteread cast the interior—this time in concrete—memorializing the house while she was formalizing it. Yet, while *Ghost* had possessed obvious real-world social implications, ultimately it was an indoor sculpture, bound for galleries and museums, thus a work that functions within the narrow sphere of the art world. *House* was another story altogether; in its brief life it functioned as public art and social commentary—a sculpture whose larger significance could not be ignored. It quickly became a lightning rod for outspoken public opinion: issues of aesthetics and public art, the perceived elitism of the art world and the philistinism of many residents of the community, and a more sweeping frustration with the state of housing in London all pressed Whiteread and her work into the public eye. When *House* was destroyed early in 1994, the furor it had caused matched that which accompanied Serra's *Tilted Arc* in 1981 and Maya Lin's Vietnam Veterans Memorial in 1982.

That paradoxical moment, combining art-world embrace and public censure in roughly equal measure, had a powerful impact on the artist. As she recently noted, "The Turner prize didn't change my life, but *House* did." Whiteread has consciously tried "to get away from the nostalgia" that she realizes is an element in some of her work, avoiding objects that she feels have a "burdensome history."[16] Her work since *House* is dominated by casts of spaces beneath desks and chairs, such as *Untitled (Twenty-five Spaces)*, 1994–95, and *Untitled (One Hundred Spaces)*, 1995 (fig. 42), the latter made for the Carnegie International 1995, Pittsburgh. In these new sculptures, Whiteread has explored a highly translucent material—resin—one with which she has added luminosity to her arsenal of formal possibilities while also negating any reference to an object's previous use or history.

Self-evidently, Whiteread's new works relate to the "cast-space" sculptures of Nauman and to the 1970s "timber" sculptures of Andre, and they are unquestionably among her most formally accomplished works to date. The blending of two spheres in Whiteread's work—represented by *Ghost* and *House* with their unavoidable social commentary, and the recent, more formal sculptures in resin—show a still-young artist balancing complex social and artistic impulses while seeking to avoid one-dimensional classification.

Notes

1. Quoted in Iwona Blazwick, "Rachel Whiteread in Conversation with Iwona Blazwick," *Rachel Whiteread* (Eindhoven: Stedelijk Van Abbemuseum, 1992), 15.
2. Quoted in *The British Art Show 1990* (London: South Bank Centre, 1990), 114.
3. Quoted in Blazwick, *Rachel Whiteread*, 8.
4. Quoted in *The British Art Show 1990*, 114.
5. Ibid.
6. Quoted in Blazwick, *Rachel Whiteread*, 9.
7. Michael Kimmelman, "Turning Things Inside Out," *New York Times*, 5 February 1991, Arts and Leisure, 1; 35.
8. Quoted in *The British Art Show 1990*, 114.
9. Quoted in Blazwick, *Rachel Whiteread*, 10.
10. Ibid., 13.
11. Ibid., 12–13.
12. Ibid., 14.
13. Ibid.
14. Ibid.
15. See James Lingwood, ed., *Rachel Whiteread: House* (London: Phaidon Press, 1995).
16. Quoted in Kimmelman, "Turning Things Inside Out," 1.

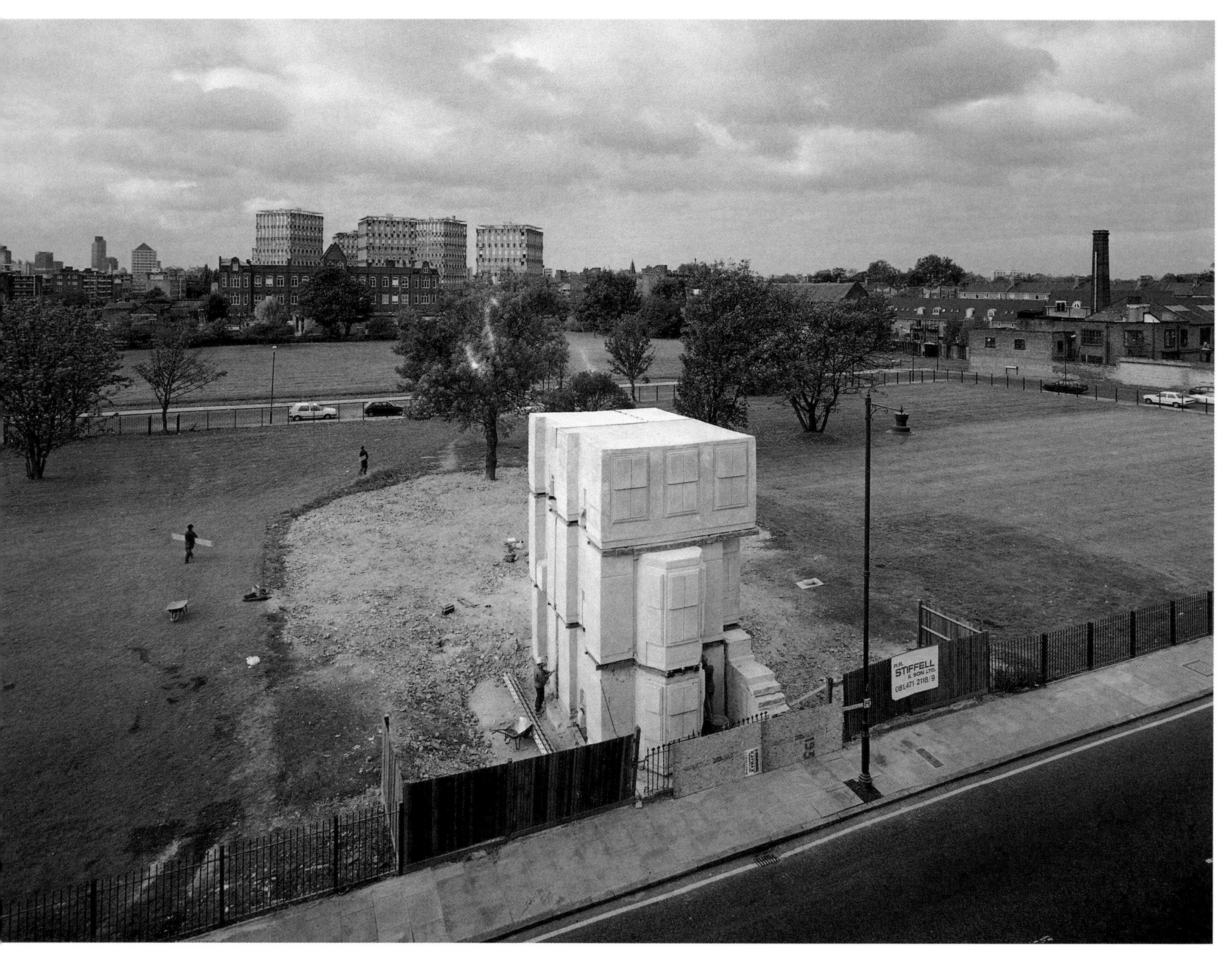

Fig. 43. Rachel Whiteread, *House*, 1993.

Biographies of the Artists

LESLIE R. RABINOVITZ

OLGA M. VISO

Mirosław Bałka

born 1958, Warsaw

lives and works in Otwock, Poland

Mirosław Bałka grew up in the small town of Otwock, near Warsaw, where he currently maintains a studio in his childhood home. He attended the Academy of Fine Arts, Warsaw, from 1980 to 1985. His graduation project, *Remembrance of the First Holy Communion*, 1985 (fig. 6), merged performance and sculpture in an installation held in an abandoned two-room house in Zuków, Poland. Until 1989, Bałka continued to create performance-based works, often in collaboration with an avant-garde performance group that he cofounded with Mirosław Filonik and Marek Kijewski.

Bałka made predominantly figural works throughout the 1980s. These were included in a number of group exhibitions throughout Europe and in "Metaphysical Visions: Middle Europe," Artists Space, New York, 1990, which was Bałka's first exhibition in the United States. By that time he had begun to create works that referred to architectural interiors. For Aperto '90 of the XLIV Venice Biennale, he displayed three-dimensional wall and floor sculptures made of wooden planks, iron plates, and concrete. Reduced to simple geometric forms, the spare objects resembled domestic furniture. On occasion Bałka would dust his installations with pine needles, ash, and salt, and he used electrical wires to heat the sculptures to human body temperature. The titles and dimensions of Bałka's sculptures also began to derive specifically from his own body parts and measurements. Works of this type were included in "Possible Worlds: Sculpture from Europe," organized by the Institute of Contemporary Arts and the Serpentine Gallery, London, 1990–91; a solo show at the Stichting De Appel, Amsterdam, 1991; and "Metropolis" at Martin-Gropius-Bau, 1991.

At Documenta IX, Kassel, Germany, in 1992, Bałka exhibited slab sculptures made of terrazzo. The same year, the artist was awarded the Mies van der Rohe grant from the Kaiser Wilhelm Museum, Krefeld, Germany, and he created "Bitte," an installation of sculptures for the Museum Haus Lange, also in Krefeld. He was given a solo show at The Renaissance Society at the University of Chicago, 1992, which traveled to the List Visual Arts Center, Massachusetts Institute of Technology, Cambridge, 1993. The title of that exhibition, "36,6," refers to the Celsius equivalent of 98.6 degrees Fahrenheit, the temperature of a healthy human body.

As the Polish representative at the XLV Venice Biennale, 1993, Bałka exhibited the sculptural installation *37,1*, the title indicating the temperature in Celsius at which fever begins in the human body. Acquired by the Lannan Foundation, Los Angeles, it was later exhibited there in the exhibition "37,1 (cont.)," 1994.

Bałka created two outdoor installations for Sonsbeek 93 in Arnhem, The Netherlands. The first, a subterranean box accompanied by two cement chairs at ground level, was located just outside a local cemetery. The second installation, resembling the size and shape of an open parachute, was a war memorial to Polish paratroopers.

In 1994 the Stedelijk Van Abbemuseum, Eindhoven, in cooperation with the Muzeum Sztuki, Łódź, organized related solo exhibitions: "Rampa" in Łódź, and "Laadplatform + 7 Werken 1985–1989" in Eindhoven. *Laadplatform* ("Soap Corridor") was installed in the central passageways of the Van Abbemuseum accompanied by a selection of earlier works. Bałka's early figurative sculptures were included in "Rites of Passage: Art for the End of the Century" at The Tate Gallery, London, 1995, which recently gave the artist a solo exhibition, "Dawn," 1995–96. Bałka also participated in the Carnegie International 1995, Pittsburgh.

Suggested Reading

Heynen, Julian. "Skizzen zu einem Vokabular" (Drafts for a Vocabulary). In *"Bitte," Mirosław Bałka*. Krefeld: Museum Haus Lange, 1992. Reproduced in English in *36,6*. Chicago: Renaissance Society at the University of Chicago, 1992, with additional essay by Peter Schjeldahl. Exhib. cat.

Mirosław Bałka: Die Rampe. Eindhoven and Łódź: Stedelijk Van Abbemuseum and Muzeum Sztuki, 1994. Essays by Jan Debbaut, Maria Morzuch, and Anda Rottenberg. Interview by Jaromir Jedliński. Exhib. cat.

Morris, Frances, "Mirosław Bałka." In Stuart Morgan and Frances Morris. *Rites of Passage: Art for the End of the Century*. London: Tate Gallery, 1995. Exhib. cat.

Morzuch, Maria. "Metamorphosis Towards Death." In *Polnische Avantgarde 1930–1990*. Berlin and Łódź: Neuen Berliner Kunstvereins and Muzeum Sztuki, 1992. Exhib. cat.

Possible Worlds: Sculpture from Europe. London: Institute of Contemporary Arts and Serpentine Gallery, 1990. Interview by Iwona Blazwick, 1990. Exhib. cat.

Marlene Dumas

born 1953, Capetown, South Africa
lives and works in Amsterdam,
The Netherlands

Until her early twenties, Marlene Dumas lived in South Africa, where she studied painting at the Michaelis School of Fine Arts, University of Capetown, from 1972 to 1975. After receiving a bachelor's degree in fine arts, she moved to The Netherlands. In Haarlem, 1976–78, she studied at Ateliers '63, a leading Dutch art school, with Carel Visser, Jan Dibbets, and Ger van Elk. Working mostly on paper, Dumas made nonfigurative, gestural drawings and mixed-media photocollages with ballpoint pen, colored pencil, and watercolor. While attending the Psychological Institute, University of Amsterdam, 1979–80, the artist had her first solo exhibition at the Galerie Annamarie de Kruyff, Paris, 1979. She was also selected to participate in Documenta VII, Kassel, 1982.

After Documenta, Dumas was given her first solo museum exhibition, "Ons Land Licht Lager Dan De Zee" (Below Sea Level), 1984, at the Centraal Museum Utrecht. She began to focus on painting and the human figure, creating a series of expressive "portrait" heads—masklike faces of individuals, friends, lovers, family members, historical figures, and strangers. She exhibited the paintings at the Galerie Paul Andriesse, Amsterdam, 1985, in the solo exhibition "The Eyes of the Night Creatures." The same year, Dumas was selected to represent The Netherlands in the XVIII São Paulo Bienal, where she exhibited the portraits.

The artist's next major group of paintings, "The Private Versus the Public," dealt with issues of individual and collective identity and were exhibited at the Galerie Paul Andriesse, 1987. In the solo exhibition "The Question of Human Pink" at the Kunsthalle Bern, 1989, Dumas displayed a variety of drawings and paintings, including a group of nudes, mostly female.

During her pregnancy and after the birth of her daughter, Helena, in 1987, Dumas created related paintings and works on paper that considered pregnancy, infancy, and motherhood. She exhibited them in early 1990 in "The Origin of the Species" at the Staatsgalerie Moderner Kunst, Munich. *The First People I–IV,* 1990 (fig. 14), consisting of four later paintings of writhing infants, were included in "Inconsolable, An Exhibition about Painting" at the Louver Gallery, New York, 1990, marking the artist's first exhibition in the United States.

A large solo exhibition at the Stedelijk Van Abbemuseum, Eindhoven, 1992, "Miss Interpreted," traveled to the Institute of Contemporary Arts, London, 1993–94. It included more than one hundred paintings and drawings, among them *Black Drawings,* 1991–92 (cat. no. 2), a wall of 112 unframed portrait heads arranged in a grid—the first of Dumas's unframed serial drawing installations. Subsequent drawing series (*Female, Garden,* and *Porno as Collage,* all 1993, and *Chlorosis,* 1994) have explored themes of female oppression, pornography, and skin color.

"The Particularity of Being Human," a major exhibition in 1995 organized by the Malmö Konsthall, Sweden, and seen subsequently at the Castello di Rivoli, Museo d'Arte Contemporanea, Turin, coupled Dumas's expressive figural paintings with those of Francis Bacon. The artist's most recent body of work, "Models," on the themes of the cult of fashion, media, and models, was presented in two related solo exhibitions coordinated by the Salzburger Kunstverein and the Portikus Frankfurt am Main, 1995–96. The artist has participated in many international group shows, including "The 21st Century," Kunsthalle Basel, 1993; "Cocido y Crudo," Museo Nacional Centro de Arte Reina Sofía, Madrid, 1994–95; and the Carnegie International 1995, Pittsburgh. Dumas represented The Netherlands at the XLVI Venice Biennale, 1995, and was also included in "Identity and Alterity" at the Palazzo Grassi and the Museo Correr.

Suggested Reading

Marlene Dumas/Francis Bacon: Det unika med att vara en människa/The Particularity of Being Human. Malmö, Sweden: Malmö Konsthall, 1995. Essays by Marente Bloemheuvel and Jan Mot, Marlene Dumas, Richard Francis, and Daniel Kurjakovic. Exhib. cat.

Marlene Dumas: Models. Salzburg and Frankfurt: Salzburger Kunstverein and Portikus Frankfurt am Main, 1995. Essays by Silvia Eiblmayr and Ernst van Alphen. Exhib. cat.

Miss Interpreted: Marlene Dumas. Eindhoven: Stedelijk Van Abbemuseum, 1992. Essays by Marlene Dumas, Selma Klein Essink, and Marcel Vos. Exhib. cat.

Parkett, no. 38 (1993). Marlene Dumas: Edition for Parkett. Essays by Ulrich Loock, Ingrid Schaffner, Anna Tilroe, and Maria Warner.

Schaffner, Ingrid. "Snow White in the Wrong Story: Paintings and Drawings by Marlene Dumas." *Arts Magazine* 65, no. 7 (March 1991): 59–63.

Robert Gober

born 1954, Wallingford, Connecticut
lives and works in New York

Robert Gober earned a bachelor's degree in 1976 from Middlebury College, Vermont, where he focused on painting and literature. After graduation he moved to New York and performed in multimedia dance productions. Inspired by his father, a factory worker, craftsman, and hobbyist, Gober created precisely detailed dollhouse constructions from 1978 to 1981. While he continued to paint, he began in 1982 to make plaster sculptures that referred to animals and the human body.

In 1983, Gober created the earliest of his signature sinks, which were first shown at the Paula Cooper Gallery, New York, 1985. From 1986 to 1988 the artist turned his attention to other domestic objects and began to conceive of his sculptures as elements in installations. A selection of works based on household furniture was shown in a solo exhibition at The Art Institute of Chicago, 1988. Later that year, Gober made a dog bed covered with a print pattern that was included in the 1989 Whitney Biennial, Whitney Museum of American Art, New York. The print pattern was developed into a wallpaper design used to line the walls of a larger installation at the Paula Cooper Gallery, also in 1989.

Gober has participated in and curated a number of joint projects with other artists, including "A Project," 303 Gallery, New York, 1988, with painter Christopher Wool, and "Utopia Post Utopia," at The Institute of Contemporary Art, Boston, 1988, with Meg Webster. The latter was reassembled for the XLIII Venice Biennale, 1988, and included Webster's *Moss Bed*, a landscape by the nineteenth-century painter Albert Bierstadt, the transcription of a joke by Richard Prince, and a door construction by Gober. For "Culture and Commentary: An Eighties Perspective," at the Hirshhorn Museum and Sculpture Garden, Washington, D.C., 1990, the artist collaborated on an installation with Sherrie Levine.

The Museum Boymans-van Beuningen, Rotterdam, organized a survey of the artist's work that traveled to the Kunsthalle Bern, 1990. There Gober exhibited a new work, *Untitled Leg*, 1989, the first of a series of dismembered wax limbs that seem to emerge from the wall. The disembodied legs and cropped male torsos became central elements in several of his large environmental installations of the early 1990s. In a solo show at the Galerie Nationale du Jeu de Paume, Paris, 1991, which traveled to the Museo Nacional Centro de Arte Reina Sofía, Madrid, 1992, Gober placed a wax torso pierced by candles and a six-foot-long cigar sculpture inside a room covered with a dense, printed pattern of forest motif. Re-created for Documenta IX, Kassel, 1992, the installation was punctuated by three sculptures of truncated male buttocks inscribed with bars of music. For the Dia Center for the Arts, New York, 1992, the artist created a complex environment of sinks with running water, stacks of newspapers, and prison windows inset in walls covered with a trompe l'oeil forest design.

Gober has participated in many group shows since the late 1980s. He has been the subject of important solo exhibitions at the Serpentine Gallery, London, The Tate Gallery Liverpool, 1993, and most recently, at the Museum für Gegenwartskunst, Basel, 1995–96.

Suggested Reading

Parkett, no. 27 (March 1991). Robert Gober: Edition for Parkett. Essays by Gregg Bordowitz, Lynne Cooke, and Nancy Spector. Interview by Ned Rifkin and Teresia Bush.

Robert Gober. Basel: Museum für Gegenwartskunst, 1995. Essay by Theodora Vischer. Exhib. cat.

Robert Gober. London and Liverpool: Serpentine Gallery and Tate Gallery Liverpool, 1993. Essay by Lynne Cooke. Interview by Richard Flood. Exhib. cat.

Robert Gober. New York: Dia Center for the Arts, 1992. Essay by Karen Marta. Exhib. cat.

Robert Gober. Paris: Galerie Nationale du Jeu de Paume, 1991. Essays by Catherine David and Joan Simon. Exhib. cat.

Robert Gober. Rotterdam and Bern: Museum Boymans-van Beuningen and Kunsthalle Bern, 1990. Essays by Trevor Fairbrother, Ulrich Loock, and Karel Schampers. Exhib. cat.

Mona Hatoum
born 1952, Beirut, Lebanon
lives and works in London

Mona Hatoum attended Beirut University College from 1970 to 1972. While she was vacationing in England in 1975, civil war broke out in Lebanon and she could not return home. Hatoum remained in London, studying at thc Byam Shaw School of Drawing and Painting, 1975–79, and the Slade School of Art, 1979–81, where she produced Minimalist-inspired process sculpture.

Hatoum became interested in performance and video and performed publicly at the London Film-Makers Co-op and Battersea Arts Center, London, 1980. In performances of the early 1980s, including *Under Siege*, 1982, and *The Negotiating Table*, 1983 (illus. p. v), she dealt with the vulnerability of the human body and themes of violence, oppression, and war.

Beginning in the mid-1980s, Hatoum turned her attention to the production of videos, most notably *So Much I Want to Say*, 1983 (fig. 21), *Changing Parts*, 1984, and *Measures of Distance*, 1988 (fig. 22). The latter addressed themes of exile and memory, human sexuality, and the position of women within patriarchal Lebanese society.

As a Senior Fellow in Fine Art at the Cardiff Institute of Higher Education, England, from 1989 to 1992, Hatoum began to create sculptural installations, including *The Light at the End*, 1989 (fig. 20)—six vertical, electrical heating rods seen against a triangular corner that emanated heat. *Alive and Well*, 1990, was installed in Victoria Tunnel, Newcastle-on-Tyne, England. Also employing electrical heating elements, the work consisted of evenly spaced vertical metal bars accompanied by a chair. Suggesting torture and imprisonment, these installations effectively destabilized the viewer's space.

A major sculpture, *Socle du Monde* (Pedestal of the World), 1991 (cat. no. 10), was first shown in "Pour la Suite du Monde" (For the Rest of the World), Musée d'Art Contemporain, Montreal, 1992, and later at the Galerie Chantal Crousel, Paris. *Short Space* and *Light Sentence*, both 1992, employed mechanized devices that introduced movement and they were first seen in the solo exhibition "Dissected Space," Chapter, Cardiff Institute. The latter was included in "Sense and Sensibility: Women Artists and Minimalism in the Nineties," 1994, The Museum of Modern Art, New York. Also in 1994, Hatoum created *Corps étranger* (Foreign Body), 1994 (fig. 23), a video installation for a solo show at the Musée National d'Art Moderne, Paris.

Hatoum also has been an artist-in-residence at Western Front Art Centre, Vancouver, 1984 and 1988; 9.1.1 Contemporary Arts Center, Seattle, 1986; and Chisenhale Dance Space, London, 1986–87; and she continues to participate in residency programs around the world. She has taught at the Central Saint Martin's School of Art and Design, London, and the École Nationale Superieure des Beaux-Arts, Paris, and she is currently teaching at Jan van Eyck Akademie, Maastricht, The Netherlands. Her work has been exhibited in many group shows, including "Cocido y Crudo," Museo Nacional Centro de Arte Reina Sofía, Madrid, 1994–95; "Rites of Passage: Art for the End of the Century," The Tate Gallery, London, 1995; "Identity and Alterity," XLVI Venice Biennale, 1995; and "1995 Turner Prize Exhibition," The Tate Gallery, London.

Suggested Reading

Mona Hatoum. Bristol, England: Arnolfini Gallery, 1993. Essays by Desa Philippi and Guy Brett. Exhib. cat.

Mona Hatoum. Paris: Musée National d'Art Moderne, 1994. Essays by Jacinto Lageira, Desa Philippi, Nadia Tazi, and Christine van Assche. Exhib. cat.

Mona Hatoum. Rome: British School at Rome, 1995. Essay by Michael Archer. Exhib. brochure.

Morgan, Stuart, and Frances Morris. *Rites of Passage: Art for the End of the Century*. London: Tate Gallery, 1995. Exhib. cat.

Pour La Suite du Monde. Montreal: Musée d'Art Contemporain de Montreal, 1992. Exhib. cat.

Zelevansky, Lynn. *Sense and Sensibility: Women Artists and Minimalism in the Nineties*. New York: Museum of Modern Art, 1994. Exhib. cat.

Mike Kelley

born 1954, Detroit
lives and works in Los Angeles

Mike Kelley grew up in a suburb of Detroit and studied fine arts at the University of Michigan, Ann Arbor, from 1972 to 1976. There he focused on painting under Gerome Kamrowski, a former student of Hans Hofmann and Roberto Matta. Kelley moved to Los Angeles in 1976 to attend graduate school at the California Institute of the Arts (Cal Arts), Valencia, where, under the influence of John Baldessari, Douglas Huebler, and Laurie Anderson, Kelley began a career as a performance-based artist.

Kelley's first public performance, *Poetry in Motion*, 1978, took place at Los Angeles Contemporary Exhibitions (LACE). His subsequent solo and collaborative performance projects were distinguished by their use of low comedy and free association of text and related objects. Kelley's most notable joint performance and exhibition projects include "Poltergeist," Foundation for Art Resources, Los Angeles, 1979; "Meditation on a Can of Vernors," Riko Mizuno Gallery, Los Angeles, 1981; "Monkey Island," performance at LACE and exhibition at Rosamund Felsen Gallery, Los Angeles, 1983; "The Sublime," performance at the Museum of Contemporary Art, Los Angeles, and exhibition at Rosamund Felsen Gallery, 1984; and "Plato's Cave, Rothko's Chapel, Lincoln's Profile," performance at Artists Space, New York, and exhibition at Metro Pictures, 1985–86. The latter project was re-created for Aperto '88 of the XLIII Venice Biennale, 1988, which introduced Kelley's work to a broad international audience.

By the mid-1980s, Kelley had begun to move away from performance to create large, multimedia exhibition projects. In 1988 at The Renaissance Society at the University of Chicago, he presented "Three Projects: Half a Man, From My Institution to Yours, Pay for Your Pleasure," independent projects made between 1984 and 1988. *Half a Man* questioned society's perceptions of gender roles and introduced the stuffed-animal sculptures for which he became widely known. Selections were included in "Directions—Mike Kelley: Half a Man," Hirshhorn Museum and Sculpture Garden, Washington, D.C., 1991. For the Carnegie International 1991, Pittsburgh, Kelley made *Craft Morphology Flow Chart*, the last installment in his stuffed-animal works. In direct reaction to his increasing association with this type of sculpture, Kelley designed tortuous bodily devices for Documenta IX, Kassel, 1992. The human-scale constructions employed stereotypically "masculine" woodworking techniques in opposition to the earlier craftwork's "feminine" aesthetic.

Between 1992 and 1994, two mid-career surveys were organized in Europe and the United States. The first exhibition, organized by the Kunsthalle Basel, 1992, re-created Kelley's major installation projects, with concurrent exhibitions at the Portikus Frankfurt am Main and at the Institute of Contemporary Arts, London, 1992. "Mike Kelley: Catholic Tastes," 1993–94, organized by the Whitney Museum of American Art, New York, which provided a more comprehensive overview of the artist's career, traveled to the Los Angeles County Museum of Art, 1994. Kelley has been included in many group exhibitions, including the Whitney biennials of 1985, 1987, 1989, and 1993, Whitney Museum of American Art, New York; "Metropolis," Martin-Gropius-Bau, Berlin, 1991; "Doubletake: Collective Memory and Current Art," Hayward Gallery, London, 1992; and "Helter Skelter: L.A. Art in the 1990s," the Museum of Contemporary Art, Los Angeles, 1992. A graduate instructor at the Art Center College of Design, Pasadena, since 1987, Kelley has also taught at the Minneapolis College of Art and Design, as well as at institutions in the Los Angeles area, including the University of California, Otis Art Institute, and Cal Arts. He continues to work collaboratively with other artists on film, video, and performance projects.

Suggested Reading

Kellein, Thomas. *Mike Kelley*. Basel: Kunsthalle Basel, 1992. Exhib. cat.

Parkett, no. 31 (1992). Mike Kelley: Edition for Parkett. Essays by Diedrich Diederichsen, Trevor Fairbrother, Bernard Marcade, and Lane Relyea. Interview by Julie Sylvester.

Sussman, Elisabeth, et al. *Mike Kelley: Catholic Tastes*. New York: Whitney Museum of American Art, 1993. Exhib. cat.

Mike Kelley. Three Projects: Half a Man, From My Institution to Yours, Pay for Your Pleasure. Chicago: Renaissance Society at the University of Chicago, 1988. Essays by John Miller and Howard Singerman. Exhib. cat.

Bartman, William S., and Miyoshi Barosh, eds. *Mike Kelley*. Los Angeles: A.R.T. Press, 1992. Interview by John Miller.

Mike Kelley, Thomas Kellein: A Conversation. Stuttgart: Cantz, 1994. Interview by Thomas Kellein.

Guillermo Kuitca

born 1961, Buenos Aires, Argentina
lives and works in Buenos Aires

Guillermo Kuitca studied painting privately with Ahuva Szlimowicz and Víctor Chab from 1970 to 1979 in Buenos Aires, and he was thirteen when he had his first solo exhibition at Lirolay Gallery in that city in 1974. In 1980 the artist traveled to Europe and worked with the innovative German dancer, performer, and choreographer Pina Bausch. Upon his return, Kuitca took the stage, always a passionate interest, as a subject for his paintings. The theatrical aspect of his stage-set paintings (created through 1987), reflects, in part, the artist's experience as a stage director in the early 1980s, when he codirected several plays in Buenos Aires, including "El Mar Dulce" (The Sweet Sea). Addressing Jewish immigration to his native country, the production had a particular resonance for the artist, the grandson of Ukrainian Jews who had immigrated to Argentina in the early 1900s. Kuitca represented Argentina in the XVIII São Paulo Bienal, 1985, with a selection of the stage-set-inspired paintings.

Kuitca's use of the figure and the narrative content of the theatrical paintings led to his inclusion in the group exhibition "New Image Painting: Argentina in the Eighties," organized by the Americas Society, New York, 1989. By the mid-1980s, however, Kuitca had begun to move toward a more conceptual type of painting involving architecture and public space. In 1987 he appropriated the floor plan of a domestic space and fragments of international road maps as resonant motifs, rendering them on canvas, as well as on actual mattresses. A selection of the map paintings and a sculptural installation of painted child-size beds were exhibited at the XX São Paulo Bienal, 1989, and in a solo show at the Witte de With Center for Contemporary Art, Rotterdam, 1990. The latter exhibition was followed by the artist's first solo exhibition in the United States, held at the Annina Nosei Gallery, New York, the same year, and a "Projects" show organized by The Museum of Modern Art, New York, 1991, that traveled. The young artist was included in Documenta IX, Kassel, 1992, where he exhibited map paintings and created a large installation of bed sculptures.

Between 1991 and 1993, Kuitca turned to family trees as source material for a group of paintings titled *People on Fire* (cat. nos. 25 and 26). He worked concurrently on "The Tablada Suite," ethereal renderings on canvas of the floor plans of large communal spaces, which he exhibited at the Sperone Westwater Gallery, New York, in 1994. The "Suite" was reassembled in part for the Carnegie International 1995, Pittsburgh. In "Puro Teatro" (Pure Theater), 1995, Kuitca returned to the theater as subject. This group of related paintings was first exhibited at Sperone Westwater in 1995.

Kuitca has been the subject of two major solo exhibitions. The first was organized by the Instituto Valenciano de Arte Moderno (IVAM), Centre Julio González, Valencia, Spain, 1993–94, which traveled to the Museo de Monterrey, Mexico, and the Museo Rufino Tamayo—Instituto Nacional de Bellas Artes, Mexico City. The second exhibition, "Burning Beds: Guillermo Kuitca, A Survey 1982–1994," was organized by the Wexner Center for the Arts, Columbus, Ohio, and the Contemporary Art Foundation, Amsterdam, and traveled to the Center for the Fine Arts, Miami, and the Whitechapel Art Gallery, London.

The artist has also participated in major group shows, including "Art of the Fantastic: Latin America, 1920–1987," Indianapolis Museum of Art, 1987; "Metropolis," Martin-Gropius-Bau, Berlin, 1991; "Latin American Artists of the Twentieth Century," The Museum of Modern Art, New York, 1993; "Art from Argentina, 1920–1994," Museum of Modern Art Oxford, 1994; "About Place: Recent Art of the Americas," The Art Institute of Chicago, 1995; and "Beyond Borders," Kwangju Biennale, Korea, 1995.

Suggested Reading

A Book Based on Guillermo Kuitca. Amsterdam: Contemporary Art Foundation, 1993. Essays by Marcelo E. Pacheco and Jerry Saltz.

Dona, Lydia. "Guillermo Kuitca Interview," *Journal of Contemporary Art* 6, no. 1 (Summer 1993): 56–63.

Elliott, David, ed. *Art from Argentina, 1920–1994.* Oxford: Museum of Modern Art Oxford, 1994. Interview by Ed Shaw. Exhib. cat.

Zelevansky, Lynn. *Guillermo Kuitca.* Newport Beach, Calif.: Newport Harbor Art Museum, 1992. Exhib. cat.

Guillermo Kuitca. Rotterdam: Witte de With Center for Contemporary Art, 1990. Essay by Rina Carvajal. Exhib. cat.

Guillermo Kuitca: Burning Beds, A Survey 1982–1994. Amsterdam: Contemporary Art Foundation, 1994. Interview by Lynne Cooke. Exhib. cat.

Charles Ray
born 1953, Chicago
lives and works in Los Angeles

The son of a commercial artist who also ran an art school in Chicago, Charles Ray took summer classes at The Art Institute of Chicago following high school. As an undergraduate at the University of Iowa from 1971 to 1975, he created indoor and outdoor sculptures based on geometric forms that relied on balance and tension for their precarious stability. In 1973 he incorporated his own body as a sculptural element. Placing his form in often painfully unnatural positions, he used planks of wood and rope to pivot and suspend his body in space. After attending various schools around the United States from 1975 to 1977, Ray completed his graduate studies at the Mason Gross School of Art, Rutgers University, New Jersey, 1977–79. At Rutgers he continued to create relationships between his body and geometry in performance-based works that were formally rigorous and often humorous.

Following the death of his younger brother in 1980, Ray moved to Los Angeles in 1981 to accept a position at the University of California, where he still teaches sculpture. Between 1981 and 1985, he created a series of "live" sculptures that presented his nude body, often painted, in opposition to hard, Minimalist geometries. Ray rented space at 64 Market Street, Venice, California, where he held his first solo exhibition in April 1993. The exhibition consisted of a sequence of timed, motionless "performances" scheduled throughout the day. Exhausted from increasing exhibition opportunities and the great physical demands of performance, Ray in 1986 ceased to use his own body in sculpture. He turned to the spectator, seeking to engage the audience in a tangible, visceral way that preserved the eventful qualities inherent to performance.

In 1987, Ray exhibited *Ink Box*, 1986 (fig. 28), at the Burnett Miller Gallery, Los Angeles, which brought him significant critical attention. The black metal cube, which appeared solid but was filled with ink, challenged audience perceptions and expectations as did many of the artist's subsequent works, including *Rotating Circle*, 1988, which was included in the 1989 Whitney Biennial, New York.

In 1990, Ray exhibited a body of new work concurrently at the Newport Harbor Art Museum, Newport Beach, and at Burnett Miller that introduced the first mannequin sculptures. For "Helter Skelter: L.A. Art in the 1990s" at The Museum of Contemporary Art, Los Angeles, 1992, he displayed *Fall '91*, a female mannequin dressed in fashionable attire. Cast larger than life, the monumental woman was a towering eight feet tall. For Documenta IX, Kassel, 1992, he created *Oh! Charley, Charley, Charley ...*, a grouping of mannequinlike sculptures cast from his body. Arranged in a disturbing autoerotic tableaux, Ray exhibited the highly controversial ensemble at Aperto '93 of the XLV Venice Biennale, 1993. For the 1993 Whitney Biennial he made *Family Romance* (illus. p. ix), a freakishly misscaled group portrait of a family of four, and a fifty-foot-long toy firetruck "parked" on the street outside the museum.

In 1994, the Rooseum–Center for Contemporary Art, Malmö, Sweden, organized a small midcareer survey that traveled to the Institute of Contemporary Arts, London. A modified version of the exhibition took place later that year with concurrent installations at the Kunsthalle Zurich and the Kunsthalle Bern. For the 1995 Whitney Biennial, Ray designed a miniature model of his own likeness that was placed inside a wine bottle (fig. 30). Ray has also been included in many group shows, including "Mechanika" at the Contemporary Arts Center, Cincinnati, 1991; "The Uncanny," curated by Mike Kelley for the international exhibition Sonsbeek 93, Arnhem, The Netherlands, 1993; and "Fémininmasculin: La sexe del'art" at the Musée National d'Art Moderne, Paris, 1995.

Suggested Reading

Barnes, Lucinda, and Dennis Cooper. *Charles Ray*. Newport Beach, Calif.: Newport Harbor Art Museum, 1990. Interviews. Exhib. cat.

Bonami, Francesco. "Charles Ray: A Telephone Conversation." *Flash Art* 25, no. 165 (Summer 1992): 98–100.

Ferguson, Bruce W. *Charles Ray*. Malmö, Sweden: Rooseum–Center for Contemporary Art, 1994. Exhib. cat.

Hugo, Joan. "Between Object and Persona: The Sculpture Events of Charles Ray." *High Performance*, no. 30 (1985): 26–30.

Parkett, no. 37 (1993). Charles Ray: Edition for Parkett. Essays by Klaus Kertess, Christopher Knight, Peter Schjeldahl, and Robert Storr.

Relyea, Lane. "Charles Ray: In the No." *Artforum* 31, no. 1 (September 1992): 62–66.

Doris Salcedo

born 1958, Bogotá, Colombia
lives and works in Bogotá

Doris Salcedo was educated at the Universidad de Bogotá Jorge Tadeo Lozano, where she received a bachelor's degree in fine arts in 1980. She came to the United States later that year to pursue graduate studies and was awarded a master's degree in sculpture from New York University (NYU), 1984. After returning to Bogotá in 1985, she served as director of the Instituto de Bellas Artes, Cali, 1987–88. She taught sculpture and art theory at the Universidad Nacional de Colombia, Bogotá, from 1988 to 1991.

While at NYU, Salcedo became interested in bodily distortions caused by warfare, exposure to chemicals, and intense emotional pain and suffering. She focused, in particular, on the experiences of Vietnam veterans through tapes of recorded therapy sessions. Although she was offered an exhibition at a New York gallery in 1985, she chose to exhibit the work inspired by her Vietnam research in her native country, feeling strongly that the subject of violence in general would have a greater resonance there. The artist's first solo exhibition was subsequently held at the Casa de Moneda, Banco de la República, Bogotá, in 1985.

For her next gallery exhibition, "El Hierro" (Iron), 1989–90, a group show at the Galería Garcés-Velásquez, Bogotá, she displayed untitled sculptures made from discarded hospital beds and stacks of plastered shirts. The shirt sculptures were motivated by a series of murders at various banana plantations in 1988. Following a period of extensive research on various cases of *desaparecidos*, Salcedo created *Atrabiliarios* ("Defiant"), 1990–91 (fig. 32), a sculptural installation about the abduction and disappearance of women. *Atrabiliarios* was first seen in the group exhibitions "Currents 92: The Absent Body," Institute of Contemporary Art, Boston, 1992; an untitled show at the Shedhalle, Zurich, 1992; and in Aperto '93 of the XLV Venice Biennale, 1993.

Salcedo also began in 1989 to make sculptures fashioned from furniture that she embedded in concrete. Various untitled furniture sculptures were included in the traveling exhibition "Ante América" organized by the Biblioteca Luis-Ángel Arango, Bogotá, 1992. In 1994 the artist was included in "The Spine," a group exhibition at the Stichting De Appel, Amsterdam, where she exhibited early sculptures. A selection of early works were recently included in "Sleeper," 1995, a group exhibition at the Museum of Contemporary Art, San Diego.

Salcedo's New York debut took place in 1994 at the Brooke Alexander Gallery in a solo show. There she introduced the first two sculptures from "La Casa Viuda" (The Widowed House; see cat. nos. 32–34), an ongoing body of work addressing the slaying of individuals in their homes and the effects of violence on children. A selection of "La Casa Viuda" sculptures were included in "Cocido y Crudo," Museo Nacional Centro de Arte Reina Sofía, Madrid, 1994–95, and in "About Place: Recent Art of the Americas" at the Art Institute of Chicago, 1995. For the Carnegie International 1995, Pittsburgh, Salcedo created a disturbing installation of more than twenty concrete furniture sculptures.

Suggested Reading

Amor, Monica. "Doris Salcedo." *Art Nexus* 13 (July-September 1994): 166–67.

Ante América. Bogotá: Biblioteca Luis-Ángel Arango, 1992. Essay by Charles Merewether. Exhib. cat.

Cameron, Dan. "Absence Makes the Art." *Artforum* 33, no. 2 (October 1994): 88–91.

Cocido y Crudo. Madrid: Museo Nacional Centro de Arte Reina Sofía, 1994. Essay by Dan Cameron. Exhib. cat.

Dermota, Ken. "Colombian Protests Violence with Sculpture." *Christian Science Monitor* (August 16, 1995): 14.

Grynsztejn, Madeleine. *About Place: Recent Art of the Americas*. Chicago: Art Institute of Chicago, 1995. Exhib. cat.

Merewether, Charles. "Naming Violence in the Work of Doris Salcedo." *Third Text*, no. 24 (Autumn 1993): 35–44.

Thomas Schütte
born 1954, Oldenburg,
former West Germany
lives and works in Düsseldorf

Thomas Schütte studied art from 1973 to 1981 at the Düsseldorf Kunstakademie under Fritz Schwegler and Gerhard Richter. As a student he created sculptural installations that engaged the architectural space. Inspired by the theater and the ways in which public space is orchestrated, Schütte in 1980 made three stage- and podium-like models for the exhibition "Westkunst," Cologne, 1981. Through the mid-1980s he continued to produce works that were based on the theater or suggested public squares. Schütte also created three-dimensional models in plaster and wood for artists' studios, 1982–83, and *Fifteen Monuments*, 1984, watercolors of hypothetical, utopian public institutions.

In *Hauptstadt* (Metropolis), 1984, the artist combined aspects of installation and painting in a series of eight painted architectural posts. These were exhibited in "Von Hier Aus" (From Here On), in Düsseldorf, 1984. Two years later, at the Galleria Tucci Russo, Turin, Schütte exhibited three sculptural installations inspired by public plazas. The large architectural constructions included small, anonymous figures in wood, which Schütte introduced to create disjunctive relationships related to scale. In 1986 he was given a solo show at the Museum Haus Lange, Krefeld.

After briefly teaching at the Hochschule für Bildende Künste, Hamburg, 1986–87, the artist began to enlarge his architectural constructions and locate them outdoors. *Schutzraum* (Shelter), 1986, a barrel-shaped bunker made of concrete, was Schütte's contribution to Sonsbeek 86 in Arnhem, The Netherlands, 1986. The following year he completed two outdoor works of more humorous bent: For "Skulptur Projekte," Münster, he sited *Kirschensäule* (Cherry Column), a sandstone column topped with two large sculpted cherries, in a public parking lot; and for Documenta VIII, Kassel, he created *EIS* (Ice Cream; fig. 36), a functioning ice cream parlor that served those visiting the exhibition.

In 1988, Schütte had a solo exhibition, "The Laundry: Mohr's Life," at the Galerie Philip Nelson, Lyon, and had a solo exhibition at the Staatliche Kunsthalle Baden-Baden. For his first solo exhibition in the United States at the Marian Goodman Gallery, New York, 1989–90, Schütte installed *Big Building*, a modular plywood structure that deconstructed the notion of grand architectural edifices and public monuments. "Sieben Felder," a survey organized by the Kunsthalle Bern, traveled to the Musée d'Art Moderne de la Ville de Paris and the Stedelijk Van Abbemuseum, Eindhoven.

For Documenta IX, Kassel, in the summer of 1992, the sculptor made *Die Fremden* (The Strangers; fig. 37), large, ceramic figures that he installed atop a colonnaded portico on the Friedrichsplatz. After Documenta, he began work on "United Enemies," 1993–94, a series of small figures bundled in rags and encased in glass vitrines. Works from this series were included in the artist's solo exhibition "Thomas Schütte [Figur]," organized by the Hamburger Kunsthalle and the Würtembergischer Kunstverein, Stuttgart, 1994. In "Thomas Schütte," a solo exhibition at the Musée d'Art Contemporain, Nîmes, France, 1994–95, Schütte exhibited three new sculptures, *Grosser Respekt, Kleiner Respekt*, and *No Respekt*, 1993–94 (cat. nos. 35–37), whose titles reflect their alternately large and diminutive scale. They are Schütte's subjects in a sculptural trilogy that pays homage to but also questions the role of public monuments in our time.

Suggested Reading

"Conversation Between Stephan Balkenhol and Thomas Schütte." *Stephan Balkenhol: Über Menschen und Skulpturen/About Men and Sculpture*. Stuttgart: Edition Cantz, 1992. English supplement. Rotterdam: Witte de With Center for Contemporary Art, 1992.

Possible Worlds: Sculpture from Europe. London: Institute of Contemporary Arts and Serpentine Gallery, 1990. Interview by Iwona Blazwick and Andrea Schlieker. Exhib. cat.

Rochette, Anne, and Wade Saunders. "Figures of Estrangement." *Art in America* (May 1995): 103–7.

Thomas Schütte. Bern: Kunsthalle Bern, 1990. Edited by Ulrich Loock. Interview by Martin Hentschel. Exhib. cat.

Thomas Schütte. Baden-Baden: Staatliche Kunsthalle Baden-Baden. Essays by Bettina Dürr, Martin Hentschel, and Bettina Hesse, 1988. Exhib. cat.

Thomas Schütte [Figur]. Hamburg: Hamburger Kunsthalle, 1994. Essays by Martin Hentschel and Uwe M. Schneede. Exhib. cat.

Rachel Whiteread
born 1963, Ilford, England
lives and works in London

Rachel Whiteread grew up in the outskirts of London in the small town of Ilford. Introduced to art by her mother, a practicing artist, she studied painting at Brighton Polytechnic from 1982 to 1985 and sculpture at the Slade School of Art from 1985 to 1987. At the Slade she created sculptures that suggested the body and also made small works employing furniture wrapped in Sellotape. British sculptor Edward Allington introduced Whiteread to casting techniques, which subsequently became her signature working method.

Whiteread's solo debut in London took place at the Carlile Gallery in 1988. There she exhibited her first poured plaster sculptures that recorded the negative spaces of existing domestic objects. Continuing to develop this domestic theme, she created a series of sculptures based on tables in 1989.

A sculpture of considerable scale and import, *Ghost*, 1990 (fig. 40), presented the hollow plaster cast of an entire room in a Victorian house in North London. The work was first shown that year at the Chisenhale Gallery, London. Also in 1990, Whiteread made plaster molds of the undersides of cast-iron bathtubs. Evoking sarcophagi with their heavy, blocklike forms, the sculptures were exhibited at the Arnolfini Gallery, Bristol, 1990. The following year Whiteread began to cast mattresses found in secondhand shops. In addition to plaster, the artist was now working with high-density foam and rubber. Whiteread exhibited a selection of mattress sculptures at the Luhring Augustine Gallery, New York, 1992, the artist's solo debut in the United States.

For Documenta IX, Kassel, 1992, Whiteread exhibited casts of mortuary slabs and the exhibition hall's wooden floorboards. Following Documenta, she was the subject of a number of solo museum exhibitions both in Europe and the United States organized by the Fundació "la Caixa," Centre Cultural, Barcelona, 1992; the Stedelijk Van Abbemuseum, Eindhoven, 1992; and the Museum of Contemporary Art, Chicago, 1993.

In 1993, Whiteread was commissioned to make *House*, her first public outdoor sculpture, of the three-story interior of a Victorian house on Grove Road, London (illus. pp. i and 114). Soon after completing *House* in late 1993, she was awarded The Tate Gallery's Turner Prize, making her the first woman to receive this prestigious honor. Meeting with tremendous public controversy, *House* was ultimately torn down in January 1994.

A survey of the artist's work organized by the Kunsthalle Basel in 1994 traveled to the Institutes of Contemporary Art in Philadelphia and Boston, 1994–95, and included new works made of colored, semitransparent polyester resin and rubber. For the Carnegie International 1995, Pittsburgh, she installed *Untitled (One Hundred Spaces)*, fig. 42, one hundred sculptural equivalents of the spaces beneath chairs set out in rhythmic order in the gallery.

Whiteread has participated in numerous other international group exhibitions, including "Metropolis" at Martin-Gropius-Bau, Berlin, 1991; "Doubletake: Collective Memory and Current Art" at the Hayward Gallery, London, 1992; "The Sublime Void: On the Memory of the Imagination" at the Koninklijk Museum, Antwerp, 1993; "Sense and Sensibility: Women Artists and Minimalism in the Nineties" at The Museum of Modern Art, New York, 1994; and " 'Brilliant!' New Art From London" at the Walker Art Center, Minneapolis, 1995.

Suggested Reading

Archer, Michael. "Ghost Meat." *Artscribe* 87 (Summer 1991): 35–38.

Lingwood, James. *Rachel Whiteread: House.* London: Phaidon Press in association with Artangel, 1995.

Parkett, no. 42 (1994). Rachel Whiteread: Edition for Parkett. Essays by Trevor Fairbrother, Rudolf Schmitz, Neville Wakefield, and Simon Watney.

Princenthal, Nancy. "All That Is Solid." *Art in America* 83, no. 7 (July 1995): 52–57.

Rachel Whiteread. Basel: Kunsthalle Basel, 1994. Essay by Christoph Grunenberg. Exhib. cat.

Rachel Whiteread. Eindhoven: Stedelijk Van Abbemuseum, 1992. Essay by Stuart Morgan. Interview with Iwona Blazwick. Exhib. cat.

Wright, Beryl. "Options 46: Rachel Whiteread." Chicago: Museum of Contemporary Art, 1993. Exhib. brochure.

Lenders to the Exhibition

BACOB Collection, Brussels
Hans Böhning, Cologne
Blake Byrne, Los Angeles
Gilbert Charpenel, Guadalajara
Emanuel Hoffmann-Stiftung, Basel, Depositum Öffentliche Kunstsammlung, Museum für Gegenwartskunst, Basel
Carlos and Rosa de la Cruz, Key Biscayne, Florida
De Pont Foundation for Contemporary Art, Tilburg, The Netherlands
Martin and Rebecca Eisenberg, Rye Brook, New York
Federation of Migros Cooperatives, Museum of Contemporary Art, Zurich
Barbara Goldfarb
Hirshhorn Museum and Sculpture Garden, Smithsonian Institution, Washington, D. C.
Penny and David McCall, New York
Dr. Marvin and Elayne Mordes, Baltimore
Musée d'Art Contemporain de Nîmes, Depot du FRAC Languedoc, Rouissillon, France
Mark and Nedra Oren
Peter Stuyvesant Collection, Amsterdam
Collection Re Rebaudengo-Sandretto, Turin
Florence and Philippe Ségalot, Paris
Dr. Uli and Rita Sigg, Switzerland
Drs. Michael and Eleonore Stoffel, Cologne
Weltkunst Collection, Irish Museum of Modern Art, Dublin
Worcester Art Museum, Massachusetts
Private collections

Catalog of the Exhibition

Mirosław Bałka

1. Work in progress at time of publication.

Marlene Dumas

2. *Black Drawings*, 1991–92
   illus. p. vii
   india ink and acrylic on paper and slate
   overall 91 5/8 x 111 1/4 in. (235 x 285 cm), each 9 3/4 x 6 7/8 in. (24.9 x 17.5 cm)
   De Pont Foundation for Contemporary Art, Tilburg, The Netherlands

3. *Groupshow II*, 1993
   illus. p. 36
   oil on canvas
   39 x 117 in. (100 x 300 cm)
   Collection Dr. Marvin and Elayne Mordes, Baltimore

4. *Cupid*, 1994
   illus. p. 38
   oil on canvas
   51 x 43 1/4 in. (130 x 110 cm)
   Collection Dr. Michael and Eleonore Stoffel, Cologne

5. *Indifference*, 1994
   illus. p. 36
   oil on canvas
   39 x 117 in. (100 x 300 cm)
   Federation of Migros Cooperatives, Museum of Contemporary Art, Zurich

6. *The Painter*, 1994
   illus. p. 37
   oil on canvas
   78 x 39 in. (200 x 100 cm)
   Collection Martin and Rebecca Eisenberg, Rye Brook, New York

7. *Cold Woman*, 1995
   illus. p. 39
   oil on canvas
   78 3/4 x 39 5/8 in. (200 x 100 cm)
   Collection Florence and Philippe Ségalot, Paris

Robert Gober

8. *Prison Window*, 1992
   illus. p. 45
   plywood, forged steel, plaster, latex paint, and lights, edition of 5
   overall 48 x 48 x 36 in. (122 x 122 x 91.4 cm), opening 24 x 24 in. (61 x 61 cm)
   Collection of the artist, courtesy Paula Cooper Gallery, New York

9. *Chair with Pipe*, 1994–95
   illus. p. 44
   wood, bronze, printed cotton fabric, and paint, 32 1/2 x 30 x 71 in. (82.6 x 76.2 x 180.3 cm)
   Emanuel Hoffmann-Stiftung, Basel, Depositum Öffentliche Kunstsammlung, Museum für Gegenwartskunst, Basel

Mona Hatoum

10. *Socle du Monde* (Pedestal of the World), 1992 (refabricated 1996)
    illus. p. 53
    wood, steel, magnets, and iron filings, edition of 2
    64 1/2 x 78 3/4 x 78 3/4 in. (163.8 x 200 x 200 cm)
    Collection of the artist, courtesy Alexander and Bonin, New York

11. *Entrails Carpet*, 1995
    illus. pp. 52 and 55 (detail)
    silicone rubber, edition of 3
    1 3/4 x 78 x 117 in. (4.5 x 198.1 x 297.2 cm)
    Created in collaboration with The Fabric Workshop and Museum, Philadelphia
    Collection of the artist, courtesy Alexander and Bonin, New York

Mike Kelley

12. *Untitled #2*, 1994
    illus. p. 58
    enamel on aluminum
    66 1/4 x 46 1/2 in. (170 x 118.1 cm)
    Collection of the artist, courtesy Metro Pictures, New York

13. *Untitled #3*, 1994
    illus. p. 58
    enamel on aluminum
    62 1/2 x 40 in. (158.75 x 101.6 cm)
    Collection Gilbert Charpenel, Guadalajara

14. *Untitled #5*, 1994
    illus. p. 59
    enamel on aluminum
    62 3/8 x 39 7/8 in. (158.4 x 101.3 cm)
    Collection of the artist, courtesy Metro Pictures, New York

15. *Untitled #7*, 1994
    illus. p. 58
    enamel on aluminum
    69 x 42 in. (175.3 x 106.7 cm)
    Hirshhorn Museum and Sculpture Garden, Smithsonian Institution, Washington, D.C.; Joseph H. Hirshhorn Bequest Fund, 1994

16. *Untitled #9*, 1994
    illus. p. 58
    enamel on aluminum
    69 x 42 in. (175.3 x 106.7 cm)
    Collection Barbara Goldfarb

17. *#1, The Birth of the New Year* from "The Thirteen Seasons (Heavy on the Winter)," 1994
    illus. p. 62
    acrylic on wood
    61 7/8 x 40 in. (158.8 x 101.6 cm)
    Collection Re Rebaudengo-Sandretto, Turin

18. *#6, The Fall* from "The Thirteen Seasons (Heavy on the Winter)," 1994
illus. p. 63
acrylic on wood
61 7/8 x 40 in. (158.8 x 101.6 cm)
Peter Stuyvesant Collection, Amsterdam

19. *#7, The Descent* from "The Thirteen Seasons (Heavy on the Winter)," 1994
illus. p. 63
acrylic on wood
61 7/8 x 40 in. (158.8 x 101.6 cm)
Peter Stuyvesant Collection, Amsterdam

20. *#11, The Giving Old Man* from "The Thirteen Seasons (Heavy on the Winter)," 1994
illus. p. 63
acrylic on wood
61 7/8 x 40 in. (158.8 x 101.6 cm)
Collection Hans Böhning, Cologne

21. *#12, Death* from "The Thirteen Seasons (Heavy on the Winter)," 1994
illus. p. 63
acrylic on wood
61 7/8 x 40 in. (158.8 x 101.6 cm)
Collection Drs. Michael and Eleonore Stoffel, Cologne

22. *#13, Art* from "The Thirteen Seasons (Heavy on the Winter)," 1994
not illus.
acrylic on wood
61 7/8 x 40 in. (158.8 x 101.6 cm)
Private collection, courtesy Marc Blondeau, Paris

23. *Liberal Paganism*, 1995
not illus.
acrylic on wood
64 x 47 in. (162.6 x 119.4 cm)
Collection of the artist, courtesy Metro Pictures, New York

24. *Prenatal Mutual Recognition of Betty + Barney Hill*, 1995
illus. p. 64
acrylic on wood
64 x 47 in. (162.6 x 119.4 cm)
Collection Blake Byrne, Los Angeles

Guillermo Kuitca

25. *People on Fire*, 1993
illus. p. 72
oil on canvas
48 1/2 x 76 5/8 in. (123.2 x 202.2 cm)
Private collection, courtesy Sperone Westwater, New York

26. *People on Fire*, 1993
illus. p. 70
mixed media on canvas
77 1/4 x 117 1/4 in. (196.2 x 298 cm)
Collection of the artist, courtesy Sperone Westwater, New York

27. *Untitled*, 1994
illus. p. 67
oil and acrylic on canvas
76 3/4 x 92 5/8 in. (195 x 235.2 cm)
Collection Mark and Nedra Oren

28. *Mozart–da Ponte I*, 1995
illus. p. 71
oil, pastel, and pencil on canvas
71 x 92 1/8 in. (180.4 x 233.8 cm)
Hirshhorn Museum and Sculpture Garden, Smithsonian Institution, Washington, D.C.; Smithsonian Collections Acquisition Program, 1995

29. *Untitled*, 1995
illus. p. 75
oil on canvas
76 1/4 x 74 1/8 in. (193.7 x 188.2 cm)
Collection Penny and David McCall, New York

30. *Untitled*, 1995
illus. p. 74
chalk and acrylic on canvas
71 x 92 in. (180.3 x 233.7 cm)
Private collection

Charles Ray

31. Work in progress at time of publication. Courtesy Donald Young Gallery, Seattle.

Doris Salcedo

32. *La Casa Viuda I* (The Widowed House I), 1992–94
illus. pp. 88 and 90 (detail)
wood and fabric
101 1/2 x 15 1/4 x 23 1/2 in. (257.8 x 38.7 x 59.7 cm)
Worcester Art Museum, Massachusetts; Gift of the Friends of Contemporary Art

33. *La Casa Viuda IV* (The Widowed House IV), 1994
illus. p. 88
wood, fabric, and bone
102 1/2 x 18 1/4 x 13 in. (259.8 x 47 x 33 cm)
Collection Carlos and Rosa de la Cruz, Key Biscayne, Florida

34. *La Casa Viuda VI* (The Widowed House VI), 1995
illus. p. 89
wood, metal, and bone
three parts: 74 7/8 x 39 x 18 1/2 in. (189.7 x 99 x 47 cm); 62 7/8 x 47 x 22 in. (159.3 x 119.4 x 55.9 cm); 62 1/2 x 38 x 18 1/2 in. (158.75 x 96.5 x 47 cm)
Collection of the artist, courtesy Alexander and Bonin, New York

Thomas Schütte

35. *Grosser Respekt*
(Large Respect), 1993–94
illus. pp. x (detail) and 101
bronze and steel
51 1/8 x 175 1/2 x 214 1/2 in.
(131 x 450 x 550 cm)
De Pont Foundation for Contemporary Art, Tilburg, The Netherlands

36. *Kleiner Respekt*
(Small Respect), 1994
illus. p. 103 (detail)
Fimo, plaster, and wood
85 3/4 x 46 3/4 x 46 3/4 in.
(220 x 120 x 120 cm)
BACOB Collection, Brussels

37. *No Respekt* (No Respect), 1994
illus. p. 102
mixed media and 31 photographs
sculpture 35 1/8 x 19 1/2 x 19 1/2 in.
(90 x 50 x 50 cm); photographs, each 35 1/8 x 23 3/8 in. (90 x 60 cm)
Musée d'Art Contemporain de Nîmes, Depot du FRAC Languedoc, Rouissillon, France

Rachel Whiteread

38. *Untitled (Black Bed)*, 1991
illus. p. 107
fiberglass and rubber
12 x 74 x 54 in.
(30.5 x 188 x 137.2 cm)
Weltkunst Collection, Irish Museum of Modern Art, Dublin

39. *Untitled (Yellow Bed, Two Parts)*, 1991
illus. p. 107
dental plaster
66 3/8 x 27 1/4 x 28 in.
(168.5 x 69.2 x 71.1 cm) and
66 3/8 x 27 1/4 x 28 in.
(168.5 x 69.2 x 71.1 cm)
Hirshhorn Museum and Sculpture Garden, Smithsonian Institution, Washington, D.C.; Museum Purchase, 1993

40. *Untitled (Amber Mattress)*, 1992
illus. p. 110
rubber
44 x 36 1/2 x 43 in.
(111.8 x 92.7 x 109.2 cm)
Private collection

41. *Slab (Plug)*, 1994
illus. p. 111
rubber
8 x 30 x 79 in.
(20.3 x 7.6 x 200.7 cm)
Collection Dr. Uli and Rita Sigg, Switzerland

42. *Untitled (Wardrobe)*, 1994–95
illus. p. 111
plaster and glass
70 7/8 x 49 1/4 x 18 1/8 in.
(180 x 125 x 46 cm)
Private collection, courtesy Karsten Schubert, London

List of Figure Illustrations

Fig. 10, p. 27
Mirosław Bałka, *St. Adalbert*, 1987, steel, wood, painted jute, oats, and neon lights, 117 x 78 x 39 in. (300 x 200 x 100 cm). Muzeum Sztuki, Łódź, Poland.

Fig. 11, p. 28
Mirosław Bałka, *260 x 120 x 194, 250 x 120 x 194*, 1995, steel, soap, linoleum, and felt, 101 3/8 x 46 3/4 x 75 5/8 x 97 1/2 x 101 3/8 x 46 3/4 in. Collection of the artist, courtesy Galerie Nordenhake, Stockholm, and London Projects.

Fig. 12, p. 31
Marlene Dumas, *The Answer to the Marriage Proposal*, 1977–78, oil, pencil, ballpoint pen, and collage on paper, 39 x 48 3/8 in. (100 x 124 cm). Private collection.

Fig. 13, p. 32
Marlene Dumas, *The Banality of Evil*, 1984, oil on canvas, 48 3/4 x 41 1/8 in. (125 x 105.2 cm). Stedelijk Van Abbemuseum, Eindhoven, The Netherlands.

Fig. 14, p. 33
Marlene Dumas, *The First People (I–IV)*, 1991, oil on canvas, four panels, 70 1/4 x 35 1/8 in. (180 x 90 cm) each. De Pont Foundation for Contemporary Art, Tilburg, The Netherlands.

Fig. 15, p. 35
Marlene Dumas, *Waiting (For Meaning)*, 1988, oil on canvas, 19 1/2 x 27 1/4 in. (50 x 70 cm). Kunsthalle zu Kiel, Germany.

Fig. 16, p. 41
Robert Gober, *Slides of a Changing Painting*, detail, 1982–83, slides, 3 sequences of 3, left to right. Walker Art Center, Minneapolis; T. B. Walker Acquisition Fund, 1992.

Fig. 17, p. 42
Robert Gober, *Untitled*, 1991, wax, wood, cotton, skin, and hair. 9 x 16 x 44 1/2 in. (23 x 41 x 114 cm.) Collection of the artist. Installation, "Robert Gober," Galerie Nationale du Jeu de Paume, Paris, 1991.

Fig. 18, p. 46
Robert Gober, installation, "Robert Gober," Dia Center for the Arts, New York, 1992–93.

Fig. 19, p. 47
Robert Gober, *Untitled (Man in Drain)*, 1993–94, bronze, wood, brick, aluminum, beeswax, human hair, chrome, pump, and water, 56 x 37 1/2 x 34 in. (142.2 x 95.25 x 86.4 cm). Collection of the artist, courtesy Paula Cooper Gallery, New York.

Fig. 20, p. 49
Mona Hatoum, *The Light at the End*, 1989, steel frame, electric heaters, and electric bulb, 66 1/4 x 55 3/8 in. (170 x 142 cm). Arts Council Collection, Hayward Gallery, London.

Fig. 21, p. 50
Mona Hatoum, *So Much I Want to Say*, 1983, still from videotape, black and white, sound, 5 minutes. A Western Front Video Production, Vancouver.

Fig. 22, p. 51
Mona Hatoum, *Measures of Distance*, 1988, still from videotape, color, sound, 15 minutes, 25 seconds. A Western Front Video Production, Vancouver.

Fig. 23, p. 52
Mona Hatoum, *Corps étranger* (Foreign Body), 1994, video installation, 136 1/2 x 117 x 117 in. (350 x 300 x 300 cm). Musée National d'Art Moderne, Paris.

Fig. 24, p. 68
Guillermo Kuitca, *Si Yo Fuera el Invierno Mismo* (If I Were Winter Itself), 1986, acrylic on canvas, 54 1/2 x 98 1/4 in. (140 x 252 cm). Javier Benítez, Monterrey, Mexico.

Fig. 25, p. 69
Guillermo Kuitca, *Porgy and Bess*, 1988, acrylic on canvas, 61 5/8 x 87 5/8 in. (158 x 224.5 cm). Stedelijk Museum, Amsterdam.

Fig. 26, p. 76
Guillermo Kuitca, *Untitled*, 1995, oil on canvas, 77 1/4 x 77 in. (196.2 x 195.6 cm). Collection of the artist, courtesy Sperone Westwater, New York.

Fig. 27, p. 79
Charles Ray, *Ink Box*, 1986, steel and ink, 36 x 36 x 36 in. (91.4 x 91.4 x 91.4 cm). Newport Harbor Art Museum, California; Purchased with funds provided by Edward R. Broida.

Fig. 28, p. 80
Charles Ray, *Plank Piece I–II*, 1973, 2 black-and-white photographs, 39 1/2 x 27 in. (100 x 68.6 cm) each. Lannan Foundation, Los Angeles.

Fig. 29, p. 82
Charles Ray, *No*, 1992, color photograph, edition of 4; 38 x 30 in. (96.5 x 76.2 cm). The REFCO Group, Chicago.

Fig. 30, p. 83
Charles Ray, *Puzzle Bottle*, 1995, glass, painted wood, and cork, 13 3/8 x 3 3/4 x 3 3/4 in. (34 x 9.5 x 9.5 cm). Whitney Museum of American Art, New York; Purchase with funds from the Contemporary Painting and Sculpture Committee and Barbara and Eugene Schwartz.

Fig. 31, p. 84
Charles Ray, *The Most Beautiful Woman in the World*, 1993, 1 from set of 9 color photographs created for *Parkett*, no. 37 (1993).

Fig. 32, pp. 86–87
Doris Salcedo, *Atrabiliarios* ("Defiant"), 1992, shoes, plywood, animal fiber, and surgical thread; shoe in niche, 11 x 7 in. (27.9 x 17.8 cm).

Fig. 33, p. 91
Doris Salcedo, *Untitled*, detail, 1995, wood, concrete, cloth, and steel, 77 1/4 x 49 x 76 in. (196.2 x 124.5 x 193 cm). Hirshhorn Museum and Sculpture Garden, Smithsonian Institution, Washington, D.C.; Joseph H. Hirshhorn Purchase Fund, 1995.

Fig. 34, pp. 92–93
Doris Salcedo, installation, Carnegie International 1995, The Carnegie Museum of Art, Pittsburgh.

Fig. 35, p. 97
Thomas Schütte, *Studio II in den Bergen* (Studio II in the Mountains), detail, 1984, cardboard and fabric, dimensions variable. Collection Hannes Rossner.

Fig. 36, p. 98
Thomas Schütte, *Eis* (Ice Cream), 1987, mortar and brick. Installation, Documenta VIII, Kassel, 1987.

Fig. 37, p. 99
Thomas Schütte, *Die Fremden* (The Strangers), 1992, glazed ceramic, dimensions variable. Installation, Documenta IX, Friedrichsplatz, Kassel, 1992.

Fig. 38, p. 100
Thomas Schütte, *Mohr's Life*, 1988, mixed media, dimensions variable. Collection D. Guichard, Paris.

Fig. 39, p. 105
Rachel Whiteread, *Yellow Leaf*, 1989, plaster, formica, and wood, 59 x 29 x 37 in. (149.9 x 73.6 x 94 cm). Museu Calouste Gulbenkian, Centro de Atre Moderna, Lisbon.

Fig. 40, p. 106
Rachel Whiteread, *Ghost*, 1990, plaster on steel frame, 106 x 140 x 125 in. (269.2 x 355.6 x 317.5 cm). Saatchi Collection, London.

Fig. 41, p. 109
Rachel Whiteread, *Ether*, 1990, plaster, 43 x 34 1/2 x 80 in. (109.2 x 87.6 x 203.2 cm). Collection Jay Jopling, London.

Fig. 42, p. 112
Rachel Whiteread, *Untitled (One Hundred Spaces)*, 1995, resin, 100 units of 9 sizes. Installation, Carnegie International 1995, The Carnegie Museum of Art, Pittsburgh. Collection of the artist, courtesy Karsten Schubert, London, and Luhring Augustine Gallery, New York.

Fig. 43, p. 114
Rachel Whiteread, *House*, 1993, concrete. Located at 193 Grove Road, London. Commissioned by Artangel, London. Destroyed.

Hirshhorn Museum and Sculpture Garden Staff

Office of the Director
James T. Demetrion, Director
Maureen Turman,
Assistant to the Director
Kathy L. Jayne,
Secretary to the Director

Administration and Museum Support Services
Bevery Lang Pierce, Administrator
Carol Parsons, Special Assistant
James Hilton,
Safety and Occupational Health Specialist
April Martin, Budget Analyst
Daria Ramirez,
Administrative Assistant
Carolyn Lewis, Office Assistant

Anna Brooke, Librarian
Kent Boese, Library Technician
Jody Mussoff, Library Technician

Lee Stalsworth, Chief Photographer
Ricardo Blanc, Photographer
Ann Stetser, Photo Coordinator

Department of Public Programs
Neal Benezra,
Director of Public Programs/ Chief Curator
Valerie J. Fletcher, Curator of Sculpture
Frank B. Gettings,
Curator of Prints and Drawings
Judith K. Zilczer,
Curator of Paintings
Phyllis D. Rosenzweig,
Associate Curator
Olga M. Viso, Assistant Curator
Anne-Louise Marquis,
Research Associate
Francis Woltz, Curatorial Assistant
E. Tina Gómez, Secretary

Jane McAllister,
Publications Manager
Elizabeth Block, Editorial Assistant

Sidney Lawrence,
Head, Public Affairs
Michèle Colburn,
Public Affairs Specialist

Teresia Bush, Senior Educator
Diane Kidd, Education Specialist
Kelly Gordon, Museum Specialist
Suzanne Pender, Docent Coordinator
Holly Marken, Education Technician

Conservation Laboratory
Laurence Hoffman,
Chief Conservator
Lee Aks, Sculpture Conservator
A. Clarke Bedford,
Object and Painting Conservator
Susan Lake, Painting Conservator
Bruce Day, Museum Technician
Roni Polisar, Museum Specialist

Office of Exhibits and Design
Edward Schiesser, Chief
Robert Allen,
Design and Production Supervisor
Jonnette Butts, Exhibits Specialist
Larry Keller, Exhibits Specialist
Albert Masino, Exhibits Specialist
Daniel Murray, Exhibits Specialist
Tibor Waldner, Exhibits Specialist
Christopher Wilson,
Exhibits Specialist

Office of the Registrar
Douglas Robinson, Registrar
Brian Kavanagh, Assistant Registrar
Penelope Brown,
Assistant Registrar for Exhibitions
Margaret R. Dong,
Assistant Registrar for Loans
Barbara Freund,
Assistant Registrar for Exhibitions
Roy Johnsen,
Art Packaging Specialist
James Mahoney,
Museum Registration Specialist
Stephen Moore,
Museum Registration Technician

Building Management
Fletcher Johnston, Building Manager
Rosetta Hawkins,
Assistant Building Manager
Robert Ellis, Exhibits Specialist
Ronald Petty, Exhibits Specialist
Charles Shields,
Maintenance Mechanic
David Cheeks, Maintenance Worker
Eugene Jones, Jr., Laborer
Arnold Kirby, Laborer
Pamela Smith, Custodial Foreman
Mary Jackson, Custodial Leader
Louis Morgan, Custodial Leader
Daniel Bryant, Custodial Worker
Angela Davis, Custodial Worker
Odell Johnson, Custodial Worker
Daniel Russell, Custodial Worker
Janet Sharp, Custodial Worker
Gene Truesdale, Custodial Worker

Photographic Credits

The authors wish to thank the artists as well as the museums, galleries, and private collectors who supplied photographs of works of art in their possession and/or granted permission for works in their collections to be reproduced as illustrations. Photographic material was obtained directly from the collections cited in the Catalog of the Exhibition (p. 127) or the List of Figure Illustrations (p. 130), unless otherwise indicated here. Additional information is also cited below.

Cover: ©AP/Wide World Photos, photo by Michel Euler; p. i, courtesy Artangel, London, photo by John Davies; p. iii, courtesy Sperone Westwater, New York, photo by Adam Reich; p. iv, courtesy Lannan Foundation, Los Angeles, photo by Susan Einstein; p. v, courtesy the artist, photo by Eric Metcalfe; p. vi, courtesy The Carnegie Museum of Art, Pittsburgh, photo by Peter Harholdt; p. viii, courtesy Paula Cooper Gallery, New York, photo by D. James Dee; p. ix, courtesy the artist; p. x (cat. no. 35) courtesy Galerie Nelson, Paris; pp. 6–7, ©AP/Wide World Photos, photo by Lionel Ciromneau; pp. 8–9, ©AP/Wide World Photos, photo by Vladis Paze; p. 13, ©AP/Wide World Photos, photo by Jeff Widener; pp. 16–17, ©AP/Wide World Photos, photo by Nabil Juda; p. 19, ©AP/Wide World Photos, photo by Charles Pereira; p. 23, courtesy Stedelijk Van Abbemuseum, Eindhoven, photo by Peter Cox; p. 24 (fig. 7) courtesy The Tate Gallery and London Projects, (fig. 8) courtesy the artist; p. 25, photo by Susan Einstein; pp. 31–32, courtesy Galerie Paul Andriesse, Amsterdam, photos by Peter Cox; p. 33, courtesy Galerie Paul Andriesse, Amsterdam; p. 35, photo by Renard Kiel; p. 36 (cat. no. 3) courtesy Galerie Paul Andriesse, Amsterdam, (cat. no. 5) photo by Peter Cox; pp. 37–38, courtesy Jack Tilton Gallery, New York, photos by Erma Estwick; p. 39, courtesy Galerie Samia Saouma, Paris; p. 42, courtesy Paula Cooper Gallery, New York; p. 44, courtesy Paula Cooper Gallery, New York, photo by Russell Kaye; p. 45, photo by Geoffrey Clements; p. 46, courtesy Paula Cooper Gallery, New York, photo by Bill Jacobson; p. 47, photo by Russell Kaye; p. 49, courtesy the artist, photo by Edward Woodman; p. 50, courtesy the artist; p. 51, courtesy the artist; p. 52 (cat. no. 11) photo by Graydon Wood, (fig. 23) courtesy the artist, photo by Philippe Migeat; p. 53, courtesy the artist and Galerie Chantal Crousel, Paris; p. 55, photo by Graydon Wood; pp. 58–59 (cat. nos. 12–16) courtesy Rosamund Felsen Gallery, Los Angeles; pp. 62–63 (cat. nos. 17–19, 21–22) courtesy Jablonka Galerie, Cologne; p. 67, courtesy Sperone Westwater, New York; p. 68, courtesy Sperone Westwater, New York, photo by Alejandro Chermiavsky; p. 71, courtesy Sperone Westwater, New York; pp. 74–75, courtesy Sperone Westwater, New York; p. 79, courtesy Feature, Inc., New York; p. 80, photo by Susan Einstein; pp. 82–83, courtesy Donald Young Gallery, Seattle; p. 84, courtesy Parkett Magazine; pp. 86–87, courtesy Alexander and Bonin, New York; p. 88 (cat. no. 32) courtesy Alexander and Bonin, New York, photo by Stephen Briggs, (cat. no. 33) courtesy Alexander and Bonin, New York; p. 89, photo by D. James Dee; p. 90, courtesy Alexander and Bonin, New York, photo by D. James Dee; pp. 91–93, courtesy The Carnegie Museum of Art, Pittsburgh, photos by Richard Stoner; pp. 97–98, courtesy the artist, photos by Thomas Ruff; p. 99, courtesy the artist; p. 100, courtesy the artist, photo by H. Mundt; pp. 101–2, courtesy Galerie Nelson, Paris; p. 103, courtesy the artist; p. 105, courtesy Karsten Schubert, London, photo by Susan Ormerod; p. 106, courtesy Karsten Schubert, London; p. 107 (cat. no. 38) courtesy Karsten Schubert, London, (cat. no. 39) photo by Lee Stalsworth; p. 109, courtesy White Cube, London, photo by Edward Woodman; p. 110, courtesy Karsten Schubert, London; p. 111 (cat. no. 41) courtesy Karsten Schubert, London, photo by Volker Naumann; p. 112, photo by Richard Stoner; p. 114, courtesy Artangel, London, photo by John Davies.

Edited by Jane McAllister
Designed by Bethany Johns Design, New York
Printed on Ikonorex by Herlin Press, West Haven, Connecticut

D.A.P./Distributed Art Publishers
636 Broadway, 12th Floor
New York, New York, 10012
Telephone 212-473-5119
Fax 212-673-2887